'Is human thinking biased or rational? Or is it simply meaningful, like other acts of human communication? In *Psychorhetoric and the Psychology of Thought* Laura Macchi demonstrates an alternative to current accounts, focusing on the interpretive gap between a question and its answer. Her approach makes sense; that is: it made me think.'

Karl Halvor Teigen, *Professor Emeritus at the University of Oslo, Norway*

PSYCHORHETORIC AND THE PSYCHOLOGY OF THOUGHT

How can a particular way of argumenting direct our thinking? How does the formulation of a question influence the answer, producing a bias or an insight? And finally, what effect does public communication have on public behaviour?

Psychorhetoric and the Psychology of Thought illustrates the role played by rhetoric and communicative heuristics in the psychology of thinking and decision making, and its effect on many areas of our daily life. It gives voice to a new and unconventional approach to the contemporary debate within the psychology of thought that has wide implications for key behavioural phenomena, including biases, creativity, decision making, and public policy. This innovative work challenges conventional wisdom by proposing that cognitive biases are not inherent flaws in human cognition, but rather outcomes of misleading communication patterns that influence our thinking processes.

This unconventional approach to the psychology of thought has significant implications for creativity, decision making, economic behaviour, and public policy development. Essential reading for students and researchers in cognitive psychology, communication studies, and behavioural economics, this volume promises to reshape our understanding of human rationality and the communicative forces that guide it.

Laura Macchi is Full Professor of Psychology of Thinking, Decision Making and Communication and of General Psychology in the Department of Psychology at the University of Milano-Bicocca, Italy. Her main co-edited publications include *Thinking: Psychological Perspectives on Reasoning, Judgment and Decision Making* (2003), *Cognitive Unconscious and Human Rationality* (2016), and *Insight and Creative Problem Solving* (2018).

PSYCHORHETORIC AND THE PSYCHOLOGY OF THOUGHT

Laura Macchi

Routledge
Taylor & Francis Group
LONDON AND NEW YORK

Designed cover image: @Raffaello Cortina

First published in English 2026
by Routledge
4 Park Square, Milton Park, Abingdon, Oxon OX14 4RN

and by Routledge
605 Third Avenue, New York, NY 10158

Routledge is an imprint of the Taylor & Francis Group, an informa business

Translated by Frances Anderson

Published in Italian Language by Raffaello Cortina Editore 2024

British Library Cataloguing-in-Publication Data
A catalogue record for this book is available from the British Library

ISBN: 9781041157175 (hbk)
ISBN: 9781041156482 (pbk)
ISBN: 9781003680895 (ebk)

DOI: 10.4324/9781003680895

Typeset in Times New Roman
by Newgen Publishing UK

To Fabio and Stefano

CONTENTS

ACKNOWLEDGEMENTS

My heartfelt thanks go to Maria Bagassi, colleague, friend, and joint author of most of the research and the theories recounted in this book, with whom I have spent countless days of pure intellectual joy, sharing an ardent spirit of research. I also wish to express my debt of gratitude to our mentor, Giuseppe Mosconi, for the innumerable instances of rhetoric, or rather psychorhetoric, that he would apply, always with the same rigour and passion, to a way of saying or a witticism, so revealing their potential, nuances, and complexities. A sincere thank you, also, to Laura Caravona, Veronica Cucchiarini, Francesco Poli, and Edoardo Zulato for their collaboration on some of the research studies discussed in this book. I am also grateful to Frances Anderson for her meticulous translation, editing, and invaluable advice, and to Livia Anderson Penati for her assistance with the illustrations and cover design.

1

INTRODUCTION

Psychorhetoric, the Interpretative Function, and the Enigma of Thought. Bias versus Insight

> There is a mystery to language:
> language says something about being.
>
> Paul Ricoeur

1.1 The Psychorhetorical Approach to the Study of Thought

Is there any point today in establishing a relationship between the art of speech and the form of thought, between rhetoric and how thought evolves and manifests? Can reflections on rhetoric be of interest for the psychology of thought?

Although rhetoric is a constitutive feature of our humanistic culture, it is not held in great consideration by the general public. It brings to mind verbosity, speech that is rich in form but poor in content, designed to sway an audience and gain consensus. Rhetoric is equated with the art of persuasion, which appeals to emotion, exploiting the irrational, and strategies that advance propaganda, rather than being grounded in facts and reasoned arguments.

Indeed, traditionally, the kinds of discourse examined by rhetoric—from Aristotle to Perelman and Olbrechts-Tyteca's new rhetoric—have been viewed with suspicion. Their content is often considered dubious or spurious, and not susceptible to analytical reasoning or to absolutely unconfutable steps, as in formal logic.

But there is much more to rhetoric than this. Dating back to antiquity, it also represented the first attempt to systematically reflect on language, especially spoken language, based on common norms and principles, with its end purpose being to structure a clear and expressive discourse capable of engaging an audience, in short, an effective discourse. From the very outset, the rhetorician's

DOI: 10.4324/9781003680895-1

inquiry into the conditions and methods required to construct discourse that would appeal to listeners was based on persuasive intent and attentiveness to the audience. Therefore, even when not explicitly addressing the specific characteristics of a given audience, rhetorical analysis was applied to the discourse with the listeners in mind, implicitly considering those general psychological mechanisms that govern whether they would consider it to be acceptable.

In this sense, it could be said that the rhetorical approach to constructing discourse anticipated a psychological perspective: it recognized that speech is goal-oriented, based on implicit presuppositions shared with the interlocutor, and consequently shaped by the fact that not everything must be said explicitly, but simply what is necessary to render the utterance psychologically efficacious. It is enough to express what is needed to make the discourse psychologically effective. In this case, the interlocutors become the reference point: it is their perspective that determines where the discourse begins, how it will develop, and sometimes even how it will end.

Presuppositions and unspoken steps are two characteristics that define the economy of the discourse (over and above the cognitive economy) that is determined by requirements of psychological adequacy; in fact, since our working memory is limited, we tend to focus on what is most relevant to the context. To understand a discourse, we must identify the functions of its various passages and where they are leading, while also processing the implicit dimension of the thought to infer its most relevant elements.

In this light, rhetoric can be seen as a centuries-old reflection on the art of argumentation, on how discourse is layered, on its depth, on the interpretative interlacing of the implicit and the explicit layers, and, indirectly, on how thought functions. Understanding a persuasive discourse and how thoughts and their relationships are structured necessitates the representation and reconstruction of the implicit processes underlying what has been rendered explicit.

This holds true for all forms of discourse, including demonstrative arguments or syllogisms, as we will see in Chapter 3. More generally, the acceptability of a discourse depends precisely on the intervention of this implicit level of communication, of which usually the interlocutor is not critically aware, and on the complex interweaving of prior knowledge (presuppositions), and of the representation of intentions of the speakers and listeners.

The creation of the neologism *psicoretorica* (psychorhetoric) by Giuseppe Mosconi is a clear indication of his intent to reconsider the enormous wealth of reflections on the subject, to direct psychological research on thought, and his innovative theory on the relationship between language and thought that derives from it. Through discourse, psychorhetoric recaptures profound intuitions regarding communication from the art of persuasion, revealing both the functioning and the organization of thought.

This book takes Mosconi's theory as its basis and follows the developments that evolved from this approach, which is still highly topical today. I am referring here in particular to the identification of the interpretative function of thought, which is adaptive and transversal not only to language and thought but also to perception, and to the consequential emergence of the cognitive unconscious in the study of insight problem solving, supplanting the dualistic theories of thought (Bagassi & Macchi, 2016; see Chapter 2).

If assuming the rhetorical point of view in research on discourse can help to clarify its mental processes, then any rigid separation between truth and opinion, between demonstration and argumentation, must be set aside. What concerns us in this psychological reappraisal of rhetoric necessarily goes beyond traditional dichotomies. On the one hand, it overcomes the opposition between rhetoric and logic in terms of content; on the other, in terms of intention and function, it moves past the contrast between persuasive and natural discourse. The analysis of how human beings think and communicate draws attention to ordinary discourse,[1] understood as the psychologically relevant level at which the general rules of thought can be identified, irrespective of whether such thought is correct, certain, probable, mistaken, and so on.

1.2 The Interpretative Function of Thought

The general aim of this volume is to propose a conception of thought grounded in the dimensions of pragmatics and psychorhetoric—a conception in which communication plays a central role—with a view to identifying and understanding a broader interpretative function that cuts across the cognitive system and underpins the conceptual abilities that make communication possible (Bagassi & Macchi, 2016).

Our view is that this interpretative function is intrinsic to all forms of reasoning and constitutes an adaptive feature of the human cognitive system as a whole. Rather than filtering out contextual elements, it leverages their potential informativity. When meanings and relationships are familiar, this function ensures cognitive economy by allowing for rapid recognition, often in the blink of an eye.

However, when meanings and relationships are unfamiliar, the process becomes more demanding. We are confronted with a novel situation in which the default interpretation no longer works. This disruption is what prompts the search for alternative frameworks. A restless effort, both conscious and unconscious, begins: a search for new relationships between parts and the whole. Eventually, through an interpretative process that functions much like a heuristic, everything falls into place, and the situation makes sense in its entirety.

This mode of functioning is readily observable in everyday experiences, such as understanding speech. Indeed, language and thought share a unitary cognitive foundation—both shaped by the interpretative function and supported by universal interactive abilities. These include: "the ability to make models of the other, to 'read' the intentions behind actions, to make rapid interactional moves in an ongoing sequence of actions structured at many levels" (Levinson, 1995, pp. 225–226). Yet this interpretative function is also evident in contexts where communication and social interaction are less prominent—for instance, in tasks that involve perceptual processing. Routine activities such as recognizing a face, admiring a landscape, or viewing a painting may appear to be mere responses to visual stimuli. Actually, these are "analytical triumphs" made possible by our ability to interpret sensory information holistically. The perception of a scene, for example, depends not only on the input itself but on the relations we establish among its constituent parts—a process through which we construct meaning.

As Gardner and Johnson observe:

> When analyzing sensory experience, it is important to realize that our conscious sensations differ qualitatively from the physical properties of stimuli because, as Kant and the idealists predicted, the nervous system extracts only certain pieces of information from each stimulus while ignoring others. It then interprets this information within the constraints of the brain's intrinsic structure and previous experience. Thus [...] sounds, words, music, [...] color, tones [...] are mental creations constructed by the brain out of sensory experience. They do not exist as such outside the brain.
>
> *(Gardner & Johnson, 2013, p. 455)*

This interpretative tendency—inevitable and profoundly adaptive—operates at multiple levels: perceptual (mimicry, for example, being a form of defence, Figure 1.1), linguistic, and social. In all these domains, our ability to rapidly

FIGURE 1.1 An example of mimetics.

interpret what we are facing—and to infer its intentions—enhances our capacity to "survive", whether in a hostile environment or within any social context.

Take the phenomenon of pareidolia, for example: here, the same adaptive mechanism that drives us to resolve ambiguity and extract meaning from signals may give way to an aimless imaginative detour. We find ourselves perceiving human faces or animal shapes in the random contours of clouds. In Figure 1.2, for example, we immediately recognize the form of a rabbit.

Another example of this is Raven's matrices. In these non-verbal tests, the task is to select the element that completes a visual pattern. The only way to solve such problems is to search for pertinent relationships—a cognitive process that mirrors the interpretative work we perform in communication, but which more broadly reflects our general way of making sense of perceptual reality.

The same mechanism connects these phenomena with our understanding of speech or text—and, if we push further, with the interpretation of dreams, as explored in psychoanalysis: from the effort to attribute communicative intent to the act of shaping our internal world—as in the case of dreaming.

This tendency to attribute meaning to such formations—to recognize gestalts—reveals a transversal cognitive mechanism, developed for adaptive purposes (see Figure 1.2), and active across both perceptual and communicative domains. In fact, it underlies the communicative domain itself. The human capacity—indeed,

FIGURE 1.2 The phenomenon of pareidolia.

the necessity—to interpret and generate meaning appears to stem from general characteristics of our cognitive system.

First and foremost, the limits of our working memory (bounded rationality; Simon, 1955) have qualitative implications for how the cognitive system operates. We are simply not equipped to process all available information fully. Even so, we do not reason randomly. If we did, we might well have gone extinct long ago. Instead, given these quantitative limitations, we rely on qualitative capacities: we draw on relevance and pertinence, evaluate options in context rather than in the abstract, and continuously search for meaningful relationships. Our goal is to resolve ambiguity as quickly as possible—not out of mental laziness or superficiality, but as an expression of the adaptive function.

As the philosopher Luciano Floridi (2011) reminds us: "In order to emerge and flourish, the mind must make sense of its environment, continuously imbuing data with meaning (…). Mental life is therefore the result of a successful reaction to an original semantic horror *vacui*".

1.3 The Logical Bias of the Psychology of Thought

The intention behind this approach to the study of thought—beginning from its profound connection to language and its development through perception in a broader interpretative function—is to move beyond the traditional conception of mind, which has long been aligned with abstract and extra-psychological theoretical models. One such model is logic, adopted in the 1920s by the psychology of thought as the exclusive point of reference for understanding reasoning processes (e.g., in logical-deductive paradigms).

This theoretical–experimental framework, however, has largely ignored crucial psychological dimensions such as the content of thought with which it is formulated, its context, the intentions, and goals. As a result, outcomes that deviate from these normative parameters (which define purely formal and abstract reasoning) have been systematically labelled as biases, errors that sometimes are committed intentionally.

This is what we refer to as the logical bias in the psychology of thought (see Chapter 2): the reliance on extra-psychological disciplines such as logic, probability theory, and utility theory as cognitive models and sole reference points for understanding and evaluating mental processes (Bagassi & Macchi, 2016). Yet this perspective fails to consider that the development of formal logic itself involved a progressive de-psychologization of logical discourse—a movement towards disambiguation and simplification in contrast to the complexity of natural language (Tarski, 1969). Modern logic has aimed consistently to eliminate psychological dimensions and resolve linguistic ambiguity.

By adopting this strictly formal framework, the psychology of thought has evaluated reasoning according to the standards of logic—thereby launching the logic paradigm and contributing to the hypertrophic focus on biases. What has been lost, however, is the complexity of psychological reality, which has been treated as a source of interference rather than a subject worthy of study. Yet thought is necessarily contextual: it is steeped in content, in implicit presuppositions and beliefs, in intentions, and in its engagement with the real world.

As Stanovich and West (2000, p. 659) explain so clearly:

> The fundamental computational bias in human cognition would be the tendency toward automatic contextualization of problem (System 1), [...] while System 2's more controlled processes would decontextualize [...] and would not be dominated by the goal of attributing intentionality nor the search for conversational relevance.

Dual-process theories (Frankish & Evans, 2009; Kahneman, 2003) share a dichotomous view of the mind, which in synthesis distinguishes two different systems of reasoning: System 1—associative (fast and automatic) and System 2—reflective, rule-based (slow and analytic). This model is highly plausible. In everyday life, we are aware of our ability to reason reflectively, to engage in deliberate cognitive processes that contrast with others that seem intuitive and do not require any cognitive effort. Most automatic modes of reasoning are effective, economical, and the result of long-established learning, and appear to escape conscious control. As a result, thought is perceived as a superior cognitive activity—uniquely human, identified with awareness, and constituting a distinct system (System 2). Consequently, everything that is intuitive and unconscious (System 1) is seen as mechanical, automatic, with little involvement in thinking as such. This dualist conception emphasizes consciousness on the one hand and abstraction on the other, with contextual processing—which has often been viewed as a source of error in classical reasoning tasks—being attributed to System 1 while logical-literal abstraction and decontextualization are seen as guaranteeing correct reasoning processes and are emblematic of System 2.

In my view, however, thought cannot be reduced to the mere application of a logic-literal register, a register as univocal as it is unnatural. Instead, thought unfolds through a multilayered process that engages not only explicit reasoning but also what has not been said and unconscious analytic thought, both of which are essential for solving problems of a creative type, the so-called insight problems.

The same applies to communicative language; speech and discourse must be recovered as utterances, as events, intentional acts of enunciation. Without this, we would be forced to rely solely on combinations of signs to interpret what is meant. Yet it is the context and subjectivity of each communicative act that shapes the richness of its meaning.

This approach has raised a number of general questions, which became working hypotheses for the empirical studies I will explore in the following chapters. How does a specific argumentative strategy influence thought? How does the formulation of a question shape the response? How can we explain the proliferation of cognitive biases in contrast to the human capacity for creative insight? Could it be that these "failures" in reasoning are actually artefacts of the experimental formulations used to study them? Finally, can virtuous behaviour such as energy-saving habits be encouraged more effectively by tailoring public communication to cognitive processes, rather than by simply providing information?

The following chapters illustrate the paradigmatical investigation into these questions that I have conducted with my colleagues over the years; the results have encouraged us to rethink the traditional concept of rationality in the psychology of thought. In this perspective, biases and errors are not considered as intrinsic features of the human cognitive system, but rather the consequence of a lack of attention to how the human mind actually functions, and therefore potentially misleading (see Chapter 2). Indeed, many well-known judgement biases may partly reflect a fundamental misunderstanding of the context of the problem posed in a research study. Participants in experiments often assume that researchers are cooperative communicators, offering informative and relevant contributions. Researchers, however, often unwittingly, present information in a form that does not adhere to such criteria but follows a different communicative register (for example, that of formal logic) without advising the participants, thus creating a misunderstanding. In fact, when words and concepts from natural language are employed by a researcher or a logician, their meaning is curtailed: non-essential attributes are stripped away, altering the meaning those same words carry in everyday usage.

If this communicative mismatch is corrected, many of the best-known biases (first and foremost, the tendency to seek confirmation rather than falsification, the confirmation bias) are weakened or may even disappear altogether, which leads to the possibility that such phenomena may be less a sign of a cognitive deficit than the result of defective communication. The classical biases of reasoning and decision making will be reappraised in Chapters 4 and 5, respectively, while, as I will mention in more detail below, in Chapter 3, we will investigate the extraordinary processes of insight problem solving and will have the opportunity to see creative thinking in action.

1.4 Psychorhetoric, the Interpretative Function, and Problem Solving

The psychorhetorical approach to the study of thought has focused on problem solving, a domain where communication and the interpretative function play an active role, both in the act of forming and of solving the problem.

Even in our everyday life, we come across situations and problems that appear unsolvable; our analytical thought seems to fail us, and we just cannot see our way out of the dead end into which we have inadvertently strayed. We know we are in difficulty, but we have no idea what to do next. We have no strategy, and failure does not come to our aid with information that could help us forge forward. In other words, we have come up against an impasse. These are situations that change our lives radically if we do find a solution; the situation, which a moment before seemed to lead nowhere, suddenly takes on a different meaning and is transformed into something completely new. The literature discusses studies in which these situations are reproduced as experimental paradigms of insight problem solving.[2]

Our research, illustrated in detail in Chapter 3, has demonstrated the central role of these problems in understanding the functioning of the human mind. In doing so, it challenges the rigid dichotomies characteristic of dual-process theories (Frankish & Evans, 2009). I am referring here to a substantially dualistic formulation approach which, in a nutshell, tends to attribute correct reasoning to abstract, logical thought and error to typically psychological features, such as context sensitivity, the tendency to respond to or to grasp what is transmitted, mostly implicitly, by content, the speaker's intention, and the use of communicative language. From this dualistic perspective, the implicit dimension of thought and language, unconscious thought, has been viewed as a "disruptive element" that interferes with abstract, conscious processes assumed to be the true guarantors of rationality.

Yet as Lamberto Maffei reminds us: "Consciousness is a late cerebral affectation, in evolutionary terms, of limited biological relevance—though paranoically grandiose for the individual" (2012). This "grandiose" faith in conscious, abstract reasoning is called into question by insight problem-solving which, when successful, depends on the ineliminable contribution of implicit thought: analytic thought indeed, but unconscious (unconscious analytic thought—see Chapter 2). In my view, the challenges these problems present lie in their capacity to reveal a general cognitive mechanism—one that explains not only why we make mistakes or reach impasses but also how we manage to overcome them.

This general mechanism that we have identified and mentioned above, which emerges from the experiments that will be illustrated in greater length throughout the book, is the interpretative function of thought, or the ineliminable tendency to look for relationships between the data and the stimuli, whether they be perceptual or linguistic, and constantly search for attributions of meaning.

Both explicit (conscious) and implicit (covert) thought processes are engaged in this activity. However, only the implicit system can operate in parallel, initiating multiple interpretative paths simultaneously, guided by relevance and pertinence. This is how we break through the blocks that require a shift in representation—a new perspective. The kind of unconscious thought involved here is goal-directed and adaptive—whether oriented toward knowledge, problem-solving, or survival. This stands in sharp contrast to the traditional view of unconscious thought as intuitive, automatic, and cognitively "lazy"—associated with learned behaviour habits (such as driving a car) or thought patterns (with a preference for familiar solutions) that have already been used in the past.

In Chapter 3, then, we will explore the hypothesis that insight problems originate in misunderstandings—glitches in communication—and that the impasse reflects a failure of the default interpretation. Restructuring, in this view, is a process of re-interpretation that draws on both explicit and implicit cognitive resources. It cannot occur through conscious effort alone, which is often constrained by fixation and a predefined interpretation—the so-called Einstellung effect. Instead, the impasse—this seemingly insurmountable difficulty in finding the solution—triggers an implicit search increasingly oriented to the goal of the problem, generating an interpretative game, a re-interpretation of the available data in light of the request and vice versa.

The *Study Window* problem is one of the most intriguing of these insight problems; it poses a genuine challenge and at first sight seems impossible to solve. It is an example of a problem that cannot be solved analytically, in which the impasse seems to be insurmountable; an incubation period is necessary, and the solution only emerges from a deep restructuring. It is formulated as follows:

> The study window measures 1 m in height and 1 m wide. The owner decides to enlarge it and calls in a workman. He instructs the man to double the area of the window without changing its shape so that it still measures 1 m by 1 m. The workman carried out the commission. How did he do it?

As shown in Figure 1.3, if the owner's instructions are to be carried out, the original window has to be a square (i.e., a geometric form) that "rests" on one of its angles, thus "becoming" a rhombus (i.e., a phenomenal form). The height and width are those of the diagonals of the rhombus (ABCD). Therefore, the workman will need to create a square window whose sides measure the same as the diagonals of the original window and superimpose it on the rhombus: the form is the same, the height and width are the same, but with the surface area of the square superimposed on that of the rhombus, the combined area is double that of the original window.[3] When we posed this problem to the participants in our study, they all declared it was impossible to solve (Macchi & Bagassi, 2014), and indeed, nobody actually solved it. In our view, the solution is blocked by the problem solvers' mental representation

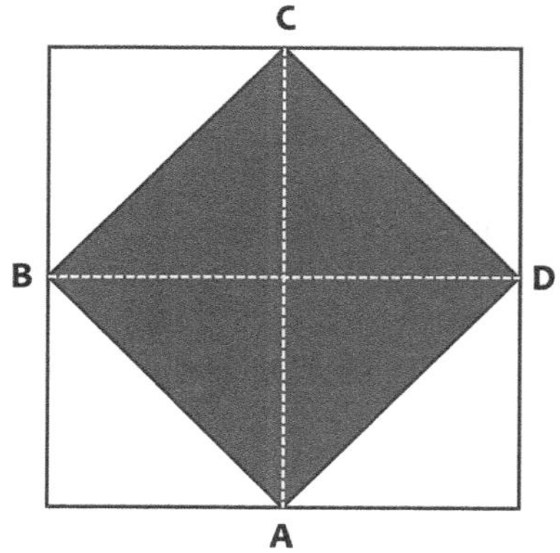

FIGURE 1.3 The solution to the *Study Window* problem.

of the window described in the text of the problem, which they will "visualize" in the usual, orthogonal orientation (with the sides parallel to the vertical–horizontal coordinates). The information provided regarding the dimensions evokes a square form. The problem solvers therefore interpret the window to be a square 1 metre high by 1 metre wide, resting on one side. Furthermore, the problem states "without changing its shape", intending the geometric shape of the two windows (square, independently of the orientation), while the problem-solver interprets this as meaning the phenomenal shape of the two windows (two squares with the same orthogonal orientation). And this is where the difficulty of the problem lies, in the mental representation of the window and the concurrent interpretation of the text of the problem, which I will discuss in Chapter 3.

In Chapter 4, following this exploration of the field of problem solving, we study the impact of the formulation of the text in classic logical-deductive reasoning tasks, while in Chapter 5 we investigate judgement in conditions of uncertainty. Chapter 6 examines choices and decision making, including its applications in the field of public communication, to test the applicational reach of the psychorhetorical approach. Chapter 7 discusses efficacy in public communication. Scientific communication, in particular, seen to be crucial during the COVID-19 pandemic and fundamental for conveying the complexities of climate change, has shown that communicating genuine data alone is not enough, as the human cognitive system must be taken into account to ensure the efficacy of the communication.

1.5 The Enigma of Thought: Bias versus Insight

The representation of the functioning of the human mind that emerges from studies of the psychology of thought contains an enigma, a contradiction, that has remained mostly latent. If it is not taken into consideration, it hinders a more integrated, comprehensive, and inevitably more complex account of the cognitive system. It becomes particularly apparent when we attempt to reconcile two major domains of research involving the psychology of thought: reasoning and decision making on the one hand, and problem solving on the other. Here we are confronted with a jarring juxtaposition: one vision presents human cognition as substantially irrational, riddled with biases and fallacies; the other highlights its creativity, adaptability, and even moments of brilliance, as exemplified in insight problem solving.

These contrasting representations have developed in isolation, without their divergence giving rise to doubts or interrogatives regarding their implication and, in consequence, the implication regarding the general representation of the human cognitive system. Such a divergence cannot be explained simply by claiming that, on the one hand, humans are obtuse and fallible, susceptible to fallacies and biases (especially regarding the principles and procedures to which the psychology of reasoning attributes particular importance), and insightful problem-solvers on the other. A deeper reflection on the theoretical and experimental approaches of these two fields is needed and could provide indications for understanding this irreconcilability.

As noted earlier, research on reasoning draws from disciplines, such as logic and probability theory—models that are extra-psychological and largely de-psychologized. By contrast, problem-solving has evolved as a field in its own right, rooted in Gestalt psychology's early investigations of perception and the tendency of the human mind to organize reality into meaningful gestalts, which was never intended to be an evaluation of the performance and characteristics of the functioning of the mind. This is the epistemological approach I have adopted in my research, illustrated in this volume; it is a contribution to the ongoing debate within the psychology of thought and decision making, addressing the mechanisms behind reasoning errors, the interplay of language and thought, and the role of the unconscious and its critical implications that challenge the dual-process theories.

In this perspective, the question of bounded rationality takes on a new light. The study of how we think reveals the principles that describe how human thought functions; it is not a question of limits, which in themselves lead to error—cognitive illusions—but of characteristics with which we perceive, think, and communicate. Take optical illusions, for example. It is the same perspectival perceptive mechanism that creates three-dimensionality from a two-dimensional painting. Images in art, like all images, do not represent reality; they represent the observers' perceptions, imagination, expectations, and their knowledge of other images recalled from memory. Art is, in part, a creation of the mind; the sensorial information is organized according to Gestalt principles so that the mind can create reality. In this sense, cognitive illusions, biases, just like perceptual illusions, could be considered as a collateral effect, the epiphenomenon of the functioning of the cognitive system that occurs in the absence of context, when there is a misunderstanding.

In the Müller-Lyer optical illusion, for example, the experimenter measures the objective bidimensional length of the two segments, ignoring the three-dimensional effect produced by the fins at the ends of the shaft (see Figure 1.4a). Art, instead, exploits the three-dimensional interpretation of the two-dimensional

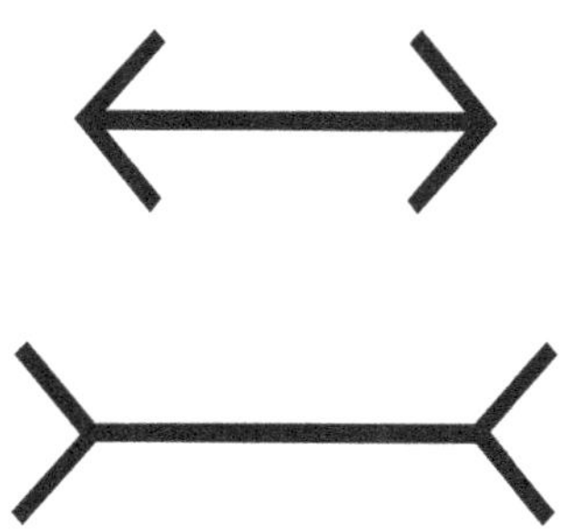

FIGURE 1.4A Müller-Lyer optical illusion.

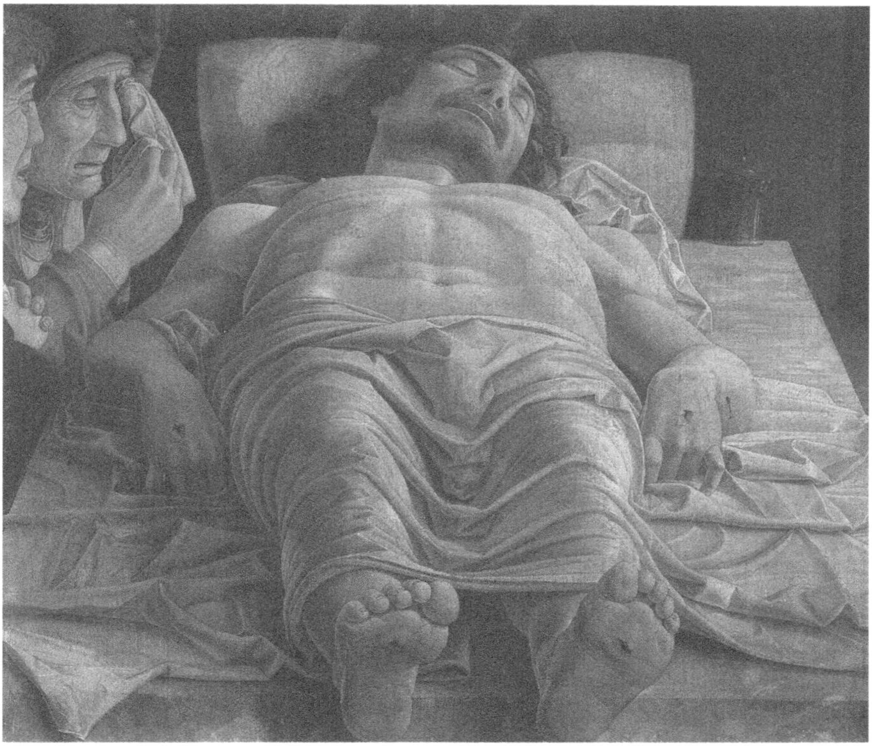

FIGURE 1.4B The *Lamentation of Christ*; Tempera on canvas (68 cm × 81 cm); Andrea Mantegna, 1475–1478.

data cooperatively. In Andrea Mantegna's painting *The Lamentation of Christ*, the body of Christ is positioned in a dilated space with the depth of a room, an incredible achievement of foreshortening of the perspective given the dimension of the canvas, a mere 68 × 81 cm. When we move while observing the painting, the perspective is maintained as in reality; in this case, the tacit collaboration between the observer and the artist, on which the artistic experience of the painting is based, creates a powerful representation of reality.

Notes

1 Discourse, rather than the individual word or phrase (Grice, 1975), would appear to be the level of communication at which the development of thought—its underlying mechanisms and the connections activated by a person's communicative intent—is most clearly identifiable.

2 How procedural problems are dealt with was first explored by Newell and Simon in their pioneering study of 1972 and subsequently developed in the ambit of the Human

Information Processing (HIP) theory. On the contrary, the processes required to solve problems that need a change of representation (insight problems) is still considered to a certain extent "mysterious", although in recent years there has been greater interest in throwing light on this mystery of insight and creativity.

3 Spatial orientation is a decisive factor in the perception of form: two identical forms, observed from different orientations, assume a different phenomenal identity (Mach, 1914).

2

THE INTERPRETATIVE FUNCTION AND THE EMERGENCE OF UNCONSCIOUS ANALYTIC THOUGHT[1]

> Consciousness is a late cerebral affectation, in evolutionary terms, and of limited biological relevance — though paranoically grandiose for the subject.
>
> Lamberto Maffei

2.1 The Bias of the Psychology of Thought

Philosophy assumes the exploration of thought in its functional and structural qualities as the starting point of its investigations; more precisely, it assumes both the exploration of the instruments that contribute to the construction of truth and the exploration of the source itself that generates these instruments and guarantees them. Thought as a living whole, creator of logical relationships but at the same time the mirror of their structure, is the subject *par excellence* of philosophical inquiry and elicits the topic of "logic" in the extended sense of the term.[2]

The aim of Aristotelian logic was to establish the truth, the ontological substance, through the study of the argument or the inference or, in other words—of what follows necessarily from certain premises, rooted in truth—as an instrument of knowledge in order to reach the truth.

After a long period of "conservatorism", starting from the beginning of the last century, logic underwent a phase of intensive development, assuming a framework similar to that of the mathematical disciplines, to the extent that it became known as *mathematical logic* or *logistics*. The renovation aimed at giving the fundamentals of mathematics a more solid and profound base. In just a century, this new mathematical logic reached a high degree of perfection and played an important role in our overall knowledge, extending far beyond the boundaries within which it had originally been created.

DOI: 10.4324/9781003680895-2

As a result of the intensive work done on decontextualizing and the formalization that followed, the criteria of validity in logic gradually excluded an intuitive approach, privileging its mechanics.

It is worth noting that the development of formal logic, in fact, became a gradual process of "depsychologization" of logical language and of disambiguant simplification compared to natural language, intentionally pursued and programmatically declared by modern logic (Tarski, 1969).

The psychology of thought has inherited this tradition. The purpose of the scientific, experimental approach to the study of thought was to describe human reasoning by identifying the criteria that ensure its correctness, for example, the criteria of validity of a deduction starting from a given set of premises. From an Aristotelian perspective, these criteria constitute a form of structure of fundamental knowledge, general and independent of accidental and contingent particularisms, a sort of deep structure of knowledge, analogous to the deep structure of language, those linguistic universals *à la* Chomsky.

This claim to find the common element, the essence of psychological reality, underlying the multiplicity of beliefs, and the multitude of situations in which thought is involved, the essence of psychological reality, has paradoxically transcended reality itself in a sort of metaphysics. What has, however, been lost is the complexity of reality, which was seen as an element of interference, clouding the general structure that underlies reasoning; whereas thought is of necessity contextualized, drenched in content, implicit presuppositions, beliefs, intentions and deals with reality in all its complexity.

2.2 Logic and Natural Language

A few simple examples will help to clarify this. Take the case of disjunction, which has had such an impact on the fields of logic and psychology. To ensure that its meaning would be univocal, modern logicians made disjunction independent of psychological factors and particularly of contextual knowledge. They therefore decided to extend the use of *or* (the inclusive or) and also to consider the disjunction of any two sentences (members) as a combination endowed with sense even if there were no meaningful connections or links between the two disjuncts.

As for disjunction, modern logic has moved away from the use of the conditional sentence in *implication* (if … then) in everyday language acceptation. Once again, we use the *if* clause only when there is a pertinent relationship between the *if* and the *then* clauses. Modern logicians adopted the same procedure used for *or* in order to comply with the requirements of scientific languages, for which logic is intended to constitute the foundation. They decided to disambiguate implication and to free it from any psychological factors, above all, a pertinent relationship between antecedent and consequent. This means that the truth of the implication has been reduced to the truth or the falsity of the antecedent and of the consequent taken individually. Therefore, modern logic uses implication in material meaning, or simply *material implication*. This is in antithesis to the use of implication in natural language, where the existence of a relationship between antecedent and consequent is a necessary condition for implication to be meaningful and true.

However, natural language is so flexible and multilayered that we can even adopt what would appear to be a totally unacceptable implication, as far as pertinence is concerned, to convey the falsity of the antecedent:

If Peter comes this evening, [then] I'm a Dutchman.

Indeed, no word, no phrase in natural language has a univocal meaning independent of the situation at hand, of the context and, the context being the same, depending on the intention of the speaker. Even the same individual can, of course, intend to say different things in different moments in time using the same words.

Take, for example, the stereotyped sayings "war is war" and "business is business". Such tautological phrases are informative insofar as they isolate and emphasize the global meaning of the term. The subject corresponds to the general concept; the predicate highlights one particular element of the general concept to the exclusion of all others. Far from simply acknowledging the identity of the concept (war = war, business = business), these phrases provide important information; they tell us that, in times of war, the rules applied are different from those applied in times of peace, and that in business, behaviour can be countenanced that would be considered unacceptable in normal, everyday relationships. Statements of this type cannot be represented as A is equal to A, but as A implies X. It is only the form of these utterances that is tautological; the message is actually informative.

Now, considering the use of negation in natural language, it can be seen that this form can also take on very different meanings, which may even be substantially opposite.[3] Imagine, for example, that you are looking for a length of cloth in a particular colour, say *antique rose*, and reject the cloth that is offered as it is *powder pink* and not *antique rose*. Or that you express your opinion about a certain action, saying: "That's not fair!" If we do not take into consideration the psychological characteristics, the *not antique rose* of the first example and the *not fair* of the second could both be considered as corresponding and codified as *not A*. However, with regard to their natural meaning, the *not A* of the first example corresponds to that which only *resembles* antique rose, whereas the *not A* of the second example corresponds to the *contrary* of fair.

These two negations are very different from one another in terms of the point of view of what the speaker actually meant. In the first case, the negation refers to the identity within the terms of the comparison and corresponds to an acknowledgement of their similarity: the colour of the cloth is *almost* antique rose, but it is not an exact match. In the second case, the negation identifies with the *opposite* of what is being negated.

One of the primary differences between the language of logic and natural language is that in logic, negation is limited exclusively to negation for "contraposition", whereas in natural language it can also be used for "differentiation". But these are not the only differences; another very crucial difference is that in natural language, the reversibility of negation by contraposition is not automatic: sometimes "not unfair" expresses fairness, but this is not always the case. An action that is defined as "not unfair" is different from an action that is described as "unfair" not because it is the opposite of unfair (i.e., definitely fair) but because it is not *completely* unfair or only unfair in some respect or just seems unfair, and so on. When logicians borrow concepts and words from natural language, they circumscribe the meaning, eliminating any attributes that are not essential for their aims, thus however deviating from the significance of these concepts and words in natural language.

Logic and natural language share a common aim, that of transmitting meaning efficaciously or, in other words, of communicating, of expressing thought. However, this objective is achieved by these two language forms in opposite ways: logic achieves a univocal communication, through simplification, eliminating any meanings that might interfere with the univocal meaning to be communicated, whereas natural language exploits the expressive richness of words, but nevertheless avoids slipping into chaos and tripping over misunderstandings, by relying on the pertinence of the meaning to the context.

In Ricoeur's words:

> We then understand what happens when the word reaches discourse along with its semantic richness. All our words being polysemic to some degree, the univocity or plurivocity of our discourse is not the accomplishment of words but of contexts. In the case of univocal discourse, that is, of discourse which tolerates only one meaning, it is the task of the context to hide the semantic richness of words, to reduce it by establishing what Greimas call an isotopy, that is, a frame of reference, a theme, an identical topic for all the words of the sentence [...] Instead of sifting out one dimension of meaning, the context allows several to pass, indeed, consolidates several of them, which run together in the manner of the superimposed texts of a palimpsest. [...] More than one interpretation is then justified by the structure of a discourse which permits multiple dimensions of meaning to be realized at the same time. In short, language is in celebration.
>
> *(Ricoeur, 1969; English Translation, 1974: p. 94)*[4], [5]

There is no hierarchical order between natural language and logical language in the sense that the former is inferior or subordinate to the latter. The two simply reflect different needs: in the first case, the need to ensure the efficacy of the communication; in the second, the need to guarantee the rigour of the inferential process. Logical discourse derives from common (or natural) discourse by a process of differentiation that, in a certain sense, establishes it as a specialist discourse. The two languages are differentiated (and in this sense different), but not in the sense of being completely separate or lacking a common basis—and even less in the sense that they represent the opposition of rationality/irrationality (Mosconi, 1990).

Two constants in the history of modern logic are the tendency toward the elimination of psychological aspects and the simplification of the ambiguity of language (a justified simplification, but one that is often anti-economic from a communicative point of view). This was the state of the art when the psychology of thought encountered logic in the 1920s. At that time, logic was configured as mathematical logic, and psychology adopted it as a framework of reference. In those years, psychology was differentiating itself from philosophy and carving out a place among the sciences; to this end, to comply with the requirements of "scientificity", it integrated the speculative approach adopted by philosophy with the experimental approach, basing this on logic, the discipline that constituted the foundation of the other sciences.

Adopting this formal point of view, the psychology of thought has evaluated human reasoning, judgement and decisions, creating the *logic-deductive* paradigm.

In fact, from the very beginning and for many decades thereafter, psychology of thought focused its research on the study of syllogisms and conditional reasoning in the pure logico-philosophical tradition. Since the early studies in the 1960s, the predominant vision has been substantially rationalistic, from the logicist theory of deductive reasoning to probabilistic reasoning, to Piaget's theory of epistemological genetics on cognitive development.

2.3 The Unexpected Counterpoint: The Dilemma of Error

The unexpected counterpoint that emerged was the dilemma of how to explain human error, or the deviation of human reasoning from the logical norm. This issue had already emerged (Henle, 1962), but it only became crucial in the second half of the 1960s and even more so in the 1970s as its frequency, transversality and generality were considered to be indicative of the structural limitations of the human mind. This tendency to make mistakes translates into the concept of *bias*, indicating a systematic deviation from the norm, inherent to the human cognitive system.

From this point on, experimental research on reasoning focused on the problem of human error, the incapacity to grasp the deep logical structure (for a review on this issue, see Frankish & Evans, 2009). Therefore, the psychology of thought was obliged to adopt as a theoretical framework that dualistic vision—already *in nuce* from its emergence—in an attempt to explain both the human capacity for abstraction and correct reasoning, but also this tendency to error, the *bias*, the so-called cognitive illusions. As a result, from the 1970s, the principal theories of thought were characterized by a dualistic vision that attributes error to thought processes that are different from those that guarantee correct reasoning.

The general denomination of these theories has brought together models that, although characterized by significant differences, share the historic dichotomy between logical and common reasoning that has always characterized the psychological theories of reasoning (Evans et al., 2007; Sloman, 1996; Stanovich

& West, 1998, 2008; Wason & Evans, 1975). All the dual models, over and above the various factors that characterize them, distinguish two diverse systems of reasoning: the associative (fast, automatic and effortless—System 1) and the rule based (slow, analytic and effortful—System 2). The associative system reflects "similarity structure and relations of temporal contiguity" and is generally unconscious. "The other is rule based and tries to describe the world by capturing different kinds of structure, structure that is logical, hierarchical, and causal-mechanical" (Sloman, 1996, pp. 3, 6).

Philosophers and psychologists have long held and shared the view that two substantially different ways of thinking coexist in the mind. This representation is very plausible: every day we experience our capacity to reason consciously, applying a reflective process compared to the other modes that would appear to be automatic, intuitive, and that appear not to require any particular cognitive effort. Most of these automatic modes are functional, economic, the outcome of ancient, consolidated learning, and seem to elude any attempt at conscious control. As a result, thought is perceived as a superior cognitive activity, particularly developed in humans, that identifies with awareness and constitutes a system in itself (S2). Consequently, everything that is intuitive, not conscious (S1), is perceived as being mechanical, automatic, and with little involvement of thought (see also pages 7 and 8.

Hence, this dichotomic view of the mind focuses on one hand on the role of consciousness and on the other on the capacity for abstraction. In particular, the processing of the context in cognitive processes would be typical of System 1 (or Type 1) and was considered one of the causes of error in classical reasoning tasks, whereas the process of abstraction and de-contextualization has been considered as being emblematic of System 2 (or Type 2), ensuring that the process of reasoning is implemented correctly. Furthermore,

> the fundamental computational bias in human cognition would be the tendency toward automatic contextualization of problem (System 1), [...] while System 2's more controlled processes would decontextualize [...] and would not be dominated by the goal of attributing intentionality nor the search for conversational relevance.
>
> *(Stanovich & West, 2000, p. 659)*

2.3.1 Paradoxical Effects of Content in Explaining Error

A paradoxical result emerges from research regarding the effect of the content on logical abstract reasoning. In fact, if we compare the research on *belief bias* and on conditional reasoning using deontic material, what seems to be an antithetical phenomenon appears, for which the dichotomic vision has no explanation. In the first case, the content provokes the bias, whereas in the latter case, the deontic and familiar material activates the inferential schema for the conditional reasoning.

According to the dualistic theories of thought (Evans, 2010; Evans et al., 1983; Stupple et al., 2011), the *belief bias* occurs when the premises conflict with logical validity, as in the example "All flowers fade. All roses fade. All roses are flowers". This constitutes evidence that two systems are involved in evaluating validity and that the system of knowledge and beliefs (S1) prevails. But what type of knowledge or belief is this, if it actually defines the categorical class inclusion, implicitly activated by the terms *roses* and *flowers*?

It is true that from the two premises, it is not possible to conclude that "roses are flowers", according to logic. However, this error from a logical point of view can be interpreted as the result of a cooperative act; concluding that roses are flowers does not add knowledge, it only allows communicative interaction, although at the lowest level of informativeness. As in the Socratic dialogue, rhetorical questions have a common basic function from which the argument will start and will be developed. Saying that "roses are flowers" is to give our own consent to obvious but shared knowledge. In a nonexperimental context, the two premises would raise a spontaneous reply such as "We know this, so what?", the natural equivalent to the logical "nothing ensues."

In 1966, Peter Wason devised a classic selection task in which, on the other hand, the realistic content would activate logical inferential schemas (Johnson-Laird et al., 1972), real counterexamples (Griggs & Cox, 1982), or pragmatic reasoning schemas (Cheng & Holyoak, 1985).

Wason's Selection Task, which will be discussed in detail in Chapter 4, consists of four cards with a letter printed on one side and a number on the other, with a conditional rule in the form "if p, then q". The rule is as follows:

If a card has a vowel on one side, then there is an even number on the other.

The problem-solver has to decide which cards to turn over to establish if the rule is true or false. According to Wason, if human beings were to think analytically, they should adhere to the rules of logic, in particular, the material implication *if ... then ...* The correct answer requires the choice of the card with the vowel and the card with the uneven number (A and 7): this is the only combination of letters and numbers that can demonstrate the falsity of the hypothesis. However, the answer that is most frequently given is the cards with the vowel and the even number. The rule, however, does not envisage what happens when the card has a letter other than

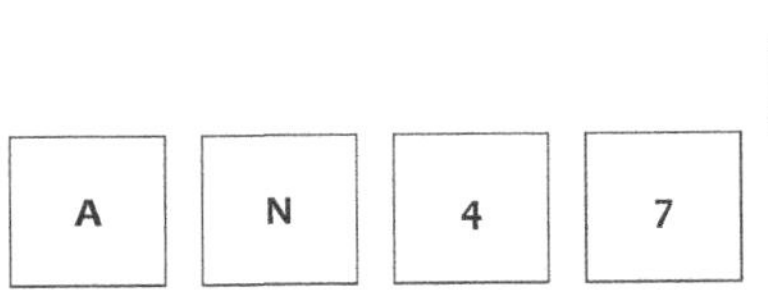

FIGURE 2.1

A; therefore, there is no point in selecting the card with the letter N (non-p). In the same way, the conditional is (in logic) unidirectional, so it is equally pointless to select the card with the number 4 (q). Notwithstanding this, the results show that less than 10% of the persons asked to undertake this task give the correct answer. This phenomenon, which was identified by Wason, is known as the *verification bias*, the erroneous tendency to check a rule using the cases that confirm it (in this case, by turning over the card marked A) and even though a further check is of no use whatsoever, turning over the card marked 4, completely ignoring the card marked 7 (counterexample of the rule) which could falsify the hypothesis. In general, as Wason noted in an article in 1983, "this provides an affirmative answer to Jonathan Cohen's question, 'Can human irrationality be demonstrated with an experiment?'" (Wason, 1983, p. 59).

Thematic materials have also been used to obtain better results in selection tasks. Johnson-Laird and colleagues (1972), for example, asked their participants to imagine they were Post Office employees, with the responsibility of distributing the mail and verifying that the letters respected the following rule:

If an envelope is sealed, then it has a 50-lire stamp

The test consisted of four envelopes, representing *non-q* (40), *q* (50), *p* (closed), and *non-p (open).*

Practically all the participants selected *p* (the sealed envelope) and *non-q* (the envelope with the 40-lire stamp).

The success rate was attributed by the authors to the realism of the experiment and the sense of familiarity with the problem, which transmitted the unidirectional logical relationship and consequent activation of the inferential logical schemes of falsification (*non-q*) and the verification (*p*).[6]

At this point it is worthwhile to reflect on the strange case of the "logical aberrations" (*not p* and *q*) demonstrated, with great spirit of innovation, by Mosconi and D'Urso (1975), using the same deontic version of the *selection* task adopted by Johnson-Laird et al. ["if a letter is sealed, then it has a 50-lire stamp on it"; selected cards: "sealed letter" (*p*) and "40-lire stamp" (*not q*)]. But this time, Mosconi and D'Urso asked the subjects to check the *inverse* rule ("if a letter is open, then it has a 40-lire stamp on it"). The cards mainly selected were again: "sealed letter"

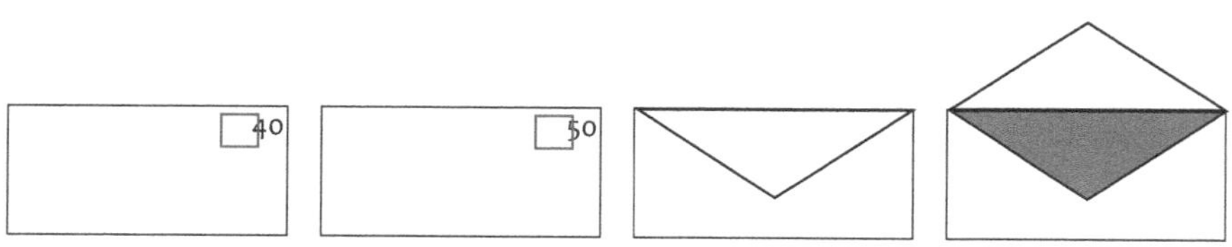

FIGURE 2.2

(*not p*) and "40-lire stamp" (*q*) but, this time, these cards (*not p* and *q*) were an aberration from a logical perspective, even though they represented the crucial cases of potential violators in that context. It is worth noting that the two most selected cards were the same as those that were chosen in Johnson-Laird et al.'s original experiment, but in Mosconi and D'Urso's experiment, they represented non-valid cases.

The paradoxical effects of content that emerge from the two fields of research illustrated above cannot be explained simply by the agreement or disagreement between content and logical validity, with content always prevailing.

Actually, what this appears to mean is that independently of their logical function (*p* and *not q* vs. *not p* and *q*), the cases that are crucial for testing the rule in this specific situation ("sealed" and "40 lire") are those that are selected based on the logic of pertinence and usefulness, rather than on formal logic. When we adopt the relevance criterion, we are processing information on explicit and implicit levels of knowledge, exceeding the logical layer of the conditional sentence. It is possible to understand these paradoxical results only if we consider the implications of the specific content and the relevant rule in that context. Just as content transmits implicit relations that render the material implication significant or not significant, so does the relation of inclusion in classes with categorical syllogisms, as we have seen in the *belief bias*.

A possible interpretation is that reasoning always goes beyond the logical level of meaning and so requires an intensive search for as much information as possible. Thus, the logical meaning is only one of possible interpretations, the least relevant and, therefore, the least likely to be assigned, if the "logic" intent of the task is not adequately transmitted.

In fact, natural language is ambiguous in itself, differently from specialized languages (i.e., logical and statistical ones), which presuppose a univocal, unambiguous interpretation. The understanding of what a speaker means requires a disambiguation process centred on the intention attribution.

2.4 The Shadow Area of Thought

Recently, certain weaknesses and criticisms of the dual theories have been discussed: what are the roles played by the abstraction processes, the meta-representational ability, and the working memory in distinguishing Type 1 and Type 2 processes? Is it possible to extrapolate essential factors in these processes? How do these two types of processes work and interact? In particular, what is the relation between implicit and explicit thought, between intuition and reflection, regarding what is emerging from the shift in the paradigm of the psychology of reasoning, on which there is an ongoing debate? (Macchi et al., 2012).

The new paradigm goes beyond the idealized logic of certainty, which was typical of both the old deduction paradigm and the dual-process theories, toward a more realistic logic of uncertainty, moving toward a general probabilistic explanation of human reasoning (Over, 2009). To deal with the inevitable uncertainties of reasoning in the real world, thought must—of necessity—process probabilities, implicit assumptions, and beliefs. This leads to a more complex view of rationality, less concerned with and less focused on the quantitative limits of conscious thought, imposed by the *working memory capacity*, and more centred on the ability to contextualize and exploit the complexity of what is real, moving toward a form of *bounded-grounded rationality*.

This has resulted in a revaluation of implicit-intuitive thought, the "shadow zone" (Macchi & Bagassi, 2012), which in the past was considered responsible for automatisms and frequently for errors in reasoning. Now, the dualistic view of thought and the logical-deductive paradigm are being questioned, and this implicit-intuitive thought is acquiring a more central position in interaction with explicit thought. Intuition can deal rapidly with numerous items of information, interpreting them in parallel (Betsch, 2007; Betsch & Held, 2012), not limited by the working memory capacity.

Contextual elements, beliefs, implicatures, and propositional attitudes are an integral part of human thought (Frankish, 2012); they contribute to conceiving the emotional response as a basis of the theory of meta-cognitive judgement, which predicts the activation of analytic processes (Thompson & Morsanyi, 2012). However, although implicit processing is losing the negative connotation that characterized it in the dual-process models, it is still subordinate to explicit processing, to which some researchers continue to exclusively attribute *cognitive decoupling* and *hypothesis testing*. Although this perspective recognizes the fundamental independence of the Type 1 and Type 2 processes (also through the role of pre-attentive contents in reflective thought), it still attributes the ability to conceive novelty to Type 2 processes and therefore to conscious thought (Evans, 2012a, 2012b; Evans & Stanovich, 2013). Even theories that support the explicit–implicit interaction (Hélie & Sun, 2010) assign the last word, the selective ability, to explicit thought; in this way, the solution search process is iterated until the outcome yields a solution. The contribution of implicit thought is almost obtained by chance, associatively, via spatial–temporal contiguity.

This phase of reflection has therefore identified the requisites for a creative process of reasoning in a conscious search, dependent on the working memory capacity or, more precisely, the capacity to manage more data and to perceive further representations of these data (take, for example, tests used to measure the working memory capacity and divergent thought). Yet again, rationality is conceived in quantitative terms and as such is measurable.

2.5 Insight Problem Solving: The Challenge of "Mysterious Events"

The legacies from the extra-psychological disciplines, such as logic, the theory of probability, and so on, have conditioned the psychology of reasoning and have had a negative impact in terms of originality and adequacy in psychological research. The research on problem solving, however, was not affected by these legacies. Given that, in a manner of speaking, any situation that involves thought processes can be considered a problem, solving or attempting to solve problems is the typical and, hence, general function of thought. This then is the scenario in which the question of the relationship between explicit and implicit thought can be reconsidered in a genuine psychological perspective.

According to the consolidated theoretical tradition that started with Simon and Newell's *Human Information Processing Theory* (Newell & Simon, 1972; Simon & Newell, 1971) and has continued through to the present day (Weisberg, 2015), the labyrinth is an appropriate abstract model for human reasoning. When faced with a problem, we move within the *problem space* just as in a labyrinth; we search for the right path, retrace our steps when we come up against a dead end, and sometimes even return to the starting point. We will form and apply a strategy of sorts, making a selective search in the problem space. The labyrinth model, which was devised for problems in which the difficulty lies in the calculation, the number of operations to be performed, and the quantity of data to be processed and remembered (e.g., the *Cryptoarithmetic* or the *Missionaries and Cannibals* problem), has also been used for particularly complex problems when a change of representation is necessary (Kaplan & Simon, 1990).

As I mentioned in Chapter 1, there are problems whose difficulty does not lie in the onerousness and complexity of the processing to be implemented, but in the capacity to consciously evaluate the merits of the various possible outcomes and to settle on a suitable strategy. The difficulty is the change in representation that does not appear to involve the working memory capacity, nor the conscious retrieval from memory of solutions or crucial parts of solutions to reproduce. It needs implicit processing—incubation—and for this reason it is a challenge to the current theories of thought, regarding the central role of consciousness, given that, in these cases, restructuring (or change in representation) is not performed consciously.

In Chapter 1, we have seen that there are situations in everyday life that involve an impasse; our analytical thought seems to fail us, and we just cannot see our way out of the dead end into which we have inadvertently strayed. We know we are in difficulty, but we have no idea what to do next. We have no strategy, and this time failure does not come to our aid with any information that could help us forge forward. In other words, we have come up against a deep impasse. These are situations that change our lives radically if we do find a solution: the situation, which a moment before seemed to lead nowhere, suddenly takes on a different meaning and is transformed into something completely new. The literature discusses studies in which these situations are reproduced as experimental paradigms of insight problem-solving.

These problems look deceptively simple (Metcalfe, 1986) in that they contain little in the way of data, and the number of operations required to arrive at the solution appears limited (for example, in the *Nine-dot* problem). However, they are not simple at all. Sometimes, taken in by this apparent simplicity, we are tempted to give the first answer that comes to mind, but it is almost always wrong, and from that point on, we are faced with a dead end, an impasse. Sometimes, we encounter it immediately, and the problem may appear impossible to solve, as in the *Study Window* problem.[7]

These problems may seem bizarre or constructed to provide an intellectual *divertissement*, but they are a paradigmatic case of human creativity in which intelligence is at its acme. Studying them provides a privileged route to understanding the processes underlying creative thought, scientific discovery, and innovation, and all situations in which the mind has to face something new. Insight problems have traditionally been considered tests of *giftedness* (see, for instance, Sternberg & Davidson, 1986). However, what type of intelligence is this, if it does not coincide with conscious analytical thought? (Macchi et al., 2006).

According to the Gestaltists, finding the solution to an insight problem is an example of creative, "productive thought". In addition to the reproductive activities of thought, there are processes that create, "produce" that which does not yet exist. This is characterized by a switch in direction that occurs together with the transformation of the problem or a change in our understanding of an essential relationship. The famous "Aha!" experience of genuine insight accompanies this change in representation, the *restructuring*.

2.6 Restructuring as Reinterpreting: The Emergence of Unconscious Analytic Thought

Incubation, which remains the core issue in the renewed interest in insight problems, is still a crucial question to be solved (Fleck & Weisberg, 2013; Gilhooly et al., 2013; Gilhooly et al., 2015; Macchi & Bagassi, 2012; Sio & Ormerod, 2009). A heterogeneous complex of unresolved critical issues underlies the research on this subject (for a review, see Sio & Ormerod, 2009) and still revolves around the controversy of the relationship between the conscious and unconscious layers of thought in the solution of insight problems.

However, the various mechanisms that have been proposed only describe the characteristics of the solution but do not explain the processes of reasoning that have made the solution possible (these include, for example, eliciting new information, selective forgetting, strategy switching, and relaxing self-imposed inappropriate constraints).

Moreover, a general characteristic that is common to the literature on insight problems in general, and in particular on the incubation–solution relationship, is the total absence of an analysis of the types of difficulty found in individual insight problems. In other words, what makes a difficult insight problem difficult? What kinds of difficulty are we facing? If it were possible to lay them out as a continuum in an ascending order of difficulty, we would see that, in fact, the difficulty correlates with the incubation, and this, in turn, with the possible discovery of the solution, thus allowing the restructuring process to occur. Therefore, incubation may offer a measure of the degree and type of difficulty of the problem, as it may vary in length, depending on the degree of gravity of the state of impasse (Macchi & Bagassi, 2012; Segal, 2004).

At this point, the question is what kind of unconscious intelligent thought operates during the incubation to solve these special problems? Through experiments in brain imaging, it is now possible to identify certain regions of the brain that contribute both to unconscious intuition and to the processing that follows. Jung-Beeman et al. (2004) found that creative intuition is the culmination of a series of transitional cerebral states that operate in different sites, such as the anterior cingulate of the prefrontal cortex and the temporal cortex of both hemispheres, and for different lengths of time. According to these authors, creative intuition is a delicate mental balancing act that requires periods of concentration from the brain but also moments in which the mind wanders and retraces its steps, in particular during the incubation period or when it comes up against a dead end.

Incubation is actually a necessary but not sufficient condition to reach the solution. It allows the process but does not guarantee success; however, if it is inhibited, for example, by compelling participants to verbalize, the solution process will be impeded. The study of the verbalization effect, indeed, offers a promising line of research to study the thought processes underlying the solution. In a recent study (Macchi & Bagassi, 2012), the "verbalization" procedure was adopted as an indirect method of investigating the kind of reasoning involved in two classical insight problems, the *Square and Parallelogram* (Wertheimer, 1925) and the *Pigs in a Pen* (Schooler et al., 1993); the investigation focused on whether concurrent serial verbalization would disrupt insight problem solving. The hypothesis was that correct solutions would be impaired if a serial verbalization procedure were to be adopted, as it would interfere with unconscious processing (incubation).[8]

According to our theoretical approach, language too has a nonreportable side in its implicit, unconscious dimension. In fact, language as a communicative device is achieved by a constant activity of disambiguation, by covert, implicit, unconscious processes, nonreportable in *serial* verbalization. While the participants in these studies were still exploring ways of discovering a new problem representation, they were not able to express consciously, and therefore to verbalize, their attempts to find the solution. Indeed, our data showed that serial "on-line" verbalization, compelling participants to "restless" verbalization, impairs reasoning in insight problem solving; this supports the hypothesis of the necessity of an incubation period during which the thinking processes involved are mainly unconscious. During this stage of wide-range searching, the solution still has to be found, and verbalization acts as a constraint, continuously forcing thought back to a conscious, explicit level and maintaining it in the impasse of the default representation. Conscious explicit reasoning elicited by verbalization clings to the default interpretation, thus impeding the search process, which is mainly unconscious and unreportable.[9]

Hence, we speculate that the creative act of restructuring implies high-level implicit thought, a sort of *unconscious analytic thought,* informed by relevance, where *analytic thought* is not to be understood in the sense of a gradual, step-by-step simplification of the difficulties in the given problem, but as the act of grasping the crucial characteristics of its structure.

The same data are seen in a different light, and new relations are found by exploring different interpretations, neither by exhaustive searches nor by abstractions, but by involving a relationship between the data that is most pertinent to the object of the problem. In this way, each stimulus takes on a different meaning with respect to the other elements and to the whole, contributing to a new representation of the problem, to the understanding of which it holistically concurs. Indeed, the original representation of the data changes when a new relation is discovered, giving rise to a gestalt, a different vision of the whole, which has a new meaning.

In other words, solving an insight problem—restructuring—means discovering a new perspective, a different sense to the existing relations. The interrelations between the elements of the default interpretation have to be loosened to perceive new possibilities, to grasp among many salient cues what is the most pertinent for the aim of the task, or in other words, to reach the insight. This type of process cuts across both conscious and unconscious thought. Recent experimental studies and theoretical models are now starting to consider the link between explicit and implicit information processing, in that continuous fluctuation of thought between the focus on the task, the data, and the explicit request, and then the withdrawal into an internal dimension, tempering the processing of the external stimuli to slip into an *internal train of thought* (stimulus-independent thought—*SIT*)[10] to permit evaluation of goals other than those that forced the thought into the impasse. This internal processing that takes place during incubation has a neural correlate in the "default mode network" (*DMN*; Raichle et al., 2001), that is, in a coordinate system of neural activities that continue in the absence of an external stimulus. Moreover, "the sets of major brain networks, and their decompositions into subnetworks, show close correspondence between the independent analyses of resting and activation brain dynamics" (Smith et al., 2009, p. 13040).[11]

It is interesting to note the close correspondence, as neural networks are activated, between the brain activity when focused on a task and that recorded during the resting state. The brain seems to work dynamically in different ways on the same task, at a conscious and nonconscious layer, as the substrate of a restless mind (Smallwood & Schooler, 2006; Smallwood et al., 2008).

During incubation, when an overall spreading activation of implicit, unconscious knowledge is under way, in the absence of any form of conscious control, *relevance constraint* allows multilayered thinking to discover the solution, as a result of the *restless mind wandering* between the implicit and the explicit levels in search of the relationship of the data that would finally offer an exit from the impasse.

Rather than abstracting from contextual and more specific elements, as in accordance with the logical approach, we exploit these elements, grasping the gist that provides the maximum of information in view of the aim (Levinson, 1995, 2013; Mercier & Sperber, 2011; Sperber & Wilson, 1995; Tomasello, 2009); we can indeed abstract, if this is the acknowledged purpose. Giving sense to something, *understanding*, does not derive from a summation of semantic units, each with a univocal, conventional meaning. These are simply inputs for that activity of thought, which is crucial to dynamically attributing the most relevant relationship to the recognized aim, in an inferential game that can result in interpretations that can be quite different from those originally intended. Depending on which (new) aim of the task is assumed, the relationship between the items of information changes; when the relationship is changed, the meaning that each element takes on changes too. Incredibly, the result is not cognitive chaos, but a sharper understanding!

2.7 The Interpretative Function of Language and Thought

The search for meaning, in view of an objective, characterizes every activity of the human cognitive system at all levels, from perception to language and to reasoning. We have called this characteristic, which cannot be eliminated from the human cognitive system, the *interpretative function.* It is extremely adaptive; instead of abstracting from the situation's contextual elements and the information it provides, this function exploits them to the maximum of their informative potential.

As syntax in itself does not give direct access to meaning, only based on the rules that discipline it, similarly, perceiving external reality is not just a question of registering stimuli; sensorial data have to be interpreted and organized, and relations created.

> When analyzing sensory experience, it is important to realize that our conscious sensations differ *qualitatively* from the physical properties of stimuli because, as Kant and the idealist predicted, the nervous system extracts only certain pieces of information from each stimulus while ignoring others. It then *interprets* this information within the constraints of the brain's intrinsic structure and previous experience. Thus, [...] sounds, words, music, [...] color, tones [...] are mental creations constructed by the brain out of sensory experience. They do not exist as such outside the brain.
>
> *(Gardner & Johnson, 2013, p. 455)*

Even when we use an object, the interpretative function comes into play, as Rizzolatti and Strick (2013) suggest:

> [...] objects usually have more than an affordance and may be grasped in several ways. How does the brain determine which is optimal? Behavioral analysis of grasping, for instance, reveals that nonvisual factors determine the choice of affordance and thus how an object will actually be grasped. These factors relate both to what the object is for and the individual's intent at that moment. [...]

> Thus, when an unconventional use of an object is intended, the prefrontal input could override the selection of *standard* affordances and select those affordances that are congruent with the individual's intention.
>
> *(pp. 421–422)*

Routine activities, such as recognizing a face, admiring a landscape, or looking at a painting, activities that seem to be nothing more than input from our visual capacity, are actually "analytical triumphs" made possible through our ability to grasp sensorial information holistically and attribute a meaning to it, so that in perceiving a scene, for example, we respond to a whole in which the relationship we establish between the individual parts is crucial.[12]

Our view, therefore, is that this *interpretative function* is a characteristic inherent to all reasoning processes and is an adaptive characteristic of the human cognitive system in general. Rather than abstracting from contextual elements, this function exploits their potential informativeness. It guarantees cognitive economy when meanings and relations are familiar, permitting recognition in a "blink of an eye" (see page 3).

This same process becomes much more arduous when meanings and relations are unfamiliar, obliging us to face the novel. When this happens, we have to come to terms with the fact that the usual, default interpretation will not work, and this is a necessary condition for exploring other ways of interpreting the situation. A restless, conscious and unconscious search for other possible relations between the parts and the whole ensues until everything falls into place and nothing is left unexplained, with an interpretative heuristic-type process.

In my view, the way the human cognitive system functions is recognizable, and it continuously occurs in the process involved in the understanding of an utterance. In fact, language and thought share a unitary cognitive activity, addressed by the interpretative function and grounded on common, universal interactive abilities: "the ability to make models of the other, to 'read' the intentions behind actions, to make rapid interactional moves in an ongoing sequence of actions structured at many levels" (Levinson, 1995, pp. 225–226).

This meta-representational ability always implies an analytic, multilayered reasoning, which works on a conscious and unconscious layer by processing explicit and implicit contents, presuppositions, and beliefs, but is always informed by relevance.[13] Tracing communicative behaviour back to its meaning is impossible to compute logically, given that what is said presupposes many plausible, possible premises; nevertheless, the absolute inferential miracle of communication continues to take place.

Sometimes, however, our initial interpretation does not support understanding, and misunderstanding is inevitable; as a result, sooner or later, we come up against an impasse. We are able to get out of this impasse by the default interpretation and looking for another one that is more pertinent to the situation, which helps us grasp the meaning that matches both the context and the speaker's intention; this requires continuous adjustments until all makes sense.

For instance, grasping a witty comment and understanding rhetorical figures of speech, such as irony and metaphor, are the result of an interpretative process adhering to or detracting from the explicit meaning as the case requires, often all in the twinkling of an eye.

This analysis allows us to consider insight problems as paradigmatic examples of *misunderstanding*, in that they arise from a *qui pro quo*, a glitch in communications. When insight problems are used in research, it could be said that the researcher sets a trap, more or less intentionally, inducing an interpretation that appears to be pertinent to the data and to the text; this interpretation is adopted more or less automatically because it has been validated by use. But in point of fact, the solution presupposes a different interpretation that is only theoretically possible, just as when someone makes a witty comment, playing on an unusual interpretation of a sentence.

Indeed, the solution—*restructuring*—is a *re*-interpretation of the relationship between the data and the aim of the task, a search for the appropriate meaning carried out at a deeper level, not by automaticity.

If this is true, then a disambiguant reformulation of the problem that eliminates the trap into which we as problem solvers have fallen should produce restructuring and the way to the solution.

2.8 Retrieved Psychological Wholeness in Creative Intelligence

Efficacious reformulation is like litmus paper, indirect evidence that the reasoning applied on an implicit level by those who found the solution during the incubation period consists of a highly pertinent disambiguation process performed by *unconscious analytical thought*. This is a mode of information processing practised by unconscious thought that differs to that traditionally characterized as associative-automatic; it is similar to the mode of conscious analytic thought that activates the function of *decoupling*, typical of hypothetical thinking.

Maria Bagassi and I found confirmation of the reformulation effect hypothesis in studies involving classical insight problems.[14] In their original version, these problems are true brain teasers, and the majority of our participants needed them to be reformulated to reach the solution; probably the few who were able to "see" the solution in the original formulation were endowed with a high level of cognitive ability of the type we call *interpretative talent*. It could be argued that they possessed a particular skill in perceiving the real aim of the task, *re*-interpreting all the informative elements of the situation, and recognizing the specific intent behind the problem, thus *re*-contextualizing the task rather than *de*-contextualizing it. This skill would activate an implicit, increasingly focused, selective search exploiting unconscious knowledge by a covert mind wandering that eludes the control of consciousness.

At this point, it could be speculated that the high-level cognitive abilities required for insight problem solving are the same as those needed to solve classic reasoning tasks. As I have previously discussed, there is a consolidated line of research that claims that the ability to abstract (*cognitive decoupling*) is a *sine qua non* condition for correct reasoning and for hypothesis testing (Stanovich & West, 1998, 2000). However, a number of interesting studies in the past ten years have shown that beliefs affect both intuitive and reflective reasoning (Verschueren & Schaeken, 2005) and that many cognitive biases are independent of cognitive abilities (Evans et al., 2007; Stanovich & West, 2008). The question of the negative effect of the content (beliefs, context) on abstract reasoning is once more a subject of debate.

Despite the significance of these findings, which show the almost ineradicable impact of beliefs on reasoning, in an updated version of dual-process theories, Evans and Stanovich (2013) consider reasoning abilities of the higher order to be still identified with hypothetical thought, which is supported by cognitive decoupling and highly correlated to working memory capacity. This all leads back to the conscious layer.

This issue can be explored by revisiting the classic studies conducted on probabilistic reasoning with people trained in logic and mathematics, inviting further speculation about the type of cognitive capabilities of those gifted people who solved the same tasks without such training. A first critical question emerges from an analysis of the results obtained by Tversky and Kahneman (1983) working with *informed* and even *sophisticated* subjects in the field of statistics. Paradoxically, when attempting to solve their well-known *Linda* problem, the majority of the participants in that study committed the so-called *conjunction fallacy*.
The problem is formulated as follows:

"Linda is 31 years old, single, outspoken, and very bright. She majored in philosophy. As a student, she was deeply concerned with issues of discrimination and social justice and also participated in anti-nuclear demonstrations". This is followed by eight statements to put in order of probability from the most probable to the least probable. These include:

"Linda is a bank teller.
Linda is a bank teller and is active in the feminist movement."

Almost all the participants considered that it was more probable that Linda would be a bank teller and a feminist. In my view, the fact that people trained in decoupling failed to recognize the inclusion rule, which is a relatively elementary logical rule, raises questions that need to be addressed.

To investigate this topic further, we conducted a further study with statistically sophisticated participants, the majority of whom solved the Bayesian *Medical Diagnosis* (MD) problem (66% of 35 participants) but were not able to solve the *Linda* problem, which is less computationally complex (only 14% of the participants did not commit the conjunction fallacy) (Macchi et al., 2019). These results suggest that these participants possessed skills that allowed them to grasp the informativeness of the data and the aim of the task in Bayesian problems but did not help them in focusing on the logical relations of the items in a *Linda*-type problem. In this case, the misleading contextualization of the task, which focused on a brief personality sketch that was completely irrelevant to the solution of the problem, hindered even statistically sophisticated participants from grasping the intention of the experimenter concerning the inclusion-class rule (see also Appendix to Chapter 5).

Analogously, in a recent experiment involving the *belief bias* and the Wason Selection Task (see Section 4.4), we found that the performance of subjects trained in logic did not differ significantly to that of naïve participants who had not received such training. The Wason Selection Task was used with abstract material: only 13% of the informed subjects gave the correct response, a very similar result to that obtained by the uninformed naive group (5%). Paradoxically, several subjects were able to execute the material implication truth table correctly but were not able to identify the only case that was crucial for falsifying the rule. The same paradoxical result occurred with the *Invalid-Believable* syllogism, showing that the influence of beliefs on reasoning is analogous in the two groups (correct responses, respectively, 10% and 4%).[15]

How can it be that subjects trained in logic or statistics had such difficulty with these tasks? One would have expected that their training would have facilitated them in decontextualizing and in abstracting, but this was not the case. In the absence of specific indications, they reasoned in the same manner as the naïve group and used the conversational rules of natural language to interpret. However, when the instructions expressly required an evaluation of the validity of the syllogism according to the criteria of logic, both the statistically trained subjects and the logically naïve group "limited" their evaluation simply to the logical validity, reducing the belief bias (respectively, 66% and 41%). Even in the paradigmatic Wason *Selection Task*, once the unidirectional sense of the material implication had been clarified simply by adding the phrase "but not vice-versa" to the rule, the percentage of correct responses increased dramatically to over 50% in both groups.

For the problem to be solved correctly, the interpretation of the task requires a "particularized" formulation (see Grice, 1975; Levinson, 1995, 2000). In the absence of an appropriate translation from the logical to the natural code or of an adequate signalling of the code used, it is only to be expected that the understanding of the syllogism as a discourse proposed by the researcher (and consequently the response to it) is based on discursive-conversational rules that do not necessarily correspond to the logical code to which the researcher is referring (even taking into account that the particular knowledge of the informed subjects may compensate for the lack of indication or "translation").

We could further speculate that the few who gave the correct answer to the *Linda* problem, the Wason Selection Task, or the syllogisms had a particular aptitude for grasping the intention of the researcher and the aim of the task rather than the ability to decouple from contents and contexts. In doing so, they revealed a form of "interactional intelligence" (Levinson, 1995).

We suggest that cognitive decoupling could be seen as a form of sophisticated interpretative ability that permits the subject to decouple, but to decouple from the default interpretation and identify that which is most pertinent to the task at hand.

Cognitive decoupling assumes continuous "fluctuations in focus between external stimuli ['on task' thoughts] and stimulus-independent thought" (Schooler et al., 2011), which is quite different from a process of distraction. It would appear, therefore, that the crucial element in decoupling is the qualitative dimension. What distinguishes a quirky representation from a representation that, even if it is abstract, still provides an explanation of the phenomenon? In my opinion, it is pertinence, as pertinence exercises a constraint, in this case, a qualitative constraint, on our thought processing. This view would appear to converge with the *Global Workspace* theory proposed by Baars (1989) and its neuronal correlates of consciousness (Dehaene & Changeux, 2011; Kandel, 2012), as well as with the concept of the restless mind, now known as DMN, which supports the idea that a coordinated system of neural processes continues to process the external stimulus while decoupling from it.

At this point in the debate, what has changed in our concept of human rationality? It could be said that, despite the quantitative constraints that characterize our thought processes, we are subtly adaptive to novelty because we use default strategies and construct new ones as required, always applying heuristic procedures to grapple with problems. Although heuristics are judged to be *weak methods* and do not guarantee success in problem solving, heuristics are the only means available, as exhaustive searching does not characterize human reasoning.

What happens when the difficulty does not lie in the computational onerousness of the problem but in the need for a new representation? In this case, our mind, free from the quantitative limits of consciousness, fluctuates between the conscious and unconscious levels in a wide-range analytical search. Paradoxically, it is due to these constraints that analytical thought can achieve scientific discovery and create poetry. As psychoanalysis predicted, unconscious processes appear to underlie almost every aspect of our conscious existence, promoting a creative and imaginative dimension capable of *re*-describing reality, revealing previously unknown dimensions.

Notes

1 This chapter draws substantially from a previously published version in *Cognitive Unconscious and Human Rationality*, MIT Press, 2016, edited by L. Macchi, M. Bagassi, R. Viale. The material has been revised and adapted for the purposes of this volume, with the consent of the co-author.

2 I am citing here the reflections of Paolo Bozzi, philosopher and psychologist of the Gaetano Kanizsa-Vittorio Benussi school.

3 The following considerations on negation come from many illuminating conversations with Giuseppe Mosconi.

4 Quand le mot accède au discours, avec sa richesse sémantique, tous nos mots étant polysémiques a quelque degré, l'univocité ou la plurivocité de notre discours n'est pas l'œuvre des mots, mais des contextes. Dans le cas du discours univoque, c'est-à-dire du discours qui ne tolère qu'une signification, c'est la tâche du contexte d'occulter la richesse sémantique des mots, de la réduire, en établissant ce que M. Greimas appelle une isotopie, c'est-à-dire un plan de référence, une thématique, une topique identique pour tous les mots de la phrase. ... Au lieu de cribler une dimension de sens, le contexte en laisse passer plusieurs, voire en consolide plusieurs, qui courent ensemble à la manière des textes superposés d'un palimpseste ... plus d'une interprétation est alors justifiée par la structure d'un discours qui donne permission aux multiples dimensions du sens de se réaliser en même temps. Bref le langage est en fête (Ricoeur, 1969; pp. 94, 95).

5 Ricoeur, 1969; English Translation, 1974: p. 94.

6 Modus Ponens (p=>q, p, therefore q) and Modus Tollens (p=>q, non q, therefore non p).

7 Macchi and Bagassi (2014, 2015).

8 This procedure is notoriously favourable for the solution of procedural problems (Ericsson & Simon, 1984).

9 With their Global Neuronal Workspace (GNW) model, Dehaene and Changeux (2011) supplied indirect evidence of these processes through the convergence of neuroimaging and neurophysiological data. Verbalization would impede axons located at a distance from GNW neurons to transmit specific neural representations to several other processors at cerebral level. Global transmission allows information to be processed more efficiently (because it is no longer confined to a subset of nonconscious circuits but can be flexibly shared by many cortical processors) and eventually to be verbally reported (because these processors include those involved in formulating verbal messages).

10 Stimulus-independent thought occupies almost 50% of waking thought (Killingsworth & Gilbert, 2010, p. 932; Schooler et al., 2011).

11 "In cognitive neuroscience, researchers have examined neural processes that occur in the absence of an explicit task (such as in the resting state) in part due to an observation of a coordinated system (including the posterior parietal cingulate, the medial prefrontal cortex (medial PFC) and the medial temporal lobes), now known as the 'default mode network' (DMN) that exhibits neural activity that often continues in the absence of an external task" (Schooler et al., 2011, p. 319).

12 "Human neuroimaging methods and electrophysiological recordings during conscious access, under a broad variety of paradigms, consistently reveal a late amplification of relevant sensory activity, long-distance cortico-cortical synchronization at beta and gamma frequencies, and 'ignition' of a large-scale pre-fronto-parietal network" (Dehaene & Changeux, 2011, p. 209).

13 The hypothesis that interpretation uses the conscious-unconscious level of thought is supported by the studies on selective spatial attention in cluttered displays of Dehaene and Changeux (2011). According to these authors, the gate to *the conscious access* (working memory) is always the outcome of a *nonconscious selection*, "[...] separation of relevant versus irrelevant information, based on its saliency or relevance to current goals [...] that regulates which information reaches conscious processing" (Dehaene & Changeux, 2011, pp. 201, 202).

14 Macchi and Bagassi (2012, 2015, 2019).

15 Valid and credible syllogisms: "All animals are mortal. All human beings are animals. All human beings are mortals". Invalid and non-credible syllogisms: "All flowers wilt. All roses wilt. All roses are flowers". Wason Selection Task: Control: "If there is a vowel on one side of the card, there is an even number on the other side". Experimental version: "If there is a vowel on one side of the card, there is an even number on the other side, but not vice-versa".

3

SOLVING INSIGHT PROBLEMS

The Cognitive Unconscious and the "Mystery" of the Creative Solution

> A problem arises when a human being has a goal but does not know how to go about reaching it. Whenever action alone is not sufficient to go from the status quo to the desired situation, then there must be recourse to thinking.
>
> Karl Duncker

3.1 Introduction

A problem arises when a human being who is motivated to obtain a goal is unable to reach it with automated or mechanical means, in other words, by resorting to instinctive action or behaviour that has been learned. In line with Duncker's view (1945), problem solving takes on a central role in thought, even identifying with it. Solving problems (or attempting to solve them) would therefore appear to be a typical, and therefore general, function of thought.

Sometimes the difficulty of a problem lies in the calculations, the number of operations involved, and the quantity of data to be processed and remembered. However, we have seen in the preceding chapters that there are problems where the difficulty is not to be found in the complexity of the processes or the ability to weigh up the advantages of various possible outcomes and the strategies to be adopted to reach one or the other; in these cases, the difficulty lies in a *change of representation*. This change would not appear to affect either the capacity of the working memory or the conscious recovery from memory of solutions or crucial parts of processes to be replicated (see Text Box 3.1).

Our research on problem solving was focused on a particular type of problem, known as insight problems, that I will discuss in depth in this chapter. As mentioned

DOI: 10.4324/9781003680895-3

before, the solution to these problems can only be found through a process of restructuring, which changes our perception, sometimes even radically, of the relationships between the facts, the images, or the words that form the problem.

As we saw in Chapter 1, some insight problems, such as the *Study Window* problem, seem impossible to solve, but others appear easy, as there are very few data and operations involved. Sometimes, beguiled by this deceptive simplicity, we tend to give the first answer that comes to mind, which is inevitably wrong, and the explicit thought ends up in a dead-end.

The following problem is a good example of this; in fact, 68% of the participants in our research gave an incorrect answer:

> *The Ties Problem*
> Peter and John have the same number of ties. Peter gives John five of his ties. How many more ties than Peter does John have now?

In this chapter, I will explain how our research reveals that these types of problems represent a real challenge to the traditional theories of the dual processes that have characterized the study of thought to a great extent.

As we saw in the Introduction, the general mechanism that we will discuss from the experimental evidence is the interpretative function of thought, the ineliminable tendency to search for data relationships, continuously attempting to attribute a meaning to what our senses perceive, exploiting both types of thought: the explicit, conscious, and the implicit, submerged. The latter type in particular appears to be able to function in parallel, to simultaneously move in various directions searching for pertinence and relevance. This allows us to change perspective and overcome "cognitive obstacles". The concept of unconscious thought that emerges is that of a thought which is always oriented to an adaptive goal, far removed from what is now the traditional concept of System 1 of the dual process theories (see page 9; Text Box 3.2).

In this sense, the concept of the interpretative function and cognitive unconscious that I am proposing is intended to extend beyond a concept that on the one hand is focused on the social-communicative dimension of thought (from Grice's conversational maxims to Mercier and Sperber's argumentative theory of reasoning) and on the other, on the perceptual functioning of Gestaltist tradition, in which language does not appear to be considered as a relevant factor.

While I accept that both these concepts have a genuinely psychological vision that can at least partially overcome the dualistic theories of mind, I still consider that it is possible to find a unique and common dynamic that is transversal to perception, language, and thought, and the experiments I will illustrate in the following paragraphs appear to support this view.

If we think back to the *pareidolia* discussed in Chapter 1, i.e., the tendency to impose forms of known natural or artificial objects on random forms, we can see that here, in contrast to the theory of conversational pragmatics, our tendency to attribute a meaning, to interpret even where is no communicative intent, indicates that this is a transversal mechanism developed in adaptive mode that extends from the perceptual to the purely communicative sphere.

On the other hand, even beyond the Gestalt vision, the fact that in numerous experiments on classic insight problems, it is evident that reformulating the text while maintaining the data unaltered also acts on the perceptual organization of the image, facilitating or impeding the perception and, consequently, also the restructuring (see the *Square and the Parallelogram*), reveals the inevitable joint venture of thought that exploits every information channel in an unceasing effort to attribute a meaning to reality (in this case, the reality of the problem).

The next step is to examine the phenomenological approach adopted by the Gestaltists to study insight problems, successively developed by psychorhetoric, which extended the research to the interpretative function, involving not only perception but also language, and proposed a review of the concept of *restructuring* as *reinterpretation*. This extension led Maria Bagassi and me to explore a special form of unconscious thought that is responsible for insight problem solving; we coined a name for it, which is rather an oxymoron, *unconscious analytical thought* (Macchi & Bagassi, 2012).

Three branches of experimental studies—the reformulation of texts, the use of verbalization, and setting incubation tasks—were used to investigate and support these hypotheses.

3.1.1 Three Branches of Experimental Studies: Reformulation, Verbalization, and Incubation

In a first series of experiments, we *reformulated* the text of a number of classic insight problems without however changing the original data, so as to work on the *misunderstanding*, the erroneous interpretation of the original text of the problem (and the diagram, when present). In all these experiments, the reformulation resulted in a disentangling of the knot of the problem and a significant increase in the number of problems solved. The fact that this linguistic reformulation also had a positive effect on how the diagram was perceived would indicate that the interpretative function permeates language and perception to the extent that modifying the text results in a relaxing of the restrictions of the Gestalt norms (the Gestalt theory does not attribute this type of power to language), revealing the involvement of the implicit layer of language, perception, and thought functioning that goes far beyond the merely literal layer of the text of the problem.

In the second series of experiments, we used *forced verbalization* during problem solving, a technique that obliges the participants to remain on the conscious level of information processing, which has a detrimental effect on their ability to find the solution. As this did not occur for procedural and non-insight problems, it is indirect evidence that the process of solving insight problems, which involves facing something completely new and unknown, is prevalently unconscious.

The third and final series of experiments focused on *incubation*, the fundamental phase in overcoming an impasse, with an attempt to throw light on the "mysterious events" and on the type of unconscious thought that comes into play during this phase.

Studies of creative problem solving (from insight problems to scientific discoveries) have often asserted that after several unsuccessful attempts, laying the problem aside for a while can result in spontaneous processing of new ideas that lead to the solution (Gilhooly et al., 2015; Jung-Beeman et al., 2004; Schooler et al., 2011). Giorgio Parisi, who was awarded the Nobel prize for physics in 2021, when describing the birth of new ideas, ascribed a preeminent role to unconscious thought and the importance of setting aside a difficult problem to let his thoughts settle, and return to it later with a fresh mind, and so find the solution (2024). Wallas (1926) was the first to define this temporary interruption of attention to the problem as the "incubation phase".

We carried out a cycle of experiments to define the type of unconscious thought activated by creative or insight problems, by setting the participants unrelated tasks to solve during the incubation phase. These tasks differed in the degree of attention and cognitive effort required, ranging from free-style drawing to simple sums, to crosswords and sudoku. The results showed that the tasks that had the most effect on the activity of problem-solving (i.e., that generated the highest percentage of correct solutions, in the shortest amount of time) were simple arithmetic tasks (sums with one or more digits, 8+9, 10+12, 133+142, …). As this type of task requires constant attention, it keeps the incubation process at the unconscious level, but being a mechanical computational process, it leaves cognitive resources free to work on the insight problem on the unconscious level.

This is the type of cognitive unconscious that comes to light when we suddenly remember the elusive word that was on the "tip of the tongue", after a period of thinking of or doing something else. And it is the same process that leads us to solve insight problems more easily and rapidly after working on completely different tasks; a cognitive unconscious that works while our attentive (or cognitive) focus is occupied elsewhere, as long as our cognitive resources are not totally involved in intensive activities.

3.2 Problem Forming and Problem Solving

If we ask ourselves how the problem is formed in our mind, and not just how to solve it, and if we try to establish not only how we can deal with the difficulty but also how we came to be involved in it, we can explore distinctions and analogies within what we can call *problem forming*. Above all, a problem-forming theory must explain not only how the problem is formed and how the solution is reached but also how the solution can elude us; it must provide an explanation of the correct answer, and with the same cognitive mechanism, explain why an answer is incorrect. Identifying how a problem is represented (problem *forming*) should contribute to understanding how the solution is reached (problem *solving*), but most importantly, to understanding where the difficulty lies.

As mentioned before, insight problems constitute a challenge to today's theories of thought, given the centrality they attribute to consciousness, as the change in representation (or restructuring) does not seem to occur consciously. Conscious thought is not able to throw light on the solution process, and if the solution is grasped, it has all the characteristics of a "mysterious event" (see also pages 24 and 25).

Although these problems may seem to be puzzles thought up as a form of intellectual *divertissement,* as we said in Chapter 2, they are in fact paradigmatic examples of human creativity, in which our intelligence comes to grips creatively with a situation that is completely new. Studying these problems offers an opportunity to understand the processes underlying thought, discovery, innovation, and the capacity of the mind to deal with something new, or in a new way. There can be no doubt that there is a form of intelligence underlying the ability to solve insight problems, but what kind of intelligence is it if, as will be demonstrated with an analysis of various research studies, it does not coincide with conscious analytical thought?

Particularly over the last few years, more and more interest has been shown in the mystery of insight and creativity, so I think it is important to go back to the phenomenological approach of the Gestaltists as a starting point from which to examine this phenomenon.

For Gestaltists like Duncker, the study of productive thought, of insight problem solving, and the study of perception was a testing ground for a theory of how the mind functions that was psychologically authentic and phenomenologically based, as it was not derived from non-psychological normative theories external to psychology (such as logic, the theory of probability, or the maximization of expected utility, depending on the field of the study of thought involved) which of necessity required different explanations from the authentically psychological. The Gestaltist theory of isomorphism between the functioning and the structure of the mind, which was partly taken up again in *embodied cognition*, in fact represented the conviction of being in the presence of fundamental characteristics of the functioning of our cognitive system.

3.2.1 The Phenomenological Gestalt Approach to the Study of Thought through Insight Problem Solving

In the past, the most important contributions to the study of insight problem solving were those of the Gestaltist theorists, Maier and Wertheimer, in the 1920s, followed by Karl Duncker in the late 1930s. Psychologists who follow the Gestalt philosophy consider that finding the solution to a problem is an example of "productive thought", a mental activity that is not merely a reproduction of the past but has the capacity to create that which does not yet exist, realizing new relationships.

A problem creates an imbalance or a tension in the cognitive field; there are two ways of reestablishing the balance, either by guessing randomly or by reaching the solution by intelligent means. The research carried out by the Gestaltist psychologists focused on establishing the phenomenology of these productive processes and the characteristics that distinguish them from those that are merely reproductive, individuating the conditions that facilitate and those that impede them up to the point of localizing the decisive moments of the process when the "light of understanding" dawns (the *Aha* moment).

The Gestaltists tackled the problem of explaining insight problem-solving starting from their studies of perception, recognizing the contribution of the subjective dimension in perceptual organization and, in more general terms, in thought itself.

Demonized as the mind had been by the materialist approach, and having eluded all attempts at measurement and quantification particularly by the Gestaltists, it was once more enhanced with all the dignity of an object worthy of scientific study; the essence of mental activity did not lie in the mere registration of an aggregate of stimuli, but rather in the ability to understand how these related to each other. In studies on visual perception, which was the Gestaltists' original area of research, visual input was identified on the basis of knowledge and then enhanced by inferential operations initiated by principles of relevance and coherence or estimates of probability. Cognitive integrations and interpolations are not isolated cases; they are the rule in our daily interactions with the world around us. Processes of *amodal completion* are those that best allow us to highlight the analogies that exist between seeing and thinking (see Figure 3.1).

There are frequently cases of genuine perceptual problem solving, of decisions taken by reasoning, evaluating the available cues in the light of knowledge and context. One such case is when we recognize a person at a considerable distance, when the briefest glimpse is interpreted to the best of our ability.

From its early years, psychology was dominated by elementaristic conceptions, inherited from philosophical associationism and the relative conviction that the study of the contents of conscience and behaviour necessarily implied that they be

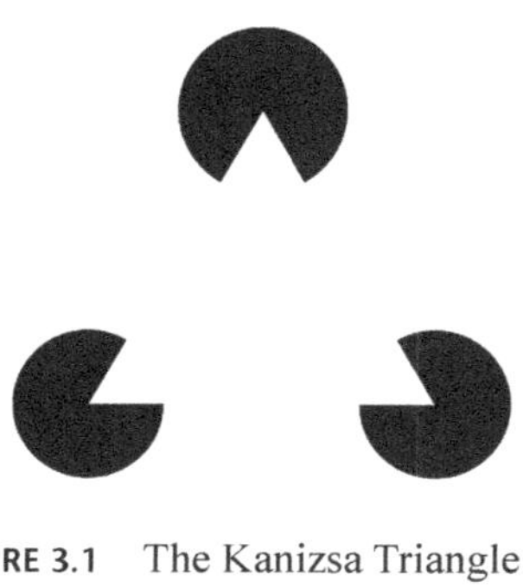

FIGURE 3.1 The Kanizsa Triangle.

broken down into their elementary parts, i.e., pure sensations, acts of elementary volition, reflexes, and so on. This approach revealed the hope of the founders of scientific psychology that applying the procedures of the natural sciences to the investigation of issues regarding the mind would have endowed the discipline with the dignity of science. Unfortunately, the analytic method adopted rendered psychological investigation sterile; it fell victim to a futile hunt for elements which, in turn, did not permit the reconstruction of the real complexity of the psychic functions in seeing, thinking, and problem solving.

Of the critical reactions to this situation, the Gestaltists were particularly outstanding for the vivacity with which they attacked the doctrine of the elements. Their phenomenological approach, if transposed from a merely descriptive level to the functioning of a hypothetic psychic activity on which representations are based, leads to the concept of "productive thought".

> What determines, for example, a certain melody are the relationships between the sounds. The phenomenal "melody" fact is independent of its phenomenal constituents, sounds.
>
> *(Kanizsa, 1980, pp. 12–13)*

For the Gestaltists, in every perception, there is a moment—the elementary and raw sensory datum—and, at the same time, another moment, realized by an act of production with which our conscience builds objects of a higher order, the structures. As Benussi stated regarding optical illusions (Figure 3.2) and the possibility of counteracting their effects, the only way this can be done is to forcedly focus attention on the individual sensorial elements, thus impeding the natural tendency to organize these elements into a totality.

We are particularly aware of this "act of production" when looking at ambiguous sketches such as the vase that can also be seen as two human profiles (Figure 3.3) or the face of an elderly woman that can also be seen as the profile of a young girl (Figure 3.4), to cite two of the best known. When we switch from one structure to the other, we have the perception of the ongoing "act of production".

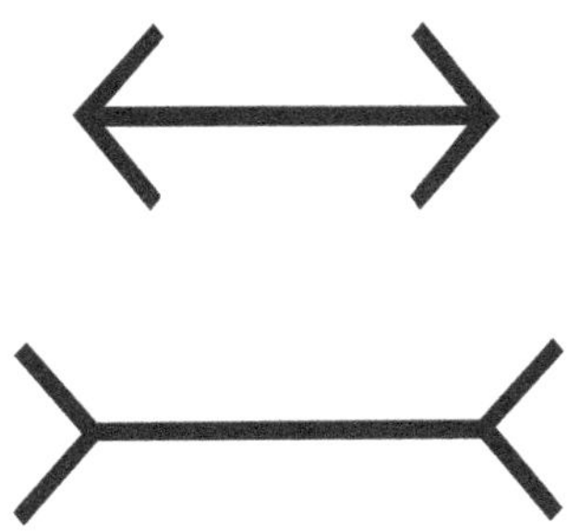

FIGURE 3.2 The Müller-Lyer illusion.

FIGURE 3.3 The figure-ground illusion.

FIGURE 3.4 The old woman–young girl illusion.

When the interpretation process establishes new links between the elements in a scene (*re-structuring*) or allows the imagination to see the object that is either hidden or covered and only partially visible (without anything truly perceptual being added), this is when the process of integration or mental completion, which generally is part of an interpretative process, takes over.

The Gestaltists considered that the concept of restructuring, to which they attributed a central role in visual perception, was also central in problem-solving. They did not often use the term "problem solving", preferring "productive thinking", as they were convinced that thinking is not merely a *re*production of the past, a *re*emergence of ideas, images, behaviours that already existed; in addition to the *re*productive activities of thought, there are processes that create and produce that which does not yet exist. The Gestalt psychologists focused their research on establishing the *phenomenology* of these productive processes and the characteristics that distinguish them from the reproductive processes; they studied the conditions that give rise to these processes or allow them to arise, and those which, on the contrary, impede them, and the decisive moments in the process when light dawns and understanding is reached. The famous "Aha!" experience of genuine insight accompanies this change in representation, the restructuring. This is characterized by a switch in direction that occurs together with the transformation of the problem or a change in our understanding of an essential relationship. It is an analytic search that "recognizes the primacy of the whole, and its dynamic nature, and its decisive role in articulating its parts" (Wertheimer, 1985, pp. 24, 25).

Thirty years later, the reaction of cognitivism to behaviourism had many analogies with the Gestaltists' reaction to associationism, to the point where Herbert Simon could, in a certain sense, be considered the heir of the second generation of the Gestalt theory, of which Karl Duncker was the most eminent scholar.

Both Duncker and Simon adopted a descriptive-phenomenological approach to problem solving (Duncker in the study of insight problem solving and Simon in his work on procedural problems; see Text Box 3.1). The boundaries (*bounded rationality*) are indeed characteristics, but characteristics without negative connotations. Just as the Gestaltists studied the principles of perceptual organization of reality, which sometimes are present when a problem comes into being, so, in Simon's theory, the basic characteristics of the human cognitive system are those that generally lead to the solution of a problem. This phenomenological approach, which is in no way conditioned by an ideal functioning model borrowed from extra-psychological normative theories, allows us to think of heuristics as expressions of our intelligence. According to Duncker, the problem solver never blunders along blindly, seeking the solution by trial and error; he proceeds by applying *heuristic strategies* and *methods*:

> the whole process, from the original setting of the problem to the final solution, appears as a series of more or less concrete proposals ... But however primitive they may be, this one thing is certain, that they cannot be discussed in terms of *meaningless, blind, trial-and-error reactions*.
>
> *(Duncker, 1945, p. 3)*

We can therefore affirm that "*insistent*" analyses of the situation, especially the endeavour to meaningfully modify appropriate elements of the goal, must be part of the essence of a solution reached by thought. Such relatively general procedures can be defined as "*heuristic methods of thinking*" (Duncker, 1945, pp. 20–21). Given that often an exhaustive search of all the possible ways to solve a problem is just not viable for a human being, the use of heuristics reduces the problem-solving process to manageable proportions.

As we will see in Chapter 5, this changes radically when considering the *psychology of reasoning*, and in particular Kahneman and Tversky's research program "Heuristics and Biases" on probability judgement. In their work, they attribute a quite different definition to heuristics, in spite of the fact that the authors explicitly state that they have taken the concept from Simon (and therefore indirectly from Duncker). Not only are their procedures simplified or abbreviated, but they are subject to their own criteria and mechanisms, completely foreign to the logic of the problem being dealt with and the decision to be taken. It is no longer a case of procedures that "do not guarantee finding the solution" due to their economy, but of procedures that will lead to the correct solution of the problem purely by chance.

> There are situations in which people assess the frequency of a class or the probability of an event by the ease with which instances or occurrences can be brought to mind ... However, availability is affected by factors other than frequency and probability. Consequently, the reliance on availability leads to predictable biases.
>
> *(Kahneman et al., 1982, p. 11)*

While for Duncker and Simon, simplification is the identification of what is salient and crucial, for Kahneman and Tversky it involves "neglect" of crucial information for probability judgement. As we have seen, a direct consequence of this theoretical framework of the psychology of reasoning is the proliferation of the *bias*, i.e., an intrinsic tendency to error of the human cognitive system.

3.2.2 Limits of the Cognitive Approach to the Explanation of Insight Problem Solving

I must however point out the limits of Simon's cognitive approach vis-à-vis insight problem-solving. He explains that in insight and procedural problems, the difficulty lies in a sort of "quantitative unmanageability", which can be caused by the excessive, "infinite" number of possible representations of the problem. I think it is more accurate to say that this way of dealing with the change in the problem space—the change in representation—describes what happens when a person solves an insight problem, rather than explaining the process leading to the solution. In fact, it is still not clear what makes people struggling with a problem concentrate on certain points they are convinced will lead them out of the impasse rather than on others. Keeping his research on the conscious level to simulate the solution process in the calculator, Simon conserves the key theoretical constructs of his theory, such as the concepts of research and process in which passages can always be reconstructed, and in which the autonoetic consciousness and deliberative connotation are of the essence (Kaplan & Simon, 1990). Although he raises the question of what actually determines the *switch*, Simon does not find the answers to his crucial questions and so ends up with a sort of explanatory circularity. In fact, wanting to decide to change the representation of the problem is not enough to resolve an insight problem.

The emphasis he places on the observability and recordability of each phase of the solution process which generates a typical protocol that can be simulated in a calculator, translates into a sort of bias when the study is dealing with insight problems; this is because, as the studies carried by the Gestaltists show, the solution to these problems is characterized by discontinuity and the transition from the impasse to the solution remains a mystery to the person trying to solve the problem. In addition, the solution can dawn after a period of incubation that can vary from minutes to weeks, during which the problem solver withdraws into himself. Not even the Gestaltists have described the hidden activity that occurs during the incubation period, and this point has been strongly criticized by cognitivists. Simon himself wrote:

> One serious difficulty in testing Gestalt theories is that the concepts that play central roles in these theories are not often defined in terms of operations or measurements, but are usually assumed to be directly understood and observable ... If we put aside our nostalgia for a rich, but largely non-operational, vocabulary, and when we focus instead on the observable processes of thought, we see that we are much further advanced in understanding these processes ... the phenomena of insight are fully visible in the behavior of today's computers when they are programmed appropriately to simulate human thinking.
>
> *(Simon, 1986, pp. 242, 254)*

When the *Weltanschauung* of cognitivism influenced psychology, and confidence in the possibility of making testable models for the functioning of the mind was at its highest, Simon wrote:

> The only solution to this problem is the hard solution. Psychology is now taking the road taken earlier by other sciences: it is introducing essential formalisms to describe and explain its phenomena. Natural language formulations of the phenomena of human thinking did not yield explanations of what was going on; formulations in information-processing languages appear to be yielding such explanations.
>
> *(Simon & Newell, 1971, p. 148)*

In that particular moment in history (1986), to keep faith with this "hard" methodology whose aim is to measure—observe—every step of the problem-solving process, Simon inevitably had to exclude insight problems as solving them requires a change in representation from his Human Information Processing research as he considered them "ill defined" for the task environment (Hayes & Simon, 1974; Newell & Simon, 1972; Simon & Hayes, 1976). He continued to maintain that "the *programmability* of the theories is the guarantor of their operationality, an *iron-clad insurance* against admitting *magical entities* into the head" (Simon, 1979). When he decided to work on these problems with Kaplan in 1990, he once again adopted the "hard" methodology used for non-insight problems, all the while embracing the reality of the Gestaltists' change in representation. In this approach, the difficulty for the person battling with the problem continues to be quantitative, and his question regarding how the change of representation comes about continues to remain unanswered if this scientific perspective focused on conscious thought is adopted.

3.2.3 Gestaltists and Cognitivists in Current Explanations: The Special Process versus Business-as-Usual

The *Special Process* view to insight problem solving borrowed certain aspects from the Gestaltists, particularly the centrality of processes that elude the control of consciousness through widespread activation of unconscious knowledge; these processes are qualitatively different from those involved in the solution of procedural problems (Jung-Beeman et al., 2004; Ollinger et al., 2008; Schooler et al., 1993). As maintained by the Gestalt theorists, the process that leads to the discovery of the solution through restructuring is mainly unconscious, is characterized by a period of incubation, and can only be described a posteriori (Gilhooly et al., 2010). However, these processes are characteristically unconscious, which has led to them being defined as automatic, spontaneous associations due to their spatiotemporal and chance contiguity (Ash & Wiley, 2006; Fleck, 2008; Schooler et al., 1993), and in this, they deviate from the Gestaltist concept of restructuring.

The other approach cited in the title of this section, *Business-as-usual*, is close to Simon's cognitivism and argues that restructuring in insight problem solving is serial and gradual, with the solution being sought step-by-step, applying a rule-based and conscious reasoning. In this way, just as when finding the way out of a labyrinth, dead ends are abandoned, and new directions attempted until the solution is reached at the end of a path, through a gradual simplification of the problem (Chronicle et al., 2004; Fleck & Weisberg, 2004; MacGregor et al., 2001; Perkins, 1981; Weisberg, 2006). This consolidated theoretical tradition maintains that conscious analytic thought can reorganize data if the initial representation fails to work, extracting information from the failure and searching for a new strategy. Weisberg rather optimistically maintained that when restructuring fails and the problem solver is up against an impasse, "a new representation of the problem can emerge [...]". However, this model does not explain how the change in representation occurs, nor the conditions that must be present for the transformation to take place. In fact, reaching an impasse and failing to solve the problem do not necessarily require changing direction or transforming data to reach a new strategy; the business-as-usual approach and the recent attempts of integrated theories (Weisberg, 2015) seem to be affected by these limits.[1]

This focus on different processes that can both be present in the solution of insight problems has legitimated the existence of these two approaches that emphasize processes that are gradually conscious rather than unconscious associative.

In my view, in fact, on the one hand, the solution process cannot be attributed exclusively to reflective, conscious thinking, since it results mainly from a covert and unconscious mind-wandering process (Baird et al., 2012; Macchi & Bagassi, 2012; Smallwood & Schooler, 2006). It implies an almost unaware restructuring process, preceded by a period of incubation which may vary in length, depending on the degree of gravity of the state of impasse[2] (Gilhooly et al., 2013; Segal, 2004).

On the other hand, however, if the solution is mainly the outcome of implicit processes, these cannot be exclusively associative, and even less so, automatic, given the correlation between insight problem solving and high cognitive abilities (take, for example, those problems which generate an almost unsurmountable impasse, such as the *Study Window* problem that we have mentioned earlier).

In this chapter, we will return to, and further discuss, the hypothesis that insight problems originate from a glitch in communication, from a *misunderstanding*, and that the impasse depends on the failure of the default interpretation. Seen in this light, the restructuring process has to be understood as a form of re-interpretation that includes implicit and explicit processing. In fact, the restructuring cannot be entirely supported by explicit thought, whose resources are tied up in fixing and predefined interpretations or *Einstellung*. The impasse, the difficulty in finding the solution, would activate an implicit search that is increasingly oriented to the objective of the problem. The result is a re-interpretation, a re-reading of the available data in the light of the text of the problem and vice versa.

3.3 Restructuring as *Reinterpretation*: From the Theory of the Dual Code to the Emergence of Unconscious Analytical Thought

I will now explore the hypothesis—mentioned in Chapter 2—that insight problems arise from a misunderstanding, a *qui pro quo* as Mosconi (1990) liked to define it, that is to be attributed to the tendency to adopt familiar and/or natural terms to interpret the text of the problem, the default interpretation. According to this view, adopting the default interpretation of the text of the problem leads to a misunderstanding, and this, sooner or later, lands the problem solver in an impasse. In the case of research, it could be said that the researcher more or less intentionally sets a trap, inducing the problem solver to apply an interpretation that appears pertinent to the data, the text, and the problem; this interpretation is adopted more or less automatically as it has been proven effective in the past. Actually, the solution requires a different interpretation that is only theoretically possible, just as when a witticism or a metaphor plays on an unusual interpretation of a phrase or an expression. The default interpretation fails, and the problem solver finds themselves in a dead-end, in other words, the impasse.

This impasse can be overcome by ignoring the more common interpretation and making continual adjustments until everything makes sense. Restructuring is just the reinterpretation of the relations between the facts given and the purpose of a task, in a search for the appropriate meaning. In this scenario, disambiguating the problem by eliminating traps and *qui pro quo* results in restructuring and clears the way towards the solution of the problem (see page 31).

The hypothesis regarding the effect of reformulating the problem was introduced and formulated by Mosconi (1974; 1990; see "Dual code"—Text Box 3.3) and was subsequently confirmed by studies using classic insight problems (Macchi & Bagassi, 2012, 2015; Gilhooly et al., 2018). In their original versions, these problems are real brainteasers, and the majority of participants needed them to be reformulated in order to find the solution ("Insight problems versus procedural problems"—Text Box 3.1 page 70).

An effective reformulation that leads problem-solvers to a successful outcome is indirect proof that the reasoning process, which takes place during the mostly implicit incubation period, consists of a disambiguation process. This is a different way of processing information that we have defined as *unconscious analytic thought* (see Chapter 2); non-associative-automatic, it would activate something similar to decoupling, the "disassociation" function that is typical of hypothetic thought, and— as I mentioned on page 31—is what happens when we interpret a witticism or a metaphor that is not immediately comprehensible. When this happens, we have to accept that the normal default interpretation will not work; this is a necessary condition for exploring alternative methods of interpreting the situation. This is followed by an unceasing search, on both the conscious and the unconscious levels, for other possible relations between the parts and the whole until everything falls into place and nothing remains unexplained. The process of understanding an utterance mirrors the functioning of the human cognitive system but is easier to analyse. Language and thought share a unitary cognitive activity, guided by the interpretative function and based on universal interactive abilities. These meta-representative capabilities always implicate a multi-level analytical reasoning that functions on both conscious and unconscious levels, always driven by the search for pertinence. A communicative act cannot be traced back to its meaning by a univocal process, because the utterance presupposes an infinite number of possible intentional premises; however, the inferential "miracle" of communication continues to take place (see also pages 30 and 31).

As explained in Chapter 2 (see pages 28 and 29), it can justifiably be hypothesized that the creative act of restructuring rests on high-level implicit thought, which must not be interpreted as a gradual step-by-step simplification of the problem but rather as the act of implicitly understanding the crucial characteristics of its structure. Seen under a different light, the same data take on different relations which, when they are seen to be more pertinent to the objective, attribute a new meaning to all the elements involved and to the totality. Restructuring—the process of solving insight problems—involves abandoning the default interpretation and moving on to a new perspective; it means finding a different sense compared to that created by the previous relations among the elements of the problem, due to a transversal process that continues to function unconsciously and in the absence of external stimulus.

3.3.1 When a Misunderstanding Challenges Our Thought: Reformulation of Problems and Restructuring

Here, I will illustrate some experiments that support our hypothesis. First of all, Maria Bagassi and I examined the *Study Window* problem, which, as we saw in Chapter 1, is particularly challenging and originates from an almost unsurmountable misunderstanding. In this case, the procedural analytic process is not an option. However, even a problem that seems unsolvable can be solved if the formulation is modified to overcome the *misunderstanding*.

3.3.1.1 The Study Window Problem (Mosconi & D'Urso, 1974)

This problem cannot be solved analytically; the misunderstanding and the consequent impasse seem unsurmountable. A period of incubation and radical restructuring of the problem are necessary to find the solution.[3] Let's take another look at the text of the problem and its graphic representation (see Figure 3.5):

> The study window measures 1 meter in height and 1 meter wide. The owner decides to enlarge it and calls in a workman. He instructs the man to double the area of the window without changing its shape, so that it still measures 1 meter by 1 meter. The workman carried out the commission. How did he do it?

When we discussed this problem in the Introduction (see page 10), we saw how important spatial orientation is in the perception of shapes (Mach, 1914). Two

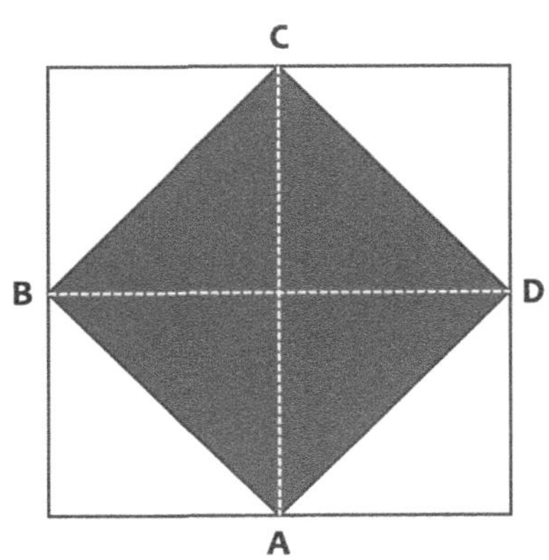

FIGURE 3.5 The solution.

identical forms seen from different angles assume a different phenomenal identity, and this leads to the *misunderstanding* that on which this problem is based. All the participants in the study we carried out in 2014[4] declared that it was impossible to solve.

We decided to see what would happen if we inverted the problem and found that it gave less trouble:

> The study window measures 1 meter in height and 1 meter wide. The owner decides to reduce it and calls in a workman. He instructs the man to halve the area of the window without changing its shape, so that it still measures 1 meter by 1 meter. The workman carried out the commission. How did he do it?

And in fact, 30% of the participants were able to solve this version of the problem. They started from the traditional representation of the square—ABCD in Figure 3.6—and searched for the solution, trying to respect the required height and width of the window, and inevitably changing the orientation of the internal square. This time, the height and width are the diagonals of the square instead of its sides (base and height).

We used yet another version, in which the orientation was not a mandatory attribute of the shape:

> The study window measures one meter in height and one meter wide. The owner decides to make it smaller and calls in a workman. He instructs the man to halve the area of the window: the workman can change the orientation of the window, but not its shape and it must still measure one meter by one meter. The workman carries out the commission. How did he do it?

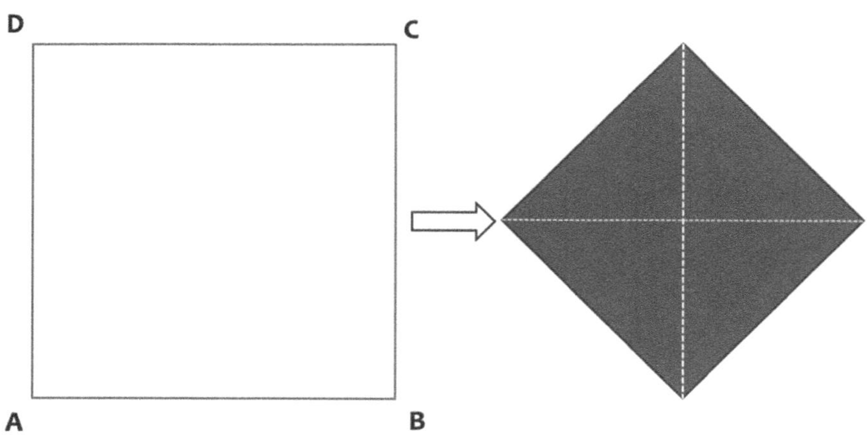

FIGURE 3.6 The solution of the inverted version.

In this version of the experiment, the majority of the participants (66%) found the solution immediately (see Figure 3.6). This confirms the hypothesis that the origin of the *misunderstanding* is an inappropriate representation of the relation between the orthogonal orientation of the square and its geometric shape.

We believe that the difficulties encountered in the next problem, the *Ties* problem that we saw earlier in the chapter, can also be attributed to a *misunderstanding.* This problem may look banal, but actually the simultaneous activation and reciprocal interference of complex cognitive processes frequently lead to error and impede the solution, as happened to 68% of our participants.

3.3.1.2 The Ties Problem (Mosconi & D'Urso, 1974)

Peter and John have the same number of ties. Peter gives John five of his ties. How many more ties than Peter does John have now?

The correct answer is obviously ten, but it seems that it is not really so obvious because it was given by only one third of the participants, while the remaining two thirds gave the wrong answer, five, which became the dominant answer (Macchi & Bagassi, 2019).

If we consider the text of the problem from the point of view of the information it transmits explicitly (i.e., what is literally said), we can see that it only theoretically supplies all the information necessary to reach the solution: (a) Peter and John possess the same number of ties; (b) Peter gives John five of his ties. In fact, people do tend to give the wrong answer. From the spontaneous explanations offered by the participants in our study who reached the wrong conclusion, it emerged that they only took into consideration the increase in the number of John's ties, neglecting to factor in the decrease in the number of Peter's ties. The following are two typical examples: "Peter gives John five ties, John has five ties more than Peter, the five that Peter gave him" and "In the beginning they both had the same number of ties, so if Peter gives John five of his, then John should have five more than Peter".

There was also a slightly different version, in which the participants took into consideration the decrease in the number of Peter's ties as well as the increase in the number of John's: "It all revolves around five ties, that move from one to the other", or "There are these five ties that pass from one to the other, so one of them has five ties more and one has five ties less" but then they reach the conclusion that "John has five ties more because Peter gave him them".

The participants who answered "10" almost always used a numeric example to justify their response or to find the correct solution after a number of failed attempts. Paradoxically, many of these participants accepted that the problem can have two solutions, one being "five ties" obtained without considering a concrete number of ties to start with, and "ten ties" obtained through numeric reasoning. So one participant, after replying "five more ties", applied the numeric reasoning and found a difference of ten ties: "Good! I think that five is more exact; this guy has five more ties, and that's it!". Another participant provided an explanation on the abstract level, "I'd be more inclined to go for another formula that gives 'five' as the answer".

Initially, approximately half of the participants who answered "five" had refused to answer at all, claiming that "we don't know the number of ties Peter and John had to start with and so we cannot say how many more ties John has than Peter", or even, "John has five ties more, and Peter has five ties less and we can't know anything more because we are missing a piece of information."

It must be said that even prior to this "operational" difficulty, the text of the problem is abstruse because the quantity by which Peter's ties diminish remains implicit (-5). This causes the misunderstanding that if the quantity of ties that passes from Peter to John is five, the difference that this causes is *only* five ties: if Peter gives John five ties, how can John have ten more ties than Peter?

This is just like saying, if a person is five years older than another, this other is five years younger, and the difference is still five years, which is perfectly acceptable in this case, but not in the case of Peter and John's ties!

The difficulty of the problem lies in the discrepancy in the number of ties that pass from Peter to John and the bidirectional effect that this quantity produces with its movement. The solution implies a restructuring of the text, "Peter gives John five of his ties (and so loses five)". This is the reasoning adopted by the participants who gave the correct answer "ten".

Given this difficulty, we created a new version of the problem, clarifying the decrease in the number of Peter's ties:

> Peter and John have the same number of ties. Peter loses five ties and John finds them. How many ties more than Peter does John have now?

In spite of this modification, the results were more or less the same as for the original version: 17% of the participants gave the correct answer and 75% a wrong answer.

Examining the spontaneous justifications, we found that the participants who answered "five" gave a similar motivation to that given by their counterparts in the original version. Just an example: "Peter loses five ties, John finds them, so John has five more ties than Peter".

The decrease in the number of ties in Peter's possession has not yet been perceived, and the discrepancy between the number of ties lost and the double effect that the movement that this quantity determines continues.

So we created a third version in which the number of ties that Peter lost has nothing to do with the number of ties acquired by John. The ties are different, and so they are not perceived as being in any way linked in order to neutralize the underlying perceptual-conceptual factor.

> Peter and John have the same number of ties. Peter loses five ties and John buys five new ties. How many more ties than Peter does John have now?

In this version, 74% of the participants gave the correct answer "ten" and only 13% "five". The participants who gave the correct answer provided the following motivation, "Peter loses five ties, John still has the five ties that Peter lost; he buys another five, that makes ten", stating that they had "added the five that John bought to the five that Peter lost", thus confirming the efficacy of the experimental manipulation.

The satisfactory results obtained with this version of the problem are not to be attributed to the use of two different verbs, which in fact proved inefficacious in Version 2, but to the separation and consequent differentiation of the two quantities (John has five more new ties). In this case, the increase in the number of John's ties and the decrease in the number of Peter's are seen as simultaneous and distinct, and their combined effect is not identified with either Peter or John but is seen as being equal to the sum of +5 and -5 in absolute terms.

The hypothesis of the reformulation effect has been confirmed in other classic insight problems such as Wertheimer's *Square and the Parallelogram*, Schooler, Ohlsson and Brooks' *Pigs in a Pen*, Frederick's *Bat and Ball*, as well in studies Maria Bagassi and I did in 2012 and 2015, all of which showed a drastic increase in the number of solutions as can be seen in Table 3.1.

In their original versions these problems are real brainteasers, and the majority of the people participating in these studies needed a reformulation of the text in order to reach the solution. The original and reformulated experimental versions of the *Pigs in a Pen* and the *Bat and Ball* problems are provided below, with explanations and a comparison of the texts.

3.3.1.3 The Pigs in a Pen Problem

Nine pigs are kept in a square pen. Build two more square enclosures so that each pig is in a pen by itself (Figure 3.7).

The difficulty here lies in how the problem is interpreted: nine pigs are to be placed each in its own pen, but only two more square enclosures can be added. The common mistake here is the interpretation given to the shape of the pens, i.e., nine pigs are to be placed each in its own "square" pen.

TABLE 3.1 Percentage of Correct Solutions Obtained from the Experimental Versions Compared to the Original Version

	Original Version (%)	*Experimental Version (%)*
Study Window	0	66
The Ties	32	74
The Square and the Parallelogram	19	80
Pigs in a Pen	38	87
Bat and Ball	10	90

FIGURE 3.7 The Pigs in a Pen problem.

This interpretation is supported by our traditional representation of the square, in its favoured, orthogonal frame of reference. According to our hypothesis, the preference for this shape is fixed by the text of the problem, which implies that the pens in which the piglets are to be individually enclosed must be square in shape. In addition, the term "enclosure" leads us to assume, erroneously, that it must take the form of a square, while the task, on the contrary, only requires that each pig be enclosed in a pen by itself (Figure 3.8).

So we created an experimental version, reformulating the problem by eliminating the word "enclosure" and so avoiding the activation of the implicit inference *that the pens are necessarily square*:

Nine pigs are kept in a square pen. Build two more squares so that each pig is on its own.

There was a significant difference between the results obtained from the experimental version and those using the original version. The experimental version yielded 87% correct answers (20 out of 23), while only 38% of the participants who attempted to solve the original version gave the correct answer (8 out of 25).

These findings were replicated in the *Square and Parallelogram* problem, in which 80% of the participants gave the correct answer in the experimental version, with most of them adopting the "two triangles" solution. In the original version, only 19% gave the correct response, and of these, only two gave the "two triangles" solution.

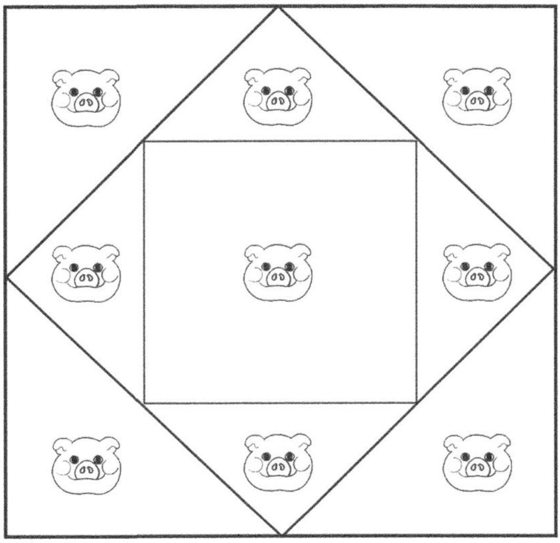

FIGURE 3.8 The solution.

The formulation of the experimental versions was more pertinent to what was required from the task and assisted the participants in interpreting the perceptual stimuli as a function of the solution. The relevance of the text and the re-interpretation of goal-oriented perceptual stimuli were shaped through a dynamic interplay of interpretations (Table 3.1).

Max Wertheimer, a first-generation Gestaltist, proposed a paradigmatic example of insight problem solution (Figure 3.9), i.e., the restructuring of the cognitive field in problems that can only be solved if there has been a change in perspective, that is, in the representation of the problem. The difficulty, in fact, lies mainly in the possibility that such a change can take place.

The Problem of the Square and the Parallelogram (Wertheimer, 1945)

Given that AB = a and DG = b, find the sum of the areas of square ABCD and parallelogram EBGD. (Correct answers: 19%)

Reformulated version (Macchi & Bagassi, 2012).

Given that AB = a and DG = b, find the sum of the areas of the two partially overlapping figures.

(Correct answers: 80%)

As the area of the square is practically a given, the difficulty lies in calculating the area of the parallelogram. This requires that the problem solver recognizes

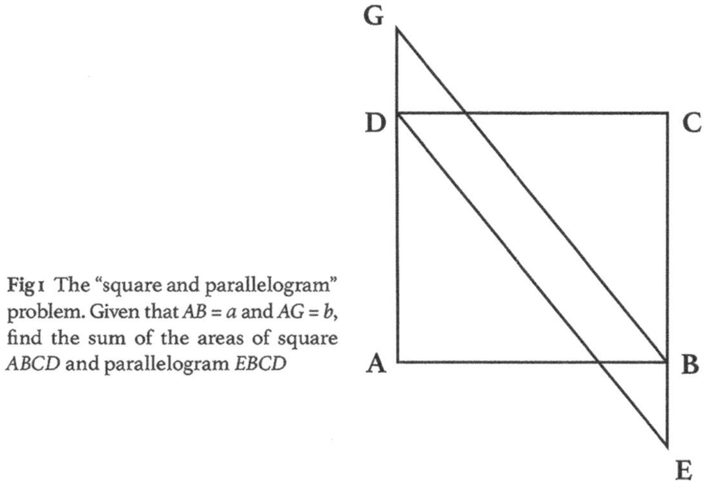

FIGURE 3.9 The Problem of the Square and the Parallelogram.

that the side of the square is also the height of the parallelogram, a reorganization of the data that is not easy to do, as it means that an element presented with a particular function (side) takes on a new function (height). The restructuring therefore consists in grasping different relations and functions between the parts of the problem, which in this case is the apparent lack of a datum (the height of the parallelogram).

Typically, problem solvers find the problem difficult and fail to see that *a* is also the height of the parallelogram EBGD (measured with respect to its shorter base DG). They tend to determine its area with onerous and futile calculations,[5] while the solution can be reached in a much more direct way with a structural reorganization, consisting of restructuring the entire shape into two partially overlapping triangles ABG and ECD. At that point, it becomes clear that the sum of these triangles is none other than the combined area of the Square and the Parallelogram, i.e., (a+ b) x a. Considering the triangles, the area is calculated as twice the base times the height divided by two. In this case, the restructuring is impeded by the resistance posed by the square, a very strong Gestalt perception, which must disappear in the new organization, giving way to the two triangles that in the original perception had no phenomenal existence. These transformations are not only perceptual however; indeed as Kanizsa so elegantly put it: "The acquisition of new functions, the emergence of new aspects, and the reorganization of figures all occur as a function of the problem itself, under the influence of a field generated by the problem in relation to the given premises"[6] and more generally, I would say, with the text of the problem.

If we consider the problem as a whole, we can see that the reference to a square and a parallelogram in the text fixes the privileged interpretation of the perceptual stimuli even more, according to those principles of perceptual organization thoroughly studied in the Gestalt theory. It firmly sets the calculation of the area on the sum of the two specific shapes dealt with in the text, while the problem actually requires that the total area of the shape be calculated, in whatever way it is organized, as the sum of two rectangular triangles, or the area of only one rectangle, just as the sum of a square and a parallelogram. The connections between the parts of the figure change in function of the question posed by the problem, which in turn changes with the restructuring, as it is no longer limited to the two geometrical figures named in the text of the problem.

3.3.2 Formulation Effect and Cognitive Abilities—The Bat and Ball Problem

The final paradigmatic example of misunderstanding in insight problems that I will analyse here is the well-known *Bat and Ball* problem:

A bat and a ball cost $1.10 in total. The bat costs $ 1.00 more than the ball. How much does the ball cost?

Of course, the answer that immediately comes to mind is 10 cents, but this cannot be correct as the problem states that the bat costs $ 1.00 *more* than the ball, which means that buying them together, the cost would be $ 1.20. For the total cost to be $ 1.10 the ball can only cost 5 cents, which is the correct answer.

The physiognomics of numbers and the apparent plausibility of the cost are traditionally considered responsible for this kind of error (Frederick, 2005; Kahneman, 2003). These factors aside, in our view, if the rhetorical structure of the text of the problem is analysed, the question as formulated concerns the ball only, implying that the cost of the bat is already known. Indeed, the way a problem is formulated provides the key to how it is to be interpreted, and, generally speaking, this is true for every discourse. The data provided, therefore, is interpreted in the light of the question. And so, "*The bat costs $ 1.00 more than*" becomes "*The bat costs $ 1.00*", by leaving out "*more than*". With this in mind, we reformulated the text as follows to eliminate any temptation to apply this misleading simplification:

Experimental Version
A bat and a ball cost $1.10 in total. The bat costs $ 1.00 more than the ball. Find the cost of the bat and of the ball.

This time, the increase in the number of correct answers was significant: 90% of the participants gave a correct answer, compared to only 10% in the original version. Reformulated, the question expresses the real aim of the task, which is to find the cost of both items and does not favour the "short circuit" of considering the cost of the bat as being $1.00, ignoring "more than".

It remains to be verified if the participants who gave the correct response in the original version have a higher-level of cognitive reflective ability compared to the "intuitive" respondents, which is how the difference in performance on the original and the experimental versions has generally been interpreted in the literature. We think it can be explained as a particular kind of reflective ability, due to which the task is interpreted in the light of the context and not abstracting from it. Resolving the difficulty which the problem implicates requires a high level of pragmatic competence to disambiguate the text more than a high level of abstract reasoning; in fact, with a simple intervention on the pragmatic level only, maintaining the number physiognomics and the plausible costs unvaried, the problem becomes a trivial arithmetical task.

3.4 Verbalization and Incubation: The Emergence of the Cognitive Unconscious

3.4.1 Verbalization

I will now return to a fundamental concept that I have touched upon in Chapter 2. Incubation is an essential, though not exclusive, condition for solving an insight problem. As we have seen earlier, it facilitates the process but does not guarantee that the outcome will be successful. That said, however, if incubation is inhibited, forcing the participants to remain on the level of conscious processing, reaching the solution will be hindered. In 2012, Maria Bagassi and I adopted a verbalization procedure to indirectly investigate the typologies of reasoning involved in two classic insight problems: *The Square and the Parallelogram* and the *Pigs in a Pen*. This research focused on the fact that serial verbalization contemporaneously with the solution process hinders the solution as it interferes with the unconscious processing by impeding incubation and maintaining the process on a conscious level. The results showed a significant decrease in the percentage of correct answers in the verbalization mode. As we have seen, when the participants in these experiments were still trying to understand how to create a new representation of the problem, they were not able to consciously describe their attempts at solving the problem. The data led us to the conclusion that serial verbalization (online) interferes with the solution process for insight problems, as it blocks the problem solver on the conscious level of information processing. This supports the hypothesis that a period of incubation is necessary, in which the thought processes involved are predominantly unconscious. During the wide-range search phase, the solution is still out of reach, and the verbalization seems to act as a restriction, continuously forcing thought to remain on the conscious and explicit level, keeping it in the impasse of the initial representation. The conscious, explicit reasoning, activated by the verbalization, remains attached to the default interpretation, impeding a deeper search (see pages 26, 27 and 28).

We will now take a more detailed look at the experiment; we adopted the revised formulation of the *Square and Parallelogram* and the *Pigs in a Pen* problems that had produced high percentages of correct answers in the previous experiments to see if serial verbalization during the incubation process interferes with solving insight problems. We hypothesized that the high percentage of solutions would diminish if serial verbalization were to be required during the experiment.

The participants were instructed to think out loud while attempting to solve the problem. As foreseen in the standard think-aloud procedure (Ericsson & Simon, 1984), they were asked to speak aloud every time there was a period of silence that lasted longer than 15 seconds, while attempting not to interrupt the solving process. They worked on both problems until either they found the solution or gave up of their own accord.

The results confirmed our hypothesis; a significantly lower success rate was recorded for the participants working in the *verbalization* condition compared to those in the *non-verbalization* condition, i.e., the percentage of the participants who solved the insight problems while recounting how they were doing it was lower than that of the control subjects who were not required to verbalize. In the *Square and the Parallelogram* problem, the percentage of correct answers in the *non-verbalization* condition was 80%, while only 37% of the participants who were asked to verbalize managed to give the correct answer. The difference was greater in the *Pigs in a Pen* problem, with only 12% of correct answers from the participants in the *verbalization* condition, and 87% from those in the *non-verbalization* condition. There was a significant difference in the performance on the *verbalization* and *non-verbalization* conditions, and similar results were obtained with other insight problems (Macchi et al., 2025).

The data show that online serial verbalization disrupts reasoning in insight problem solving, supporting two hypotheses: first, that the thought processes involved in problems of this type are neither serial nor gradual and the procedure being adopted to solve the problem cannot be articulated while ongoing; second, verbalization acts as an anchor, locking reasoning to the default interpretation of the problem and so impeding the search, which is partly unconscious and so cannot be verbalized (see also pages 27 to 29).

Schooler and colleagues (1993) also studied the negative effect of language on insight problem-solving, suggesting that language can compromise the solution and therefore thought. They sustain that "insight involves processes that are distinct from language" (p. 180), given the non-verbal characteristic of perceptual processes. This point of view follows the traditional dichotomous theory, which asserts that language, considered extraneous to higher-level cognitive processes involved in the search for the solution, would disrupt the thought involved in the processing of perceptual stimuli. We believe that unconscious thought uses the same interpretative processes as language in a unitary cognitive activity; therefore, in the experiment with the reformulation of the problem, the solution involves implicit, unconscious (perceptual and verbal) processes and activates appropriate reasoning processes.

In fact, this is not language as such; it is rather a particular type of (serial) verbalization that imposes a form of step-by-step thinking that confines the thought in a conscious path, disrupting a more or less unconscious interpretative search.

TABLE 3.2 Problem

	Non-verbalization (%)	*Verbalization (%)*
The Square and the Parallelogram	80	37
Pigs in a Pen	87	12

Unlike Schooler and colleagues (1993), we maintain that language too has a layer that cannot be reportable, in its inevitable pragmatic dimension, which is its main characteristic. Language is constantly involved in disambiguating through hidden, implicit, and unconscious processes that cannot be reported in the serial verbalization (Table 3.2).[7]

3.4.2 *Incubation Tasks and Unconscious Analytic Thought*

After a year fixated on using platinum for the filaments of his light bulbs, Thomas Edison suddenly thought of using carbon. After many fruitless attempts to find a method of distributing ink uniformly on his printing machine, Gutenberg had an illumination, an insight, watching the press in wine making, a similar process. The role of the incubation phase that preludes the change of representation, the discovery, in the solution process continues to remain a central question, even now in the renewed interest in insight problems (Fleck & Weisberg, 2013; Gilhooly et al., 2018; Bagassi & Macchi, 2016). Research on the subject is based on a heterogeneous complex of unsolved critical points (see Sio & Ormerod, 2009 for a review) and still revolves around the controversial activity of unconscious thought in the solution process. However, as we have already mentioned, the various incubation mechanisms that have been proposed seem to describe the characteristics of the solution (including selective forgetting, change of strategy, and the relaxing of self-imposed restrictions), rather than explaining the reasoning processes that have made the solution possible (see also page 26).

A classic laboratory paradigm, the *Delayed Incubation Paradigm* (Segal, 2004) has frequently been used to investigate the effects of incubation. In the incubation condition, the participants work on an insight problem for a certain period of time, known as the *preparation period* (the duration of which depends on the difficulty of the problem), after which they are assigned another task or activity for a predetermined period, called the *incubation period.* In the final phase, the *post-incubation period*, the participants return to the insight problem, which was left pending. The effect of the incubation period on the solution process is verified by comparing the results obtained with those of another group of participants working on the same problem, for a period of time equal to the sum of the *preparation period* and the *post-incubation* period. Various tasks can be set during the incubation period, mainly differing in the levels of cognitive effort required. Tasks with high cognitive requirements include mental rotation, countdown, memory tests, and their aim is to completely occupy the participant's attention and processing ability; low cognitive demand tasks, such as drawing, do not require that all the participant's conscious attention be focused on the incubation task.

Several authors have proposed different hypotheses to explain the effects of incubation on solving insight problems. The *selective forgetting hypothesis* (Simon, 1966; Smith & Blankenship, 1991) contends that for the participant to elaborate a "new view" of the problem, it is necessary to actuate a radical attention shift from the insight problem. This should have the effect of weakening the activation of irrelevant concepts that cause fixation and block the solution process. According to the *fatigue dissipation hypothesis* (Seifert et al., 1995), the pause simply allows the problem-solver to recover from the mental fatigue of attempting to solve the problem, while Segal (2004) introduced the *attention withdrawal hypothesis* which maintains that no processes take place during the incubation period as its sole function is to distract attention from the problem, unhitching the mind from the initial erroneous *organizing principle.* Following the theory sustained by the Gestalt psychologists, Segal maintains that problem solvers tend to fixate on a false assumption, but after having come up against an impasse, they usually shift their attention from the erroneous representation of the problem. Problem solvers need an organizing principle in order to have a mental representation of the problem, because it connects all the elements, so the task can be understood and processed. However, if the organizing principle is misleading, the solution cannot be reached. Once the problem solver is free of the misleading hypothesis, the elements of the problem can be restructured in a configuration that fits the solution. At this point, Segal introduces the *returning-act hypothesis*: when the problem solver returns to the problem after the period of incubation, it is unlikely that they will adopt the initial organizing assumption because it did not function earlier. They will therefore tend to apply a correct organizing assumption to the elements of the problem to construct a complete structure that will allow them to find the solution. However, what leads the problem solver to the organization remains a mystery.

In addition to this, as Sio and Ormerod (2009) brought to light in their meta-analytic review, the results obtained from the experimental studies they analysed confirm that, in general, the incubation period has a positive effect, but they also indicate procedural moderators, such as the nature of the problem, the types of *incubation task*, and the duration of the incubation, that influence the problem-solving processes during this phase of suspended activity on the task. Indeed, it is interesting to note again that if it were possible to arrange the problems along a continuum in ascending order of difficulty, we would see that the difficulty is correlated with the degree of incubation implicated, and this, in turn, is correlated with the possible discovery of the solution (see page 27). It follows, therefore, that the incubation can offer a measure of the degree and type of difficulty inherent to the problem, as it can vary in length according to the "gravity" of the impasse (Macchi & Bagassi, 2012).

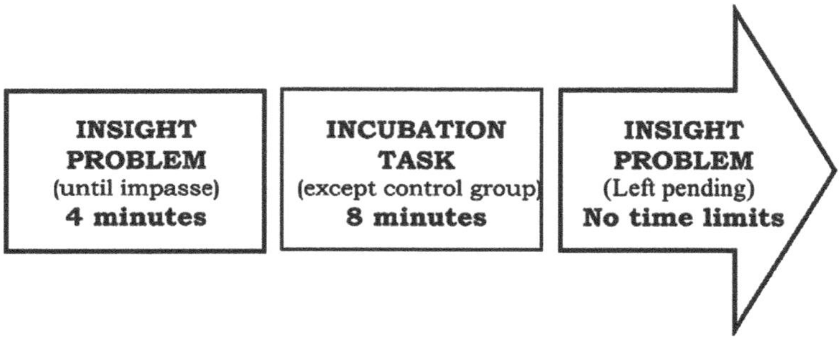

FIGURE 3.10 Timeline structure of the incubation task.

In a recent study (Caravona & Macchi, 2023), we compared three incubation tasks, differing in nature and degree of difficulty, in relation to the level of attention and degree of cognitive effort required. Figure 3.10 illustrates how the study was structured:

In ascending order, the least demanding task was "draw a castle" or "the landscape of your dreams". This task is defined as *non-demanding* because it does not appear to require focused attention or cognitive effort, allowing the processing of the problem to continue at conscious level, also while the incubation task is being tackled, until an effective process of unconscious thought can start.

The next task in ascending order of difficulty was a routine mathematical calculation which involved adding two three-digit numbers as follows:

123 + 254 = _____
472 + 226 = _____
253 + 143 = _____
[…]

or single-digit numbers in a second experiment:

3 + 4 = ___
2 + 7 = ___
5 – 2 = ___
[…]

This task was considered *low-demanding*, as while it does require constant attention, it is sufficiently routine in nature as not to exhaust the cognitive resources needed to work in parallel on an insight problem during incubation on the unconscious level.[8]

The third and final task, a difficult crossword puzzle, was considered to be *high-demanding* as, in addition to requiring constant attention, it also needs a considerable amount of cognitive effort. We hypothesized that, as this task needs more cognitive resources, it would impede unconscious processing of the insight problem.

The results obtained from these experiments suggest that working on a low-demanding task, such as carrying out arithmetical additions during the incubation phase, improves reaching the solution of an insight problem. In particular, a significant difference in the percentage of correct solutions was noted only between this condition and the control group (46.8% *vs.* 14.6%, respectively); in addition, the post-incubation time required to reach the solution was shorter in this condition (Figure 3.11).

In the other two experimental conditions, the percentages of successful solutions did not differ substantially from those of the control group. This would seem, therefore, to support the hypothesis that the insight problem solution process is at least partially unconscious, as otherwise it could not develop in parallel to the execution of the arithmetical sums. A high-demanding task, such as the crossword, on the other hand, would appear to impede the solution as it does not leave sufficient cognitive resources free to process the insight problem.

The solution would also appear to be impeded by the non-demanding task (castle or landscape drawing), as it does not interrupt the conscious processing of the insight problem during incubation. We ran another study in which we compared tasks of increasing difficulty, equivalent to those described above, but

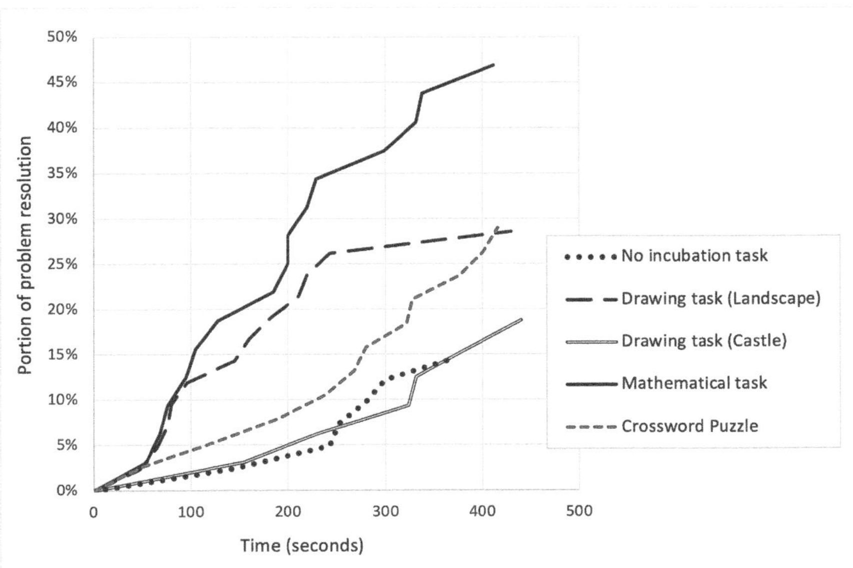

FIGURE 3.11 Percentage of correct responses compared to problem response times.

all of the same nature (three mathematical tasks), which produced results in the same direction, indicating that the incubation effect does not depend on the nature of the task but on its characteristics (high attentional focus and low cognitive effort) that permit at least a partially unconscious processing of the solution to the problem.

3.4.3 Unconscious Analytic Thought Requires Available Cognitive Resources: The Execution of Simple Arithmetic Tasks Increases the Solution of Insight Problems

As stated above, our data suggest that an incubation task requiring attention but only a very low or moderate expenditure of cognitive resources (high attentional focus and low cognitive effort) allows the appropriate problem-solving process to develop. In fact, when comparing tasks with different levels of demandingness, the best results were obtained when the participants were set low-demanding incubation tasks (simple arithmetical tasks) that still required attentional focus. In accordance with the unconscious analytic thought theory (UAT), the insight problem-solving process seems to indicate an unconscious processing of the solution; the mathematical tasks executed during the incubation period absorbed the participants' attentional resources, leaving no opportunity for conscious attempts to solve the insight problem while working on them, but, given the mechanical nature of the simple algorithmic procedure, these tasks did not exhaust the participants' unconscious cognitive resources that therefore remained available to activate the unconscious analytic thought.

The analytic nature of this process can also be deduced from the fact that no incubation effect was found when the high-demanding incubation tasks (the crossword or the sudoku of a later experiment) were used, indicating that the participants' performance suffered when the task was too demanding. This suggests that the level of difficulty of these incubation tasks exhausts the participants' cognitive resources at both the conscious and the unconscious level, which would seem to be indirect proof of an unconscious thought processing that is not only associative by chance, but also analytic. In fact, unlike merely associative processes, the unconscious analytic process requires resources that are not available when they are being used by high-demanding incubation tasks.

Moreover, the brevity of the time subsequently needed by those participants who solve the insight problem when it is submitted to them again immediately following the incubation phase seems to indicate that the solving process developed mainly during this phase, with the solution having been processed and almost available when the problem solver returns to the problem. If, on the contrary, the solution process was associative by chance, as proposed by the Special Process approach, the time required to reach the solution would be variable and mostly unpredictable. The results would have been obtained by chance, and the associations made during the incubation phase would not necessarily have led to the correct solution.

The incubation task that produced the worst performance was the low-demanding drawing task, which does not impede conscious processing of the problem. This would not seem to support the "business-as-usual" approach: in fact, if a conscious solution processing had been adopted, it should have been facilitated by this experimental condition, as the participants would have been able to work consciously at the problem while they were drawing their castle or landscape.

Our results are also in contrast with the *returning-act hypothesis*, which holds that the role of the incubation phase is to distract the participants from the influence of an incorrect solution; it follows that a demanding task, with a high distraction value, would enhance the incubation effect, while a low-demanding task should produce no effect at all. On the contrary, as we have shown above, the participants in our study obtained better results with low-demanding incubation tasks (simple arithmetic calculations), while the worst results were obtained when they were set a high-demanding incubation task (the crossword).

To conclude, our data do not appear to even support the *selective forgetting hypothesis*, which maintains that the incubation phase should weaken activation of ideas that lead to incorrect solutions; hence, a longer incubation phase should result in a stronger incubation effect independently of the type of task executed during the pause. Quite to the contrary, in fact, the incubation effect seems to depend on the characteristics of the task executed during the incubation phase.

3.5 Conclusions

My objective so far in this journey of twists and turns between language and thought, floating between the conscious and the unconscious, has been to show that the psychorhetorical and Gestalt approach to the study of insight problem solving represents a general paradigm in the sphere of the psychology of thought, as it is genuinely psychological, able to describe the phenomenology of thought without an overlay of formal theories that are inevitably distant from effective thought.

In my opinion, which is supported by the data obtained from the above experiments, this method of reasoning is very close to the process of understanding an *utterance*: we abandon the default interpretation (the *fixation* in insight problem solving) in favour of "restructuring", to capture the meaning that is pertinent to the context and the intention of the communicator. In this way, our reasoning also involves implicit and parallel processes. The restructuring cannot be entirely supported by the working memory, which is occupied by the fixation and a default interpretation or *Einstellung*.

In particular, the form of unconscious thought illustrated in the solution process entails a revaluation of that shadow zone of thought that in times past was always considered responsible for automatisms and, in many cases, errors of judgement.

Recently, from different perspectives, various researchers have sustained that it can process information very quickly through a parallel process. According to the neurological model formulated by Bowden and colleagues (2005), the solution process for insight problems entails the passage from conscious semantic activation of information that is not correlated to the solution to the unconscious activation of information that is critical to finding the solution. However, even when the working memory does not exert conscious control, a search for pertinence and relevance seems to point the unconscious solution process in the correct direction, guaranteeing a solution based on reasoning and not merely associative or found by chance.

This *search for pertinence* could be the Ariadne's *clew* that guides us in the overall activation of the diffusion of knowledge. This selective search becomes a heuristic to capture the idea, among the many salient points, that is the most pertinent to the objective of the task; we have called this the "interpretative heuristic" (Macchi & Bagassi, 2014). This characteristic is present in all insight problem-solving processes, and, in general, it is an adaptive characteristic of the human cognitive system, which is always on the lookout for the maximum yield (of information) for the minimum effort (Levinson, 1995, 2013; Mercier & Sperber, 2011; Sperber & Wilson, 1986; Tomasello, 2009). With insight problems, we are not dealing only with quantities; it is a question of understanding the sense of the task, the interdependence between the parts and the whole. The interpretative function guarantees cognitive economy when the meanings and relations are familiar, allowing them to be recognized. However, this same process becomes much more difficult when the meanings and the relations are not familiar, and we are faced with the unknown. When this happens, we have to come to terms with the fact that the usual predefined interpretation will not work, which is a necessary condition for exploring other ways of interpreting the problem. There is nothing mysterious about this; it is the result of a constant search at both conscious and unconscious levels for possible relationships between the parts and the whole, using a heuristic-interpretative process that continues until everything falls into place and nothing remains to be accounted for.

In this perspective, contextual processing (which is always oriented to relevance) is considered to be transversal for intuitive and reflective-analytic thought. Processing the context, the "situations", as Barsalou (2009) would say, seems to improve cognitive processing by increasing the "breadth and specificity of the inference". Rather than searching through all the knowledge stored in the long-term memory, all the system needs to do is to concentrate on abilities and knowledge that are relevant to the situation in question. Reasoning is the ability to produce specialized representations and their relations that support the pursuit of the objectives in the specific context.

In my view, this manner of thinking is very similar to the process of understanding an utterance: in every communication, explicit meanings are accompanied by implicit meanings that are reciprocally shared by the speaker and the listener. When a default interpretation does not contribute to our understanding and a more appropriate meaning has to be chosen to resolve the *misunderstanding* (the "impasse"), we abandon the predefined interpretation (the "fixation") to "restructure" to find a meaning that appears to be more pertinent to the context and to the speaker's intention.

Taking a look at non-insight problems, we see that the message that passes between the experimenter on the one hand and the participant on the other is univocal both in the implicit and the explicit content; in other words, both the experimenter and the participant understand the meaning in the same way, unless there are accidental errors of comprehension. As Simon maintains, "Subjects do not initially choose deliberately among problem representations, but almost always adopt the representation suggested by the verbal problem statement" (Kaplan & Simon, 1990, p. 376). Take the case in which a problem solver is given a jigsaw puzzle to solve and implicitly agrees with the experimenter that none of the pieces of the puzzle is to be broken. In this case, both the problem solver and the experimenter share an implicit presupposition. On the contrary, insight problems possess a characteristic that an external observer might think is an accidental misunderstanding, but actually the problem is couched by the experimenter in terms that are different from those commonly used. Take Mary Elizabeth Bulbrook's *String of Pearls* problem, for example (1932). She showed her participants a string of white and yellow pearls, threaded in the following order: one yellow, two white, one yellow, two white, and so on, until at a certain point there were five white pearls, one after the other, between two yellow pearls. She asked her participants to rearrange these pearls into the original sequence, without undoing the string or breaking it. Just as in the case of the jigsaw, the participants assumed that the pearls were not to be damaged, but it turned out that this was, in fact, the solution to the problem. Bulbrook had banked on the very fact that this element had not been stated specifically.

It is evident that this is not a banal misunderstanding between the experimenter and the participants; it is a *misunderstanding* created by social conventions and defined by conversational rules, and, in this case, it was the essential condition for the *formation* of the problem. In fact, if the necklace had been made of walnuts and hazelnuts, the problem would not have existed (as no stigma is attached to breaking nuts, quite the contrary), and no one would have experienced any difficulty.

Notwithstanding the numerous problem classifications that are based on certain characteristics to the detriment of others that are so general as to be generic, and therefore not able to pick up the fundamental difficulties of a problem, a criterion for distinguishing insight problems from others could be their susceptibility to a non-misleading reformulation.

Together with Maria Bagassi, I explored the effect of such a reformulation on the following problems: the *Study Window*, the *Ties*, and two classical insight problems such as the *Square and the Parallelogram*, the *Pigs in a Pen*, as well as Kahneman and Frederick's famous *Bat and Ball* problem (Macchi & Bagassi, 2012). According to our hypothesis, the difficulty of these problems is never objective or computational; it is subjective and interpretative. It is the way that the problem is formulated that creates the difficulty, as it activates a predefined interpretation that obscures the solution. Reformulating the text in which the problem is couched, rendering it more pertinent to the goal of the task, eliminated the gorgon knot at the heart of the problem. In this case, language and thought worked in unison in an interconnected interpretative "game". Therefore, the importance of the formulation of the problem should never be underestimated, both with regard to how the problem forms in the mind and how it is solved.

Therefore, as mentioned in Chapter 2 , the creative act of restructuring implies implicit high-level thought, a sort of *unconscious analytic thought* where, however, analytic thought should not be perceived as a gradual, step-by-step simplification of the difficulties of the problem as might be the case in non-insight problems, but rather as the act of seizing the crucial and relevant characteristics of the initial structure of the problem so as to be able to substitute it with another in which the difficulties are no longer present and the misunderstanding that was the cause of the impasse has been cleared up.

Coming up against an impasse is essential if we are to explore other ways of interpreting the situation. Restructuring requires multilayered analytic reasoning operating on both conscious and unconscious levels to process implicit and explicit content, presuppositions, and beliefs, but always informed by relevance. As we have seen, therefore, when our initial interpretation does not support understanding, a misunderstanding is inevitable. If we are to escape from the impasse, we have to ignore the predefined interpretation and search for another that is better suited to the situation and intercepts the intention of the speaker. Hence, problems of comprehension can be taken as paradigmatic examples for the study of communication and the functioning of the mind in general (see page 31).

The gestaltist and psychorhetorical approach adopted describes the beauty—and also the simplicity—of the workings of human intelligence, which is able to change representations, to discover misunderstandings, and to restructure.

TEXT BOX 3.1 DIFFERENCES BETWEEN INSIGHT AND NON-INSIGHT (PROCEDURAL) PROBLEMS

Non-insight (procedural) problems: Here, problem solvers start from a fact which is certain, from which they extract a conclusion or another certain fact, after which, respecting and utilizing the imposed constraints, they proceed gradually to successive determinations based on what they have already established. A serial step-by-step search is applied to find the solution.

In these problems, the representation formed at the beginning of the task remains unaltered, and the search is carried out exclusively within the limits of this problem space.

Insight problems: if the element that is causing the impasse is not removed, all attempts at solving the problem will be in vain. They will remain just that, attempts, incorrect attempts that do not connect up to progress towards the solution, which can only be found by restructuring or overcoming the critical point.

In these problems, the solution can be found only after a change of perspective (i.e., of the representation of the problem), and the difficulty corresponds mainly to the difficulty of making this change.

TEXT BOX 3.2 SYSTEM 1 VERSUS SYSTEM 2

The *Special Process* and *Business-as-Usual* approaches return to the classical dichotomy of two different systems of reasoning: the associative (swift and automatic—System 1) and the reflective and rule-based (slow and analytic—System 2). See pages 7 and 8 for an in-depth analysis of this dichotomous concept of the mind that focuses on, on the one hand, on the role of consciousness and, on the other, the capacity for abstract thinking that is typical of the human mind.

TEXT BOX 3.3 GIUSEPPE MOSCONI'S DUAL CODE THEORY

According to Giuseppe Mosconi's dual code theory, "the change in how we understand the terms of the problem depends on the change of the code used to read the message [...]. The initial understanding (or primary decodification) is produced by applying the natural code (the code we use in normal conversation). The next level of understanding (or secondary decodification) results from the application of a different, sophisticated or formal code that he called the legal code (that in the case of the 9 Dot problem permits a purely literal interpretation of the phrase being considered)" (Mosconi & D'Urso, 1974). The asymmetry between the codification and the decodification is the basis of the problem. Its realization is variable, in the sense that it varies from problem to problem.

Mosconi took the problem below, which appears contradictory, as a perfect example of dual coding (the currency has been updated). The difficulty here lies in the fact that the unfolding of what appears to be a perfectly acceptable narrative discourse leads to an unacceptable conclusion.

Three friends go to a restaurant. The bill amounts to 60 euros. They each pay 20 euros but ask for a discount. The owner of the restaurant gives 10 euros back to the three friends, who then leave 4 euros for the waiter and keep 6 euros. At the end, each friend has paid 18 euros, which multiplied by 3 makes 54 euros. The waiter has taken 4 euros. This amounts to 58 euros. Where are the 2 euros that are missing?

The error in this reasoning is that the 4 euro tip given to the waiter is considered as being over and above the overall bill for the meal paid by the friends. This representation leads to the erroneous computation:

54 euro + 4 euro = 58 euro

which in turn directly leads to the statement that there are 2 euros missing.

This problem is a genuine brainteaser that baffles most people, and for many it remains unsolved. The formulation of the problem (the account given of the situation and the question) is very clearly biased and erroneous.

There are at least two expressions in the text that contribute to the difficulty of solving this problem: "pay" and "leave 4 euros for the waiter". In this context, "pay" is usually understood in the sense of "paying the bill" and indicates only the sum of money paid directly to the restaurant, the amount indicated on the bill excluding an eventual tip. In situations such as this, the verb "leave" is usually combined with the term "tip"; hence, "leave a tip" implies a free donation, added to the bill. It would therefore seem quite natural to suppose that the use of the verb "leave" in this text gives the impression that the 4 euros left for the waiter are to be added to the amount paid (which did not include the tip).

The problem was then reformulated as follows:

> Three friends go to a restaurant. The bill amounts to 60 euros. They each pay 20 euros but ask for a discount. The owner of the restaurant gives 10 euros back to the three friends, who then **have** to leave 4 euros for the waiter for his **services** and take 6 euros. At the end, each friend **has disbursed** 18 euros, which multiplied by 3 makes 54 euros. The waiter has taken 4 euros. This amounts to 58 euros. Where are the 2 euros that are missing?

Nearly all the participants found the solution. "Some of the participants were even confused by the simplicity of the problem; they had expected to have to overcome a number of difficulties and were worried that they had overlooked them" (Mosconi, 1990, p. 251).

Notes

1 With regard to the relations between the Gestalt theory and HIP, it is interesting to note that in the 1990s, in an article replying to Michael Wertheimer, son of the well-known Gestalt psychologist Max Wertheimer, for the first time Simon admitted that insight problems, which need a change in representation for the solution to be found, "fall outside the limits of the Information Processing Theory of problem-solving and accounting for this requires an essential extension of that theory" (Kaplan and Simon, 1990, p. 338).
2 In our view, the fact that there are various types of incubation effect (Sio and Ormerod, 2009) would indicate that the impasse has various levels of difficulty. This can be clearly seen comparing the Candle problem (Duncker, 1945) with the problem of the Square and the Parallelogram (Wertheimer, 1925).
3 In their meta-analytic review of research studies carried out on the effects of incubation on problem-solving, Sio and Ormerod (2009) observed that these effects supported both the diffusion of activation processes (remote association tasks known as RAT) and restructuring after the impasse (visual problems).
4 Macchi and Bagassi (2014).
5 The participants insisted on calculating the preferential height of the parallelogram, internal to the figure and the longer side.
6 Kanizsa (1973), p. 46—our translation.
7 Unlike Schooler and colleagues (1993), Gilhooly et al. (2010) reported a lack of interaction between the insight factor and the verbalization condition on the percentages of solved problems. They accept the "business-as-usual" view, rejecting the "Special Process" view, even though their results show that verbalization has a beneficial effect on non-insight problems that on the contrary supports the "Special Process" view proposed by Schooler et al. (1993).
8 This classification was confirmed in a pre-test.
9 In a research study in 1974, Giuseppe Mosconi and Valentina D'Urso showed that this behaviour responds to a fundamental psychological need: that the operation of falsification follows a verification or is carried out on a plausible rule. Anyone who uses common sense only when a rule is sustained by positive examples may feel the necessity of making sure that the rule is always true, subjecting it to a falsification test. In short, we start from positive cases to formulate a hypothesis or a rule that describes them in general terms (tendency to verify or acknowledgement of the presence of positive cases). Only when a rule is present can there be the necessity of checking its absolute generalness by means of the falsification test.
10 According to this approach, universals would exist in interactional organization, compatible with a theory of biological basis for interactional competence: (a) studies with children suggest that there is a rapidly maturing innate base (in the adaptive function), indeed Trevarthen notes that by two months the child has "a rich repertoire of expressive behaviours combined with ready orientation of the gaze to or away from the mother's face and immediate response to her signs of interest and her talking" (Trevarthen, 1979: 541); (b) in addition, our hearing is particularly sensitive to language wave lengths, while that of other animals is attuned to their prey.

Appendix

Cooperation, Heuristics, and Communicative Principles

The importance of the relation between thought and communication emerged in the psychology of thought in the 1960s with Giuseppe Mosconi's concept of psychorhetoric, and almost contemporaneously in the philosophy of language with Herbert Paul Grice's pragmatic theory of conversational implicatures.

These two theoretical concepts had many points in common, in spite of having been developed autonomously and with different intentions in two different disciplines. Mosconi balanced the holistic view, which is characteristic of classical rhetoric, against the predominant dichotomous vision represented in psychological research on the one hand by psycholinguistics and on the other by "psycho-logic", the former dealing with language and the latter with thought. This confirmed the need to transcend the Chomskyan vision, which holds that the purpose of language is essentially to express thought. Mosconi's view of language was quite different; he maintained that rather than simply expressing thought, language is necessary for thought. United by this innovative vision, his scientific production evolved in fields of research that were strongly interrelated, from studies on linguistics on both the micro- and macro-structural level of discourse, to studies on thought, in the areas of reasoning and also of problem solving. His research program took form from his first studies with children in the mid-1960s, as Rudolf Arnheim acutely noted in his diary on August 21, 1971:

> Once again, the children remind us of how much our formalistic logic has damaged our thinking. The Italian psychologist Mosconi, wanting to find out how children interpret the concept *diverso*, presented them with six pictures, five of animals—a lion, an elephant, a horse, etc. and one of a boat. He asked which picture was "the most different" from that of a sheep, which he also showed. An educated adult would have selected the boat, but almost none of the children did. To them, nothing can be compared but what has a common base, making the comparison sensible. Nothing can be called different but what in some ways could be called the same.
>
> *(1989, p. 147)*

As we have seen in Text Box 3.3, according to Mosconi's dual code theory, the change in our understanding of the terms of the problem depends on the change of the code with which we *read* the message. The initial understanding (or primary decodification), produced by applying the natural code that we use in normal conversation, is supplanted by a secondary decodification obtained by the application of a different, more sophisticated, or formal code, which Mosconi called the legal code. In this perspective, the asymmetry between the codification and the decodification is the basis of the problem, but it is different in each case.

On the other hand, specularly, Grice, with his pragmatic theory of conversational implicatures in the field of the philosophy of language, was moving beyond a purely semantic analysis of language to give meaning to how content communicated by linguistic acts conveys much more than what is said literally. Therefore, the notion of *conversational implicatures* assumes a central role as this is how the listener integrates the meaning, which is not directly expressed, with implicit knowledge conveyed by the communicative context. Grice's theory of conversational implicatures asserts that often, when we are having a conversation, we want to say more than what our words signify literally, or we want to say something different to the literal meaning of the words we are using. The notion of the *implicature* would have the task of connecting what *we are actually saying* to what we *intend to say* and, so doing, would explain how it is possible to do what we continuously do when speaking, i.e., *communicate more than what our words mean literally*. Generally speaking, our linguistic exchanges do not consist of a series of observations that are lacking in reciprocal connections; indeed, that would not be rational. Typically, they collaborate, at least to a certain extent; and to a certain extent each participant recognizes in them a goal, or a collection of common goals. At the very least, they recognize a common direction. In every moment of a conversation, certain moves are excluded as being out of place. Grice therefore formulated an approximate general principle that participants in a conversation are expected to observe, the Cooperative Principle: "Make your contribution such as is required, at the stage at which it occurs, by the accepted purpose or direction of the talk exchange in which you are engaged". The Cooperative Principle is made up of four conversational maxims that speakers usually respect:

- The Maxim of Quantity is based on the tacit agreement that everyone contributes no more and no less information than is required by the purpose of the interaction.
- The Maxim of Quality is based on the tacit agreement that everyone makes a truthful contribution, that is, they do not say what they believe to be false or for which they have no supporting evidence.
- The Maxim of Relation is based on the tacit agreement that everyone makes pertinent contributions.
- The Maxim of Manner is based on the tacit agreement that everyone tries to be clear, avoiding obscurity of expression, ambiguity, unnecessary verbosity, and proceeding with order.

What Grice is trying to explain is not the conventional meaning, but that which an individual speaker, in any given circumstance, wants to express with a given sign or word. This is the concept of meaning, the *speaker's meaning*, that precedes linguistic meaning and not vice versa. If someone violates the maxims drastically and dramatically, the meaning can still be interpreted, and the cooperation will continue to take place, albeit on an underlying level.

Dan Sperber and Stephen Levinson, two of Grice's most dedicated followers, expanded on his theory; on the one hand, Sperber developed the argumentative function of thought, and on the other, Levinson developed the concept of *interactional intelligence*.

Sperber, a cognitivist philosopher, developed a theory together with Hugo Mercier, sustaining that cooperation, an ability that is not easy to put into practice and even more difficult to maintain, is the principal advantage that humans have compared to other species. Our ability to reason, of which we are so proud, did not evolve for the purpose of solving abstract problems of logic, of drawing original conclusions from new data, but rather to solve problems arising from group collaboration and cooperation. "Reason is an adaptation to the hypersocial niche humans have evolved for themselves", wrote Mercier and Sperber in 2011. According to these authors, the "confirmation biases" therefore would not be accidental errors but the expression of our evolutionistic tendency to confirm our opinions and reject any challenge to them that puts us at a disadvantage in the group. It is for this reason that the authors prefer to talk about "myside bias". According to this hypothesis, generally speaking, we are by no means gullible; we are quick to individuate the limits and defects of others but are selectively blind when it comes to our own.[9]

Stephen Levinson held that our intelligence is substantially interactional; in his view, there is a systematic bias in the human mind in the direction of interactional thinking (Gardner, 1985, Multiple Intelligences; Levinson, 1995). Like the great linguistic philosopher that he is, he used a semi-syllogistic form to explain his reasoning:

1. Communication is logically impossible: in fact, it is not possible to trace a conclusion (a communicative expression) to the premise from which it is derived, as it may have been generated by an infinite number of premises.
2. Nevertheless, we humans can communicate.
3. Therefore, we must use non-logical heuristics and a special form of reasoning to bridge the gap (a reasoning able to detect the communicative intention from the communicative context).
4. For communication to work routinely, these heuristics must be dominant in our thinking at all times.
5. Therefore, these heuristics spill over to bias our thinking in non-communication domains. (Levinson, 1995, p. 221)

Hence, the intentionality of every communication and the impossibility of a unique decodification system. The subject and the context are central to detecting the communicative intention.[10]

> Human interaction is clearly characterized by an inordinate concern with the implications that an actor's actions have for other actors' expectations, emotions,

> self-esteem, social status—in short it takes place within a highly structured and often restrictive set of social relationships which permeate the most intricate details of interactional patterning.
>
> *(Levinson, 1995, p. 225)*

Notwithstanding this, Levinson still abstracts from the social matrix to pose questions about the underlying conceptual abilities that make social interaction possible.

He revisited Schelling's (1960) informal experiments to show how we can almost always coordinate our plans/purposes even without communicating directly. He asked two people in different rooms who had no means of communicating with each other to say where they would go and at what time, to meet with another person who was being asked the same question.

> Go to a given place in a city to which the other person will go, simply knowing that both of you are trying to choose the same place and the same time for an appointment.

As the experiment took place in New York, most people gave New York Grand Central Station at 12 noon as their answer, as this is a typical time and place for New Yorkers to meet. We replicated this experiment in Milano and noted a significant concordance for Piazza Duomo at 18:00 (a time when most people would be leaving the office).

This certainly has the appearance of being a mystery! But let us take a look at what underlies this "mysterious" event. (a) *Mutual salience*: the situation gives only one specific clue to help with the coordination; (b) *mutual calculation of the mutual salience*: a potent characteristic of reflective thought inevitably comes into play. We have to do what the other person thinks we are most likely to do. "This is a very adaptive ability to interpret the environment..."

Comparing Psychorhetoric and Pragmatics in Insight Problem Studies

On Insight Problem Solving

In spite of the undeniable affinities that characterize the various theoretical-experimental research studies briefly described in the preceding paragraph, a certain divergence can be observed through the study of insight problem solving. For example, the formulation of a problem can conform to the Gricean maxims, but it could still be misleading if it does not take into consideration the cognitive mechanisms and psychological needs of the interlocutor.

- *When vagueness is preferable to precision.* Precision, the peak of informativeness and as such fitting perfectly into the Gricean maxims, should be preferable on the communicative level. However, taking Wertheimer's problem of the *Square and the Parallelogram* as an example, the terms "square" and "parallelogram" as adopted in the original version of the problem are more precise and therefore more informative compared to the vaguer "figure" used in the reformulated version and so, according to the Gricean maxims, should constitute a more effective communication. However, in practice, these more precise and informative terms (square and parallelogram) were limiting for the problem solvers, who were not able to conjure up a more plastic representation of the figure, impeding the restructuring process.

- *The interpretative function in perception* (not only in communication). The importance of the interpretative function extends beyond the linguistic-communicative level and is already evident at the perceptual level. In Maier's *Nine Dot* Problem, for example, a form of auto-limitation arises in the solution process, independently of how the problem text is interpreted. This can be ascribed to the Gestalt mechanism of perceptual organization, which tends to connect elements in accordance with the attribution of meaning and relational structure, leading to a visual interpretation of the nine dots as a virtual square—an interpretation that constitutes the principal obstacle to finding the solution. On the perceptual level, there are cases of "perceptual" generalized implicatures that in Grice's theory were only considered linguistically. Take, for example, the case of the indefinite article, the use of which implies an absence of familiarity with the object that is being spoken of: when we say, "a house" or "a car", we are excluding that we are speaking of "my house" or "my car". In the same way, certain terms determine a preferential representation on the perceptual level: in the *Study Window* problem, there is a spontaneous tendency to represent the window orthogonally (so causing the impasse).

On Demonstrative Discourse

In the next chapter, I will illustrate an experiment that Mosconi conducted on Euclid's First Theorem. We will see that, without prior knowledge of the rules, the demonstration of this theorem represents a violation of the Gricean maxims. However, if it is stated from the start that the rules of Euclidean geometry are being followed, i.e., that nothing can be asserted unless it has been demonstrated by what precedes it, the Euclidean demonstration of the First Theorem would be adequate for communication from the point of view of Gricean maxims. However, given the psychological demands of thought highlighted by Mosconi's experiment, this alone is not sufficient to make the demonstration an acceptable discourse, one that is both comprehensible and memorable. What is lacking is the ability to anticipate the direction of the discourse and to understand the role played, in that sense, by each step in the demonstration! Adhering to the Gricean maxims alone does not appear to be sufficient.

4

CRITICAL THINKING BEYOND BIASES

Demonstrate, Draw a Conclusion, Falsify

> All men are mortal.
> Socrates was mortal,
> So, all men are Socrates.
>
> Woody Allen

According to Norberto Bobbio, the process of argumentative reasoning is an antidote to the opposing temptations of fanaticism and scepticism, as it tends to justify and guide choices. These temptations, for opposing reasons, tend to reject the value of non-binding reasoning, which is not based only on demonstrative tests. Between absolute truth and non-truth, there is space for truths that are subjected to continuous critical revisions, weighing up the pros and cons.

We could describe critical thinking in the following terms "the competence to engage productively in the generation, evaluation, and improvement of ideas that can result in original and effective solutions, advances in knowledge, and impactful expressions of imagination" (Van Damme & Zahner, 2022). It is a matter of reasoning and argumentation, distinguishing between facts and opinion as well as knowing how the reasoning is structured. Fostering the formation of critical thought can supply instruments for thought, for forming opinions based on facts and trustworthy sources, accepting that there can be many ways of perceiving the same point of view, and developing deliberative abilities. Critical thinking has been taught for a number of years in Anglo-American schools, where it is conceived as a discipline that provides general knowledge borrowed from logic, scientific methodology and cognitive psychology. The objective is to make students more careful when accepting or rejecting arguments, to improve their ability to contribute to discussions and debates, and to detect fallacies and rhetorical tricks in public discussions.

DOI: 10.4324/9781003680895-4

With this purpose in mind, from my perspective, it is essential that this competence, which traditionally coincides mainly with an ideal of logical-scientific thought, also be reviewed in a psychorhetorical light of thought, regardless of whether it is engaged in critically evaluating the validity of an idea or a hypothesis or a conclusion. Indeed, I consider this psychorhetorical dimension to be transversal to various types of discourse, from argumentative to logical to demonstrative, from which I will start.

4.1 Demonstrate

If every discourse has a rhetorical dimension, this should also apply to demonstrative or scientific discourse, since the distinction between demonstrative and persuasive discourse, between genuine and dubious content, should not be relevant from the rhetorical and psychological point of view.

As geometrical demonstrations have always been considered a form of reasoning typically devoid of rhetorical aspects, it is important to verify empirically that it does not elude rhetorical or psychorhetorical requirements (if anything, it follows different rules).

One of the criteria traditionally adopted by mathematicians in constructing geometric proofs, or at least in presenting them, is to never make an assertion that is not supported by previously provided elements. Consequently, nothing is anticipated during the demonstration, and frequently, the propositions directly relevant and pertinent to the development of the reasoning are preceded by long digressions intended to introduce and deal with the elements that legitimize them. As a result, the recipients of the discourse often find themselves in the situation of "being led towards the final conclusion, rather like a blind person who, although aware of the destination, does not *fore*-see the path, but can only control their progress along the way, step after step and has difficulty working out the itinerary" (Mosconi, 1990, p. 35).

The demonstrative discourse can be organized following a different criterion, prioritizing the psychological needs of the person to whom the discourse is addressed, being careful to organize it taking into consideration the functioning of the mind, what can promote understanding and facilitate recall; in particular, the need to be aware of what is happening at every moment during the demonstration (also including the psychorhetorical dimension of the demonstrative discourse) should be considered.

In the following paragraphs, I have summarized the results of an elegant experiment conducted by Mosconi (1990), concerning the demonstration of Euclid's First Theorem (Figure 4.1).

> In a right-angled triangle, the square constructed on one cathetus is equal in area to the rectangle formed by the projection of that cathetus onto the hypotenuse.

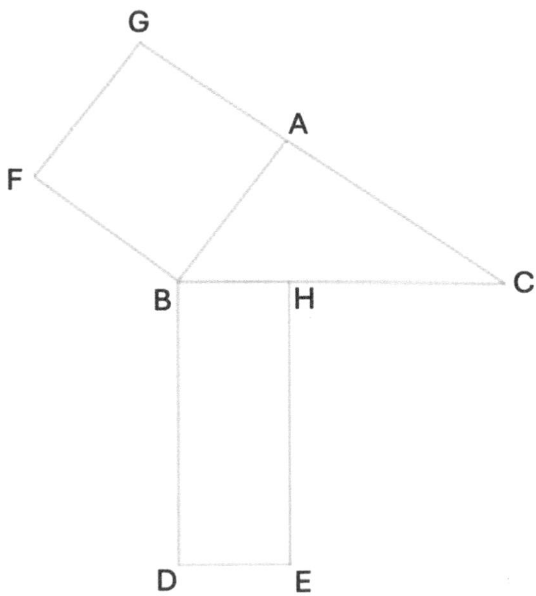

FIGURE 4.1 Euclid's First Theorem.

Euclidean Demonstration: Text

1. Construct the square (ABFG) and the rectangle (BDEH).
2. Draw the connecting lines AD and FC.
3. Given that angles BAC and BAG are right angles, the two lines AC and AG, which lie on opposite sides of the line BA, form with BA adjacent angles whose sum is equal to two right angles. Therefore, AC lies on the same straight line as AG.
4. Since the angle DBC is equal to the angle FBA, and both are right angles, and angle ABC is common to both, angle DBA is equal to angle FBC.
5. Since BD is equal to BC, FG is equal to AB, and ABD is equal to FBC, triangles (ABD) and (FBC) are congruent.
6. *Rectangle (BDEH) is twice the area of triangle (ABD), since they share the same base and lie between the same parallels BD and AE.*
7. *Square (ABFG) is twice the area of triangle (FBC), since they share the same base FB and lie between the same parallels FB and GC.*
8. Things that are double of things that are equal are equal to one another. Therefore, rectangle BDEH is equal in area to square ABFG. *Quod erat demonstrandum.*

Psychorhetoric Demonstration: Text

1. Construct the square (ABFG) and the rectangle (BDEH).
2. Draw the connecting lines AD and FC.

3. Rectangle (BDEH) is twice the area of triangle (ABD), since they share the same base BD and lie between the same parallel lines BD and AE.
4. Square *(ABFG) is twice the area of triangle (FBC), since they share the same base FB and lie between the same parallel lines FB and GC.*
5. GA and AC lie on the same straight line because, given that angles BAC and BAG are right angles, the two lines AC and AG, which lie on opposite sides of BA, form adjacent angles with BA whose sum is equal to two right angles.
6. Triangles (ABD) and (FBC) are congruent, since BD is equal to BC, AB is equal to FB, and angle ABD is equal to angle FBC: DBC is equal to FBA, both right angles, and angle ABC is common to both.
7. Things that are doubles of things that are equal are themselves equal. Therefore, the rectangle (BDEH) and the square (ABFG) are equal in area—*quod erat demonstrandum*.

The psychorhetorical version of the demonstration was drawn up keeping in mind that, as the steps of the proof proceed, the terms they contain, which are placed in relation to one another, must appear to be directly connected to the objective of the demonstration, and the direction must be indicated at each step. To investigate whether these changes would make the psychorhetoric version easier to follow than the original version, Mosconi formulated a prediction task and a comprehension task.

In the prediction task, after stating the theorem and the first two steps of the demonstration that provide instructions regarding the construction of the two triangles, the participants were asked to predict, in broad terms, how the demonstration would develop. If they were in difficulty, they were told to read the next step (3) and so on.

This experiment showed that when following the Euclidean demonstration, most of the participants had to reach step 6 before being able to predict how the demonstration would develop, while when using the psychorhetorical version, most of the participants were already able to complete the task from step 3.

The prediction test was accompanied by a comprehension test, which was constructed as follows: the experimenter recited the theorem and the entire demonstration, after which the participants were asked to explain, in broad terms without any detail, how the demonstration would develop. If they were unable to do this, the theorem and the demonstration were read out again. Most of the participants had to ask for a second reading of the Euclidean demonstration text, but only a third asked for a re-reading of the psychorhetorical version.

In conclusion, with regard to the function of the two triangles, the alignment of AG and AC, as well as the equivalence of triangles FBC and ABD, the Euclidean demonstration text seemed to make the participants focus on sub-proofs, and a "blurring" of their connecting function. The psychorhetoric text, on the other hand, emerged as better able to identify the demonstration's principal points and their reciprocal connections in regard to the theorem itself.

4.2 Drawing a Conclusion

If cold spells occur, then there is no global warming.
Cold spells occur.
Therefore, there is no global warming.

Whatever your opinion may be regarding this specific topic, the reasoning is valid from a logical standpoint (the conclusion necessarily derives from the premises), but it is based on the first premise that is not supported by scientific evidence. Cold spells are themselves a collateral effect of the increase in drought. In this case, we have drawn a valid conclusion that however is factually false.

The opposite can also occur. We may accept conclusions that are invalid but believable (or factually true),[1] like the following example:

All flowers fade.
All roses fade.
Therefore, all roses are flowers.

This is an example of the so-called *belief bias*, which can be defined as the systematic tendency to evaluate a syllogism through the credibility of its conclusion, by our preconceptions, or previous knowledge, rather than through the principle of logical necessity. As a consequence, we repudiate conclusions that are factually false but valid, and vice versa, and accept true syllogisms that, however, are invalid.

In this chapter, in addition to the *belief bias,* we will investigate another paradigmatic bias, the *verification bias*, fundamental to our reasoning processes and critical thinking. This bias consists of the erroneous tendency to test an idea, a hypothesis, or a rule, exclusively with cases that confirm it, without submitting it to cases that could potentially falsify it, the so-called "counterexamples".

"The principles by which hypotheses are discovered, or invented, are little understood, but the testing of hypotheses is a more tractable matter". To test a hypothesis,

> it is necessary to determine which particular observations from a large number of possibilities would constitute a crucial test of the hypothesis in question [...]. This is obviously analogous to the scientist's question about those individual observations which would be a crucial test of his hypothesis. The fundamental psychological issue is to discover how the individual is prone to tackle such tasks, and the practical problem is to devise a laboratory study which mirrors the logic of the situation
>
> *(Wason & Johnson-Laird, 1972)*

Wason's experimental problem is well-known, given the importance it has acquired in the field of the psychology of thinking. I am referring to the *selection task*, which will be discussed further later in this chapter (see page 92).

In both cases, we are dealing with inferential processes that are present in many instances of scientific and daily thought in which conclusions are drawn from a fairly wide set of premises. These conclusions do not increase the amount of information in the premises, but they do reveal implicit relational properties.

As explained in Chapter 2, research on deductive reasoning initially focused on the explanation of the competencies that emerged from the early studies on solving of syllogistic tasks (theory of mental logic that explained the results by hypothesizing that the human mind is equipped with natural inferential schemas) and on the question of inferential errors (i.e., the difficulty experienced by most of the participants and that dominated research on deductive reasoning) and the understanding of the influence that the contents of the premise could bring to bear on the reasoning process (the form-content relationship).

The theory I intend to develop takes into consideration a different aspect of the question; in my view, it will be able to explain the errors of deductive reasoning recorded in literature and the correct method. Even recently published handbooks tend to overlook a preliminary but fundamental step in the reasoning process: a correct understanding of the text and the objective of the task. Given the discrepancy described in Chapter 2 between natural language and the language of logic, can we really be sure that the "man in the street" who is unlikely to have had training in formal logic will interpret the task in the same way as the researcher who has conceived it?

What has emerged from the studies I have conducted with colleagues over the years is that frequently the participants' interpretation of the text of the problem or even their representation of the task overall is quite different from that of the researcher. This obviously has serious consequences for the validity of the results of these experiments and therefore contributes significantly to the frequent claims of human irrationality that are based on them.

The interpretation of natural language depends on the conditions in which the communication takes place. As I have mentioned before, the context, the identities of the speakers and the listeners, the knowledge they have in common, and the speaker's intentions all contribute to determining the interpretation of an utterance through sophisticated (but natural, adaptive) inferential processes of attribution of meaning.

What relevance does this preamble have in a chapter dedicated to reasoning? Human reasoning could be conceived as an essentially autonomous and egocentric process. Given the premises, the mechanism for reaching a conclusion or making a decision should be constituted entirely by the processing of information in our minds. This is true, but it is only a part of the truth. It overlooks the interaction between the reasoner and the context. Mostly, human reasoning has a verbal input in natural language and, contrary to formal languages, phrases do not have a univocal interpretation. In synthesis, as we have seen in the preceding chapters, the idea that the verbal input to mental activity is as clearly defined as in formal logic is an idealization. The consequences on the study of reasoning, judgement, and decisional processes are immediate. No experimental paradigm, no task, should be designed and applied without having conducted a psychorhetoric analysis of how the participants may interpret the problem.

For reasons of space, I will take just a few experimental studies of deductive reasoning to illustrate my theory, to show that, frequently, too frequently in fact, after submitting the problem to this type of analysis, it can be seen to be different, sometimes dramatically different, from its creator's original idea. As said before, this has important consequences on the evaluation of our capacity to reason correctly, and on human rationality in general.

4.3 Belief Bias: An Error of Logic or Simply Failure to Understand the Task?

Deductive reasoning is pervasive and commonly used in everyday life; starting from certain premises, it allows us to establish one (or more) conclusions that necessarily derive from them. Therefore, it allows us to establish the consequences of our beliefs. Take the following statement, for example:

> If all my friends greet me when they meet me (Premise 1) and John is a friend of mine (Premise 2), then I expect John to greet me when he meets me (Conclusion).

This kind of syllogism allows us to build expectations regarding reality and, so, helps us to guide our behaviour.

It also reveals implicit knowledge that we can express in the inference. For example:

> If catching a certain virus is contagious, and Marco has caught it, then Marco will be contagious.

In logic, it is possible to establish with certainty whether deductive reasoning is valid or not. Psychology borrowed this approach from logic, mistakenly believing it could provide a complete account of human reasoning, as though it were a natural formal logical system (Henle, 1962; Piaget, 1953).

That said, although under certain conditions human beings are capable of reasoning, applying logical criteria, under others this seems to produce biases or systematic errors of reasoning (see, for example, Wason, 1966; Johnson-Laird et al., 1972).[2]

An emblematic example of such biases is the *belief bias* that can be defined as the systematic tendency to evaluate an inferential argument or a syllogism through the believability of its conclusions rather than through the principle of logical necessity (Evans et al., 1983; Evans & Curtis-Holmes, 2005).

TEXT BOX 4.1 EXAMPLES OF CATEGORICAL SYLLOGISMS

The following examples (Ball & Stupple, 2016) depict how logical validity and the credibility of the conclusion are usually manipulated in studies of the *belief bias*:

(1) *Valid-Believable syllogism:*

All birds have wings
All crows are birds
Therefore, all crows have wings

Easy to accept.

(2) *Valid-Unbelievable syllogism:*

All mammals can walk
All whales are mammals
Therefore, all whales can walk

Difficult (or impossible) to accept: The premises are false, but the reasoning is correct.

(3) *Invalid-Believable syllogism:*

All flowers fade
All roses fade
Therefore, all roses are flowers

Difficult to refute! The premises are true, but the reasoning is flawed.

(4) *Invalid-Unbelievable syllogism:*

All meat products can be eaten
All apples can be eaten
Therefore, all apples are meat products

Easy to refute!

The findings in the literature generally show that most people consider the *Valid-Believable* syllogisms as valid, but not the *Valid-Unbelievable* syllogisms (see Text

Box 4.1). This is in spite of the fact that they share the same logical structure and so are both valid, given that in both cases the conclusion follows logically from the premises. Moreover, people generally consider *Invalid-Believable* syllogisms to be valid, but, according to logical criteria, they are not (the fact that roses fade doesn't make them flowers). Therefore, the *credibility* of the conclusion affects the *validity* evaluation of the conclusion: syllogisms with the same structure are considered valid or invalid depending on the content of the premises and the conclusions.

Typically, the validity judgement given by the participants deviates from the logical validity in two cases: when the syllogism is logically invalid, but the content makes it believable (*Invalid-Believable*); and when the syllogism is logically valid, but the content makes it unbelievable (*Valid-Unbelievable*).

Dual-process theories of thinking have been put forward to explain this type of bias. They are characterized by the distinction between two different systems of reasoning (System 1 and System 2) that we saw in the previous chapters. The general term "dual-process theories" encompasses a wide number of models, which can be divided into different classes (Evans et al., 1983; Evans & Stanovich, 2013; Oakhill et al., 1989; Sloman, 1996; Stupple & Ball, 2008). Independent of which specific model is preferred, all are characterized by the presence of a System 2 that can abstract information from the context, thus producing valid solutions (abstraction, cognitive decoupling) and by a System 1 that, instead, automatically contextualizes the information and thus bases its response predominantly on the content of the syllogism, rather than on its logical validity. Hence, according to the dualistic approach, the error is to be attributed to a lack of abstract thinking, which is caused by the dominance of System 1 and the lack of activation of System 2. The apparently most convincing evidence links the activation of System 2 to a better performance in belief-biased problems. Such evidence has been obtained by correlating general cognitive abilities with the ability to solve tasks, leading to biases. Sá and colleagues (1999) found that relatively higher cognitive ability (measured with the Scholastic Assessment Test, SAT[3]) is associated with a reduced probability of committing a *belief bias* (Stanovich et al., 2016). These abilities are synthesized in the capacity for abstraction. Actually, given that the SAT is composed of two equal parts, one that assesses logic and the other reading comprehension, in my view, it does not necessarily follow that high scores reflect a particular competence in logic, rather a pronounced interpretative ability or even simply proficiency in both areas.

To the best of our knowledge, the studies that have attempted to improve performance in belief-biased tasks show it is hard to overcome the bias: experimental manipulations always resulted in absent or weak effects (Evans et al., 1994; 2001; Handley et al., 2011).[4] More forceful triggering of analytical abilities was seen as one way of improving performance, but its role in previous research was overrated.

A study conducted by Stupple and colleagues (2011) helps to understand which factors could trigger analytic reasoning: their participants tended to answer more quickly in situations that posed no conflict, i.e., a *Valid-Believable* or an *Invalid-Unbelievable* syllogism, compared to conflict situations, i.e., an *Invalid-Believable* or *Valid-Unbelievable* syllogism. This effect was particularly evident for the high-performers, although the low-performers also showed the same pattern, which suggests that at some point in the processing of the problem, all the participants were more or less aware of the conflict between logical thinking and knowledge of the world. This finding is very intriguing for a variety of reasons (see Ball & Stupple, 2016), but especially because it suggests that individuals may indeed be capable of logical thinking—but only if it is made clear that this is what is being asked of them.[5]

4.3.1 Experts versus "Naïves"

In 1983, Tversky and Kahneman created their well-known *Linda* Problem (which we will examine in the next chapter), which led them to discover that not only their naïve participants (participants with no formal training in statistics) but also the participants who had had such training or were already experts in statistics failed to recognize the conjunction rule (i.e., the probability of two events occurring together is always less than or equal to the probability of either event occurring alone), so committing the *conjunction fallacy*. Some years later, Maria Bagassi and I investigated the questions raised by the fact that trained statisticians and experts in the field of abstract logical reasoning failed to recognize this elementary inclusion rule (Bagassi & Macchi, 2016; Macchi & Bagassi, 2018). As I pointed out in Chapter 2 (see also Dulany & Hilton, 1991; Mosconi & Macchi, 2001), the misleading contextualization of the task, which was centred on an irrelevant personality sketch from a logical perspective, hindered even statistically trained participants from grasping what the experimenter intended to communicate and evaluate concerning the inclusion class rule. Analogously, when conducting an experiment involving the Wason Selection Task (see Section 4.4), we found that the performance of participants trained in logic did not differ significantly from that of participants who had not received such training (see Chapter 2, see pages 32 to 34). When faced with the original Wason Selection Task, only 13% of the expert participants and 5% of the naïve group gave the correct response. Paradoxically, a great number of the participants were able to use the material implication correctly but were unable to identify the only case that was crucial for falsifying the rule. Once again, we were faced with the question as to why people trained in logic or statistics experienced the same degree of difficulty with these tasks as the naïve participants. We would have expected that their training and experience would have facilitated them in the logical reasoning required by this task, but this was not the case. A similar issue could be raised when considering *Invalid-Believable* syllogisms, such as the one below, that frequently recur in the literature:

All flowers fade
All roses fade
All roses are flowers

Advocates of dualistic theories of thought would argue that people accept the invalid conclusion because beliefs tend to prevail over logic in cases of conflict. However, the terms "roses" and "flowers" can be seen as two classes, the one included in the other by definition; therefore, it can be implicitly deduced that "all roses are flowers" (which is the conclusion of the *Invalid-Believable* syllogism). That said, this error from a logical point of view can be interpreted as the result of a communicative cooperative act: concluding that roses are flowers does not add any new knowledge; it only furthers communicative interaction, albeit at the lowest level of informativeness. As in Socratic dialogue, the function of rhetorical questions is to supply a basis from which the argumentation will start; stating that "roses are flowers" is to assent to a point of obvious but shared knowledge.[6]

4.3.2 A Dialogue of the Deaf

The following experimental hypotheses can be drawn from the theoretical assumptions described above:

1. When the instructions do not clearly convey the exact nature of evaluation of the inference, and so it is not possible for the participants to understand whether they are supposed to apply the rules of natural language and common knowledge of the world, or the rules of logic, the strength of the *belief bias* will be independent of the degree of expertise in logic. In other words, not even those who have been trained in logic will be able to solve the problem if they fail to understand that, in that particular context, they are required to think according to the rules of logic. Therefore, in experimental terms, we would have expected that the degree of acceptance of *Invalid-Believable* syllogisms (which is an index of the strength of the *belief bias*) would have been high for both the expert and the naïve participants.
2. Subtle modifications to the instructions, if specifically aimed at making the aim of the task clearer, can lead to significant changes in performance. The experimenter must convey a message to the participants that communicates the expectation that they will not follow the rules of natural language (i.e., reasoning, taking factual truth into account) but which must convert to the rules of logical language (i.e., reasoning considering necessity). Indeed, with such modifications, the performance of the group of "experts" trained in logic did not differ significantly from that of the "naïve" group.

The question remains, how is it possible that people trained in logic had such difficulty with these tasks? We would have expected that their training would have facilitated them in decontextualizing and abstracting, but that was not the case.

4.3.3 Does Training in Logic Provide Protection from Logical Biases?

In 2019, my colleagues and I designed a first experiment to further explore the experimental hypothesis that the performance of a group of "experts" would not differ from that of a group of "naïves", whenever it was not clear whether the proposed conclusions were to be evaluated from the point of view of logical validity or factual truth (Macchi et al., 2019). We used the conclusion-evaluation paradigm that consists in having the participants evaluate the validity of a given conclusion based on the premises.

We asked each participant to perform a paper-and-pencil task comprising the two different syllogisms below, presented in random order.

> THE VALID-BELIEVABLE SYLLOGISM:
> *All animals are mortal. All humans are animals. All humans are mortal.*
>
> THE INVALID-BELIEVABLE SYLLOGISM:
> *All flowers fade. All roses fade. All roses are flowers.*

Both syllogisms were followed by the question: "*Does the conclusion follow from the premises*?" We found a highly significant difference between the performance on the *Valid-Believable* and the *Invalid-Believable* syllogisms in both the naïve and the expert groups.

- In the *Valid-Believable* syllogism, 94% of the naïve group and 96% of the expert group responded correctly.
- In the *Invalid-Believable* syllogism, only 4% of the naïve group and 10% of the expert group responded correctly.

The performance of the naïve group was comparable to that of the expert group on both *Valid-Believable* and *Invalid-Believable* syllogisms (there was no statistical difference between the two groups of participants). These data do not want to suggest that the degree of expertise in logic has no influence on reasoning skills; what they do suggest is that performances of participants who have taken a complete course in logic will be similar to that of those who have not (the naïves), when it is not possible for the participants to infer from the instructions that they are required to activate their logical competences.

4.3.4 Transparency of Questions: We Can Reason in Logical Mode If the Instructions Are Clear

We then ran a second experiment, Experiment 2, designed to test the second experimental hypothesis according to which pragmatic manipulation of the instructions may change how the participants understand the experimenter's intentions and the aim of the task, consequently improving performance.[7]

After a class exercise on other questions of logic, each participant received an *Invalid-Believable* syllogism (the same used in the first experiment). We manipulated the instructions given in Experiment 1 in two ways, with the intention of communicating to the participants that they should apply the *principle of logical necessity*. The new instructions were: "Does the conclusion necessarily follow from the given premises?" (the *Necessarily* instruction) and "Can you infer the conclusion from the given premises according to the *Criteria of Logic*?" (the *Criteria of Logic* instruction).

The two forms were similar, but they stressed different aspects; the former communicates the principle of logical necessity directly, stressing the type of relationship that must exist between the premises and the conclusions, thus explaining the essence of logical, deductive thinking, while the latter communicated, more indirectly, that the participant was expected to adhere to logical rules while judging the validity of the syllogism. This refers to a concept well-known to logicians and informs those without such knowledge only that the type of reasoning to be applied is different from that which they usually use. Consequently, an improvement in performance would be seen here only if the participant had at least a vague idea of how logic works. We therefore made another further prediction: that the *Necessarily* instruction would lead to a similar improvement in performance in both the expert and the naïve groups, whereas the *Criteria of Logic* instruction would lead to a greater improvement in the performance of the experts, as they were better versed in the logical criteria to be applied.[8]

In the test accompanied by the *Criteria of Logic* instruction, 41% of the naïve group and 67% of the expert group gave the correct answer to the *Invalid-Believable* syllogism. The difference between the two groups was statistically significant. In the test on the same syllogism accompanied by the *Necessarily* instruction, 66% of the naïve group and 77% of the expert group answered correctly. As expected, there was no significant difference between the two groups.

The results of the experiment show that manipulating the instructions to clarify the perspective to be used when evaluating the syllogisms led to a strong improvement in the performance of both the naïve and the expert groups. With the *Necessarily* instruction, which clearly and concisely stresses that there must be a relationship of logical necessity between the premises and the conclusion, performance was greatly improved independently of the participant's level of expertise in logic. A similar, albeit lesser, improvement was found in both groups for the *Criteria of Logic* instruction.

4.3.5 Conclusions

A consolidated line of research claims that *cognitive decoupling*, the ability for abstraction, is an essential condition for correct reasoning. However, from a pragmatic point of view, it might be argued that this ability is not essential for the participant who performs syllogisms correctly without falling into the *belief bias*. Indeed, as anticipated in Chapter 2, it is more important to possess what could be called "interpretative talent", the skill of perceiving the real aim of the task, improving the contextualization of the information rather than de-contextualizing it. In fact, to perform the task correctly, the participant needs to understand (a) the experimenter's communicative intention and (b) that what is requested is to change their natural language interpretation to an interpretation based on a different parameter of evaluation of the relationships of the propositions, in other words, a logic-based interpretation.

In line with this hypothesis, there are a number of interesting studies which show that beliefs affect both intuitive and reflective reasoning (Verschueren et al., 2005) and that many cognitive biases are independent of cognitive abilities (Evans et al., 2007; Stanovich & West, 2008).

To summarize, clarifying the aim of the task significantly improved both the performance of the experts and the naïves. These results suggest that what in the literature has been considered as a typical error in logical thinking is, in fact, the consequence of a task that does not clarify that the level of evaluation required is different from that required in the common sense, distinguishing between factual truth and logical validity. We improved the performance of the naïves by activating their analytical skills; skills they already possessed, but that the original instructions did not make clear should be activated. Taking into consideration the communicative inferences typically made in everyday contexts led to a change in how the message was formulated and processed.

4.4 Verify and Falsify

4.4.1 Testing Ideas and Hypotheses

In the 1960s, Peter Wason sought to explore the question of human rationality by designing an elegant and concise experimental task, later known as the "Selection Task" (Wason, 1966). This became a fundamental experimental paradigm for addressing a crucial theoretical question that remains partly still open: in everyday life, are we capable of reasoning scientifically—that is, of testing the soundness or validity of an idea or hypothesis, both by verifying and by attempting to falsify it?

We have already seen Wason's verification bias experiment in detail in Chapter 2. Wason himself highlighted the broad negative implications of this phenomenon, not only for scientific reasoning but also for our ability to critically examine our ideas, not just by verifying them, but by identifying potential counterexamples.

In the decades that followed, experimental evidence gathered by Wason and many other researchers showed that performance on the Selection Task improved when the content of the task was altered. This initially led to the rather intuitive hypothesis that realistic content, in and of itself, facilitated formal reasoning (Johnson-Laird et al., 1972; Wason & Shapiro, 1971; Wason & Johnson-Laird, 1972). The results of these studies appeared to confirm the hypothesis, but they also produced some paradoxical effects regarding the relation between form and content in reasoning, which are discussed below.

4.4.1.1 A Psychorhetorical Approach to the Selection Task

How the instructions for a task are formulated and then imparted is crucial for the participants to execute it correctly. Instructions that are unclear, fallacious, or even misleading negatively impact performance. The original version of Wason's task made it difficult for participants without a background to understand that the conditional rule "if ... then ..." should be interpreted in a logical sense, i.e., unidirectionally, rather than bidirectionally, as often occurs in natural language.

An example will help to clarify this: if you say to someone, "If you mow the lawn, I'll give you 5 euros", it seems obvious that you mean, "I'll give you 5 euros if, and only if, you mow the lawn". From the logical point of view, however, this reversal is not justified. You might give them 5 euros for some other reason, even if they don't mow the lawn, though in this case, you would use a different expression.

The bidirectional interpretation of material implication in natural language would induce participants to form the pairings *p/q* and *not-p/not-q*. In other words, the rule is understood as "when p is present, q must be present, and when not-p is present, not-q must also be present".

As a result, participants tend to give incorrect responses, selecting A (p) and 4 (q), which, considering how we imagined they would interpret the task, is also a partially correct answer (Klauer et al., 2007; Mosconi, 1990).

The hypothesis that how instructions are formulated plays a crucial role in the correct understanding of the Selection Task has been supported by several experimental studies (Ahn & Graham, 1999; Fairley et al., 1999; Weidenfeld et al., 2005). These findings also fit well into a psychorhetorical framework; task instructions are effective when they clearly communicate the true aim of the task.

To sum up, Wason's strong initial claims were weakened by later evidence, showing high rates of correct responses in the selection task. Other studies suggested that, instead of realistic material, the presence of deontic content or pragmatic schemas (Cheng & Holyoak, 1985) was a key factor in obtaining these improvements in performance. However, the evidence from the experiments reviewed below shows that none of these factors appears necessary for a better performance.

In particular, our research aims at demonstrating that performance can improve when the conditional rule is expressed in natural language in a way that effectively conveys the meaning of material implication as defined in logic.

4.4.1.2 The Importance of Rendering Explicit the Material Implication in Natural Language

We developed a new version of the Selection Task (Figure 4.2) with the objective of demonstrating that the participants' performance would be improved by enabling them to understand that they should use the rules of logic to perform a given task, even in the absence of a realistic scenario.

A deck consists of cards that have one number on one side and a color on the other side, in the following way:

Every time that there is a 3 on one side then there must be the white color on the other side, but not necessarily vice-versa. **Instead, if there is a 5 on one side then on the other side the color can be indifferently white or black.**

Of these four cards, turn only those necessary to check that they have been made in the way indicated.

FIGURE 4.2 Experimental Condition 1.

Each participant[9] was tested individually and was randomly assigned to one of the two conditions below:

- *Experimental Condition 1* (*relevant rule*): In this version, the expression "not necessarily vice versa" was introduced after the first part of the conditional rule to specify that the relation between p and q is unidirectional: only *p* implies *q* and not vice versa, making the material implication explicit. Moreover, the content of *p* and not-*p* was changed into two odd numbers, making it less likely that the participants would arbitrarily couple *p* with *q* and *not-p* with *not-q*.
- *Experimental Condition 2* (*standard rule*): This version corresponded to Wason's original test (1966), as it did not include the second part of the rule of Experimental Condition 1, stating only that *p* is associated with *q*, while it was not stressed that the presence of q does not necessarily imply the presence of *p*. The instructions and the stimuli were identical to those of Experimental Condition 1.

In Experimental Condition 1, 55% of the participants answered correctly, selecting the cards *p* (number 3) and *not-q* (black reverse side), while only 8% gave the correct answer in the version representing Wason's task (Experimental Condition 2).
The difference in performance between the two Experimental Conditions shows that the number of correct answers increases even when participants cannot rely on a realistic scenario that encourages them to search for counterexamples. Rather, the improvement is to be attributed to the clarification that the material implication is valid in the direction p → q but not in the opposite direction, q → p. They appear to suggest that new manipulations were successful in improving the clarity of the instructions. In particular, the crucial element appears to be the clarification of the unidirectionality of the material implication by the addition of the wording "not

necessarily vice versa", since the rest of the rule is almost identical in the two conditions.

The correct communication of how the rule is to be interpreted plays a fundamental role. The unidirectionality of the material implication was not conveyed in the original version of Wason's Selection Task, but it was implicitly clear in Johnson-Laird et al.'s *Post-office worker* task. However, if the information regarding the material implication is efficiently communicated in natural language, a clear improvement in performance will be seen, regardless of whether a realistic setting is used or whether there is an explicit request for counterexamples. It is important to note that our Experimental Condition 1 is not intended as a simplified version of the task, but rather as a less ambiguous version of the conditional rule.

4.5 Conclusions

Our main aim in the study described above was to show that when a conditional rule of logic (which belongs to a specific domain of knowledge) is expressed through the conversational rules of natural language in a way that clarifies its unidirectionality, it can be understood even by those who do not have a specific training in logic. The unidirectionality of the material implication is clarified simply by adding the sentence "not necessarily vice versa" which by itself is crucial and sufficient to greatly improve performance, independently of the introduction of a realistic scenario. Most of our interpersonal relations are based on communicative exchanges, and throughout life we accumulate a vast experience on how to communicate information correctly. Moreover, even infants, as young as one year of age, have a basic understanding of pragmatic principles in communication (Behne et al., 2012; Esteve-Gibert et al., 2017), flexibly modifying their behaviour based on the pragmatic context of a communicative act (Tomasello & Barton, 1994). In spite of this, researchers frequently have difficulty in communicating their intentions clearly (Bagassi & Macchi, 2016). The reason for the discrepancy between our innate communicative abilities and their poor application in the lab can perhaps be found in the attempt of psychology to differentiate from philosophy, to carve out a place among the sciences. Hence, it complies with the requirements of "scientificity", integrating philosophy's speculative approach with an experimental approach based on logic, the discipline that constituted the foundation of the other sciences. Cognitive psychologists tend to use a form of technical communication that is perfectly comprehensible for the research community but difficult to understand, unless a specific indication is given that the natural language is not being used (see Bagassi & Macchi, 2016; Macchi, 2000; Macchi et al., 2019). Regardless of the underlying reasons, this breakdown in communication between experimenters and participants results in the latter interpreting the task in a sense that does not correspond to the experimenters' intent. Consequently, participants end up struggling to solve a task that is not what the experimenter had in mind and is frequently harder or even nonsensical.

Human beings possess extraordinary analytical abilities, but they are not always able to demonstrate them. If they are in the correct context and the formulation of the instructions is pertinent to the aim of the task, our chances of tapping into their cognitive abilities will be much greater.

In this chapter, we have proposed a new way of looking at an old problem. Instead of focusing on our participants' analytical abilities in experiments on the psychology of thought, we concentrated on the communication of the experimental task itself. By subtly modifying the instructions of the task, we were able to obtain a marked improvement in the performance of both our naïve participants and the experts in logic. The current theoretical models of deductive reasoning should be expanded to include the interpretation of the task as an essential part of processing the problem.

TEXT BOX 4.2 LOGIC AND THE REAL WORLD

According to Mosconi and D'Urso (1975), even when participants give the correct answer in the *Post-office worker* version of the Selection Task, it is not because they have applied logical inference schemas such as *modus ponens* or *modus tollens*.[10] In Mosconi's view, in fact,

> the participants were solving a real-world problem and their responses were mistakenly interpreted as evidence of deductive reasoning ability. If the "logic" of real-life situations did not happen to align with the logic of rule falsification, then this level of correct responding would not persist—even if the material was always realistic.
>
> (Mosconi, 1990, p. 195)

To test this hypothesis, Mosconi (1990) and Mosconi and D'Urso (1975) conducted an experiment using the same instructions, postal regulations, and realistic materials used by Johnson-Laird and colleagues (1972), with only one exception: the value of the stamp in the not-*q* condition. In this case, not-*q* was represented by an envelope carrying a "100-cent stamp", i.e., a higher value than the required 40 cents.[11]

As predicted, none of the participants selected the not-*q* envelope, explaining that it made no sense to check an envelope with a 100-cent stamp, since the postal service is not concerned with stamps of greater value than 50 cents, as they do not violate the rule. This experiment demonstrates that even when realistic material is used, responses may diverge from strict logical reasoning. It also shows that the correct choices made in Johnson-Laird et al.'s experiment (the "sealed envelope" and "40-cent stamp") were not the result of logical inference (i.e., the activation of *modus ponens* and *modus tollens*), as otherwise the participants would have selected the envelope with the 100-cent stamp (which, logically speaking, is a "not 50 ", i.e., not-*q*).

Participants were not merely interpreting the task literally; they were also drawing on implicit knowledge: letters with insufficient postage must be taxed, while those with the correct postage or with a higher-value stamp comply with the regulations. In logical terms, any case representing not-*q* should be selected. However, cases that appear irrelevant or perfectly acceptable from a real-world standpoint—such as the 100-cent stamp whose value exceeds that required by the postal regulations—tend not to be selected, because they appear to be completely acceptable.

Notes

1 This syllogism has the same logical structure as Woody Allen's nonsensical quips. In this case, however, most people accept the conclusion as it represents an obvious truth.

2 It is interesting to note, however, that logic has served as a reference point both for proponents of the theory of mental logic and for those who, through the study of biases and fallacies, have emphasized a more irrationalist view of human nature. According to the former, everyday reasoning follows a kind of natural logic that employs inferential patterns similar to those found in classical logic (Braine, O'Brien, Henle). The second approach, by contrast, questions this assumption, arguing that inferential patterns are used appropriately only under certain conditions: when dealing with realistic material (Wason & Shapiro, 1966/1971; Johnson-Laird et al., 1972), or when there is no conflict between content and formal rules (Frankish & Evans, 2009). Outside of these conditions, our cognitive system appears to show a structural tendency to violate such principles. In all of these approaches, the explanation of correct reasoning is attributed to the patterns of formal logic, which is nonetheless taken as the unquestioned reference model for understanding human reasoning.

3 Computer-based standardized test used predominantly in the USA as a university admission test.

4 In general they share strategies for improving performance in *belief bias* tasks: in the first place, as System 2 would appear to be initially inactive (or at least, less active than expected), it should be activated somehow. In addition, the objective should be to inhibit automatic adhesion to System 1. The previous studies that tried to improve performance on tasks of this type were based on these premises.

5 De Neys (2012) reported similar findings for other types of bias.

6 Taking these two premises out of an experimental context, the likely response would be, "we know that, and so what?"—the natural language equivalent of the logical expression *nihil sequitur*.

7 Given that our objective was to observe improvements in performance, we focused on the *Invalid-Believable* syllogism, which generally is characterized by very low rates of correct responses.

8 The syllogism was followed by the *Necessarily* instruction for 50% of the participants, while for the other half it was followed by the *Criteria of Logic* instruction. As in the first experiment, instructions were always followed by the question "Why?".

9 About 78 students of both sexes and ages raging between 19 and 25 years, attending the Humanistics faculty of the University of Milan-Bicocca, participated in the test.

10

Modus ponens	*Modus tollens*
Given these two premises:	Given these two premises:
If p, then q.	If p, then q.
p.	Non-q.
Therefore, q.	Therefore, non-p.

11 The original task was presented in Italian lire, the currency used for postage rates in Italy in the early 1970s.

5

THINKING UNCERTAINTY ACROSS POSSIBLE WORLDS

Statistical Illiteracy or Misleading Communication?

> Words are poor vehicles for discussing inverse probabilities.
>
> Robyn M. Dawes

5.1 Day-to-Day Uncertainties and Probabilities

Uncertainty characterizes a goodly part of our daily life and the reality in which we live. During the 2019–2020 pandemic, uncertainty became an inevitable factor of our existence; we were obliged to live under a cloud of uncertainty and find ways of managing it and of estimating the probability of the events that were taking place. Uncertainty relates to the future just as much as it does to the past and the present, when our knowledge of what is happening is incomplete, which is, basically, practically always the case. We live with uncertainty and try to give it expression, narrowing its indeterminacy through the use of probabilities—whether in predicting the outcome of future events (such as the prognosis of a disease, environmental risks, and the result of an exam) or in formulating hypotheses about past events, where we can only assess, in probabilistic terms, how things unfolded or which factors may have caused a given event. Another example is when a judge is called to evaluate the guilt of a person accused of a crime: this involves a probabilistic judgement of the evidence and its relation to the responsibility of the accused.

In addition to the possible difficulty of statistical (il)literacy inherent to probabilistic reasoning, there is also the question of the communication of the probabilistic information involved in the reasoning process.

I will start with some examples of misunderstandings of scientific communications and the disclosure of probabilistic data, and the sometimes dramatic consequences

DOI: 10.4324/9781003680895-5

that ensued. One such was the warning issued in England and Wales in 1995: "The third-generation birth control pill increases the risk of thrombosis by 100%". This communication, with its apparently clear message, threw adolescents into such a state of panic that many stopped taking oral contraceptives, with a consequent increase in unwanted pregnancies and abortions (over 13,000 cases), as can be seen in Figure 5.1.

This would probably never have happened if the communicator had kept in mind that a non-expert public needs a baseline (the data to which the percentage refers to) to understand the significance of the percentage referred to in the message. If the warning had been phrased as the danger of thrombosis to women taking the third-generation pill compared to the previous version, so increasing from 1 in 7000 to 2 in 7000, or from 0.014% to 0.028%, this collective wave of panic would probably not have happened. The "increase of 100%" simply represents a doubling of the probability, but this, on its own, is not informative, as the dimension of the phenomenon depends on the base sample. Given the increase in abortions following the announcement, it appears that for those without expertise in statistics, the "increase of 100%" meant that the chances of falling victim to the feared collateral effect were almost a certainty.

	Frequency	*Percentage*
Previous pill	1 in 7000	0.014%
Third-generation pill	2 in 7000	0.028%

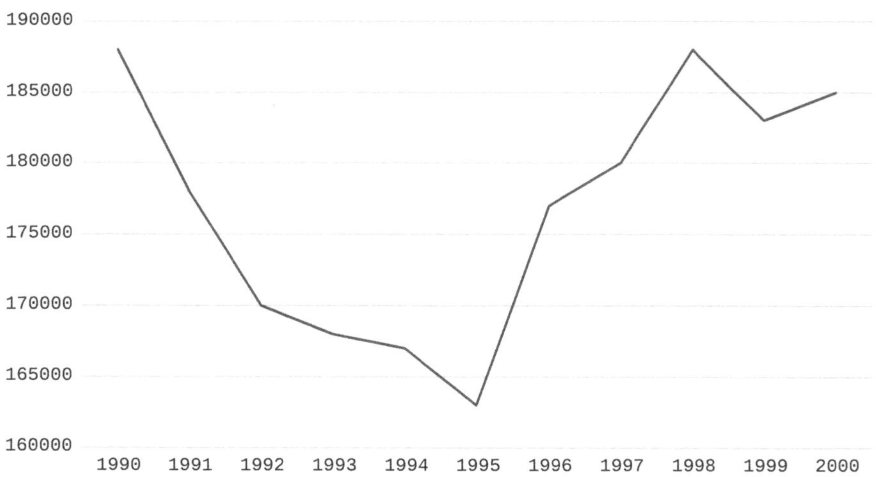

FIGURE 5.1 Inversion of the decreasing trend of abortions in England and Wales after the "pill scare" in 1995.

Another, more recent example comes from the COVID-19 pandemic. Up to November 2021, the number of people in intensive care units who had been vaccinated and those who had not was practically the same (Figure 5.2).

This was often used to support the theory that there was no point in getting vaccinated. But the question that we should have been asking was this:

> Does the number of vaccinated and non-vaccinated patients in intensive care units prove that the vaccine is useless?

The answer is negative. The percentage of hospitalized vaccinated patients calculated on the entire vaccinated population is much lower than the equivalent percentage for non-vaccinated patients, which is evident if the data is being considered correctly.

Here too, for the data on intensive care admissions to be understood correctly, it must be recognized that the same absolute number (an equal number of patients in intensive care) may correspond to very different percentages (24% vs. 74%), depending on which reference population is being considered (unvaccinated vs. vaccinated). As can be seen in Figure 5.3, although at first glance it may appear otherwise this actually demonstrates the effectiveness of vaccination in preventing the most serious outcomes of the disease.

Another example deals with feminicide, an issue that, of late, is frequently in the news, from the judicial angle. If a man is accused of killing his companion, can

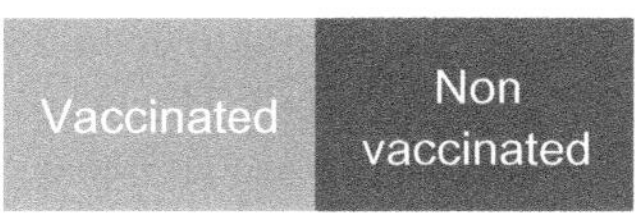

FIGURE 5.2 Vaccinated and non-vaccinated.

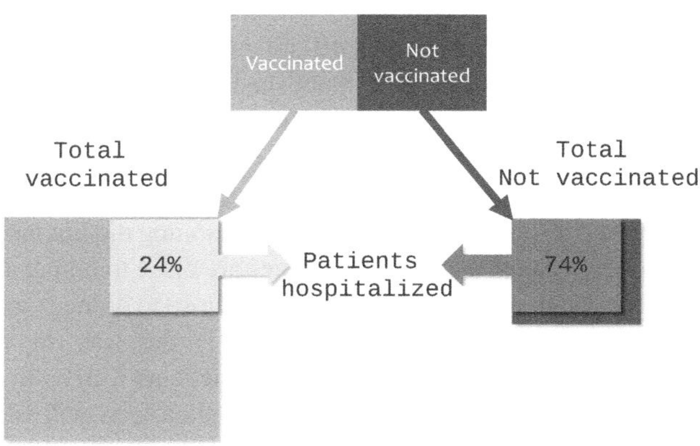

FIGURE 5.3 Total vaccinated versus total non-vaccinated.

the fact that he has been known to be violent to her be admitted as proof in the case against him?

According to Alan Dershowitz, who defended O.J. Simpson, a legendary football player and famous actor, the answer is no. O.J. Simpson was accused of murdering his wife, whom he had regularly abused. Dershowitz argued that the majority of women who are killed, are killed by a man with whom they have a relationship, regardless of whether the man has physically abused them. Only one-tenth of the 1% of men who abuse their wives actually kill them. Simpson was acquitted in a very controversial trial.

This statement caught the attention of I.J. Good, University Emeritus Professor of Statistics of the Virginia Polytechnic Institute and State University, who argued against it in an article on *Nature*, published on June 15, 1995, under the title "When batterer turns murderer". He noted that the "probability of greater relevance for legal purposes would be based on the knowledge that the woman was both battered by her husband and also murdered by somebody". He explained that P = the probability of (Guilt|Battery) = one-tenth of 1% of men who batter their wives and then kill them, but the probability of a man murdering his wife, *if he battered her and she was killed by someone* – becomes P (Guilt|Battery and Murder) = 50%. Indeed, in one case out of two, it turns out that it is the husband himself who is the culprit. Unfortunately, even if it had been used in court, the demonstration used by Good to reach this conclusion, decidedly unfavourable to the accused, would probably have been incomprehensible to anyone who was not an expert in statistics.

Finally, we will take a look at two other cases of misleading communication that R.M. Dawes (1988) identified in disseminative articles that led him to conclude that "words are poor vehicles for thinking about inverse probabilities". The headline of an article on drug use in high school on an American newspaper declared that "Most on marijuana are using other hard drugs", but the article itself actually reported that "Most secondary school students who use hard drugs also use marijuana", which significantly scales down the phenomenon of double drug use. Using soft drugs does not imply a high probability that the person will also use hard drugs, while vice versa, it is highly probable that users of hard drugs will also use soft drugs (Figure 5.4). Dawes mentioned another article, published in *This Week* magazine in 1967, this time regarding road safety, whose headline claimed "This quiz could save your life next weekend".[1] According to the author of the article, the further you drive from home, the safer you will be, as the greatest number of deaths occur within 25 miles of the place of residence. Obviously, this reasoning did not take into account that this is true only because our usual itineraries are close to home, and so the probability of being involved in an accident in the area close to home is greater.

What emerges from these examples of journalism is the way in which probabilistic data is used in common discourse (press articles), as well as in cases where the judgement is specialistic in nature—legal or medical—as will be seen in the case below. Percentages are given without the overall context to which they refer (an increase of 100% is an example of this), or confusing inverse events, such as the probability of "having breast cancer when the mammogram returns a positive result" with the probability "of the mammograph returning a positive result when the person has breast cancer".

Confusion between inverse probabilities often stems from a similar lack of clarity: what is frequently omitted (and should rightly be demanded when we receive this kind of information) is a clear statement of the event to which the percentage refers. Without this, the percentage remains a vague indication—a mere semblance of information. A further example can be found in advertising claims which, cloaked in the appearance of scientific credibility that percentages always seem to convey, tell us that a particular diet product contains 90% less sugar (less than what?), or that a cream reduces wrinkles by 30% (and once again we should be asking: compared to what?).

5.2 Diagnostic Reasoning and Probability

Of course, we make predictions—there is no way we could get by without them—and evaluate the probability of events of which we are uncertain. But how do we, the majority of the population untrained in such matters, fare when estimating probability? And how do we do it? Most researchers think that we tend to err when judging probabilities (Kahneman, 2003). They attribute these errors to the fact that we use a limited number of heuristics, which reduce the complexity of the tasks of evaluating probability and predicting values to the simplest of judgements, with the result that we lose sight of crucial information and effectively distort our judgement.

Diagnostic reasoning is a paradigmatic example of probabilistic reasoning studied in the medical field. A well-known example of this is Eddy's (1982; Gigerenzer & Hoffrage, 1995; Macchi, 2003) experiment with 100 experienced doctors, who were asked to estimate the probability that a woman might have breast cancer after receiving a positive result from a mammography. Only five gave the correct answer.

The data provided to the participants in the experiment were as follows:

> A forty-year-old woman undergoes routine screening for breast cancer—a disease which, based on existing epidemiological data, has an incidence of about 1 in 100 (1%) in the relevant population.

This is therefore the *a priori* probability (also referred to as the "base rate") that the woman in question has breast cancer. If someone were to ask us to estimate the probability that a woman from this population has the disease—without any additional clinical information—we could reply: "1%".

We know that one of the clinical tests included in routine screening is mammography. Let's suppose that the woman receives a positive result from the test. What is the probability that she actually has breast cancer?

Expressing this in more technical terms, we would formulate the question as "what is the *posterior probability* that the hypothesis 'the woman has breast cancer' is true, *given that the mammography was positive*?"

If we assume that the mammography always provides an accurate diagnosis—in other words, it always detects the disease when present (*true positive*) and never flags it as present when it is absent (*false positive*)—then we could conclude that a woman who receives a positive diagnosis is indeed ill.

But if the mammography can make a mistake (as is generally the case in the real world), then we must consider this eventuality when making our assessment. *For the sake of argument, we will assume that the mammography correctly identifies the disease in 80% of women suffering from breast cancer (true positives) but also incorrectly indicates its presence in 10% of women not affected by the disease (false positives).*

Now that we have this information, we can calculate the probability of a woman receiving a positive result both when the disease is present and when it is not.

Let's start by calculating the probability of a mammography correctly diagnosing *the presence of disease*: we must consider that 80% of women with breast cancer (who make up 1% of the total—in other words, 10 women out of 1,000) will test positive (i.e., 8 out of 10).

If we want to calculate the probability of the mammography testing positive *in the absence of disease*, we have to consider that also 10% of the women who are not affected by the disease (99%, or 990 out of 1000) will however test positive (99 out of 990). This means that in our hypothetical sample of 1,000 women, a total of 107 (8 + 99) will test positive, of whom only 8 actually have the disease.

At this point, if we want to calculate the probability that one particular woman is indeed suffering from breast cancer, we must divide the estimated probability of a *positive result being given to a woman suffering from the disease* by the estimated total probability of a *positive result being given, whether the disease is present or not.*[2]

$$\text{Posterior probability} = \frac{(0.8)(0.01)}{(0.8)(0.01) + (0.1)(0.99)}$$

This is equal to 0.008/0.107 = 0.07.

If we apply the correct Bayesian reasoning (Text Box 5.1) to solve the problem, the answer is 7%, which was the answer given by 5 of the 100 doctors participating in Eddy's study. The remaining 95 had estimated the probability of a woman with a positive mammogram actually having a tumour to be 75–80%. This shows that the base rate was neglected, as was, for the most part, the data on true positives. When dealing with cases like this, it is advisable to take all the available information into account to avoid making errors of judgement, especially when, as in our specific case, there is a very low incidence of the disease involved. The understanding and application of this kind of information have been a significant topic of study and theoretical debate.

TEXT BOX 5.1 PROBABILITIES

For a more formal representation of this intuitive reconstruction of probability estimation, we must refer to Bayes' theorem (Thomas Bayes, 1702–1761), which is one of the fundamental statistical principles concerning how to estimate the probability that a given event will occur based on all the information known before the event actually takes place, and on any further information we may obtain afterward.

The calculation of the conditional probability of an event is illustrated by Bayes' theorem:

$$p(H|D) = p(H)p(D|H) / p(D)$$

where,
$p(H|D)$ is the posterior probability;
$p(H)$ is the base rate;
$p(D|H)$ is the probability that the datum will emerge when the hypothesis is true (true positives);
$p(D)$ is the probability that the datum will always emerge, i.e., both when the hypothesis is true (true positives) and when it is false (false positives).

5.2.1 The Base-Rate Fallacy

One of the most well-known and widely studied phenomena in this field concerns the neglect of prior probability in judging the likelihood of conditioned events (*base- rate fallacy*, Kahneman & Tversky, 1973; for reviews, see Barbey & Sloman, 2007; Koehler, 1996; Pennycook et al., 2022). Many of the core discussions in the debate on decision-making revolve around this paradigm, as this phenomenon can lead to serious distortions of judgement and decision-making.

The most widely known explanation of the *base-rate fallacy* can be found in Kahneman and Tversky's Research Program on Heuristics and Biases. Heuristics are described as cognitive shortcuts that simplify the complexities inherent in assessing the probability of an event, but according to Kahneman and colleagues (1982), they mainly lead to "serious and systematic errors", i.e., *biases*.[3]

According to this theory, most people assess the probability of an event by focusing only on specific information—that is, information relating to individual cases or subgroups within the reference population (for example, in the medical diagnosis scenario mentioned earlier, the result of the diagnostic test would be prioritized)—at the expense of the base rate, which refers to the probability for the entire population (for example, the incidence of the disease in the population in question), even when this base rate is explicitly provided. In this type of task, the heuristic principle involved would thus be that of *specificity* (i.e., greater importance is given to specific information) and/or *causality* (for instance, the perception that the base rate is not causally relevant and can therefore be disregarded).

Bar-Hillel claims that: "The genuineness, the robustness, and the generality of the base-rate fallacy are matters of established facts" (1980, p. 215). According to Kahneman and Tversky (1973):

> The failure to appreciate the relevance of prior probabilities in the presence of specific evidence is perhaps one of the most significant departures of intuitive judgment from the normative theory of prediction. (...) One of the fundamental principles of statistical prediction is that prior probability, which summarizes what is known about the process before the arrival of specific evidence, remains relevant even after such evidence is obtained.

However, studies exploring probabilistic reasoning produce results that appear to follow a cyclical pattern, which has led to the emergence and subsequent disappearance of phenomena once thought to be fundamental to a theory of intuitive probabilistic reasoning, as in the case of the classic biases.

While this might seem discouraging, the trend has, in fact, made it possible to further clarify the conditions under which these phenomena occur and so to identify not only the limits but also the potential of this type of reasoning.

5.2.2 The Statistical Format: Frequencies versus Percentages

For decades, it has been argued that the human mind encounters serious difficulties in probabilistic reasoning, falling prey to biases and fallacies as mentioned earlier. Indeed, even when probabilistic data are available, most people are not able to exploit them fully. According to Gigerenzer (2000), although the concept of probability has a long cultural tradition dating back to the 17th century (Hacking, 1975), only from the second half of the 20th century onwards has it become rooted in everyday language, expressed in its mathematical form to represent degrees of certainty in judgement. While mathematical terms have become part of ordinary communication in this relatively short time, especially in certain fields (healthcare, economics, meteorology, and environmental risk), the key question at this point is whether enough time has passed to allow a correct assimilation and understanding of probability, which is mostly expressed in percentages. Not according to Gigerenzer and Hoffrage (1995), who considered that the difference in prediction between correct probabilistic inference and incorrect intuitive inference is to be attributed to the percentage format with which data are mainly presented, which is comprehensible only to a small group of experts in statistics.

According to this theoretical approach, the human mind, having evolved in harmony with a given environment, would have the ability to make naturally probabilistic estimates only from data in frequentist format (considered by the authors as an ecological format), i.e., the natural format of observation of a sequence of events, and not by percentages (the format typically adopted by Tversky and Kahneman), which are fairly recent forms of representing uncertainty (Goldstein & Gigerenzer, 2002). They supported their hypothesis by converting the data from the classic problems used in their "heuristics and biases" research program into a frequentist format, obtaining a significant reduction in biases (Text Box 5.2).

TEXT BOX 5.2 A COMPARISON OF THE FORMULATIONS OF THE MEDICAL DIAGNOSIS PROBLEM

The Medical Diagnosis Problem (Eddy, 1982)
The probability that a woman aged 40 who participates in routine screening has breast cancer is 1%. If a woman has breast cancer, the probability that her mammography will be positive is 80%. If a woman does not have breast cancer, the probability that she will also get a positive mammography is 10%. Now imagine that a woman in this age group who participated in the routine screening had a positive mammography. What is the probability that she actually has breast cancer?

Standard Frequency Format (Gigerenzer & Hoffrage, 1995)
Ten out of every 1,000 women at age 40 who participate in routine screening have breast cancer. Eight of every ten women with breast cancer will get a positive mammography.

Ninety-five out of every 990 women without breast cancer will also get a positive mammography.

Here is a new representative sample of women at age 40 who got a positive mammography in routine screening. How many of these women do you expect to actually have breast cancer out of ...?

Partitive Formulation (Macchi, 2003)
The probability of breast cancer is 1% for women at age 40 who participate in routine screening.

80% of women with breast cancer will get a positive mammography.

10% of women without breast cancer will also get a positive mammography.

What percentage of those who get a positive mammography actually have breast cancer?

As I see it, however, it is equally true that using percentages expresses and satisfies the need for cognitive economy, for saving cognitive resources, which constitutes the basis of the functioning of inductive thought: the need to generalize from particular cases. The percentage allows us to extend a characteristic from a limited number of cases, individuals, or observations (in this case, 10 out of the 1000 40-year-old women observed) to the general population from which they have been extracted (i.e., 1% of 40-year-old women). There is an undeniable advantage here for the mind: a saving of cognitive resources and an increase in knowledge that lies in the possibility of being able to make inferences and forecasts with samples to which we do not have direct access, as long as said samples belong to the same population to which the percentage refers. In my view, both frequencies and percentages are comprehensible but only when relativized to the baseline or sample: if we talk about 2 or 2% without explaining which sample we are referring to, this 2 or 2% will practically be useless and may well create confusion or misunderstanding with the statistical formats, frequencies, or percentages.

5.2.3 From **Homo Heuristicus** *to* **Homo Loquens**

5.2.3.1 The Hypothesis of the Confusion of the Inverse Probabilities

At this point, for the sake of clarity, I will take a step back to the answer that practically all the doctors gave when faced with the diagnosis problem. As you will remember, 95 doctors out of 100 neglected the base-rate probability in the calculation, erroneously taking the probability of the true positives as the answer. Generally speaking, it is not unusual to confuse the conditional probability p(H|D) with the inverse probability p(D|H), as we have seen in the real-life examples illustrated in the previous paragraph. The phrases below seem to say the same thing because both associate a positive mammography with breast cancer:

- 80% of the women who have breast cancer got a positive mammography: p(M+|T);
- 80% of the women who got a positive mammography have breast cancer: p(T|M+);

However, they are stating two very different concepts: the percentage in the first phrase refers to women with breast cancer (T), while in the second phrase it refers to women who received a positive mammogram (M+).

According to the "confusion" hypothesis (cf. Braine et al., 1990; Cohen, 1981; Eddy, 1982; Dawes, 1988), subjects confuse the conditional probability of the accuracy of a specific item of information (i.e., the probability of observing a particular datum given that one hypothesis is true, P(D/H)), with the inverse conditional probability, (i.e., the probability that one hypothesis is true given that a particular datum has been observed, P(H/D)).

These authors attribute the confusion to our inherent inability to understand the difference between these two conditional probabilities. However, as generally we are capable of distinguishing these two types of probability in many other contexts (cf. Bar-Hillel, 1990; Thüring & Jungermann, 1990), it can be argued that the confusion may depend less on a natural tendency to err and more on an ambiguous transmission of information due to the structure of the text (cf. Lindley, 1985). If there is a fundamental confusion in our cognitive system, a textual variation that does not alter the nature of the conditional probability should not have any effect on the final evaluation of the subjects.

5.2.3.2 Partitive Formulation or Nested Sets

In the past, I have written several articles, two in particular (Macchi, 1995, 2000),[4] regarding the use of the base rate; in them, I suggest that neither heuristic nor frequentist factors can explain why the base-rate fallacy occurs or is eliminated. My perspective is that what is crucial for this phenomenon is the absence or presence of what I have called the *partitive formulation* (Macchi, 1995) of specific information (*true positives* or *likelihood*). A partitive formulation clearly defines the set to which the data refers (in terms of percentages or frequencies), thus relativizing its numerical content. So, for example, when we say "80% of the women who have breast cancer got a positive mammography", the 80% defines the proportion (or subgroup) of the population suffering from the illness (*the base rate*) and that has particular properties (a positive mammogram). Importantly, this formulation indirectly clarifies the relationship between the probabilities (and the corresponding sets) and ensures that the inverse probabilities—(p(H|D) versus p(D|H)—are not confused.

In my view, the improvement in the outcomes resulting from the use of the frequentist formulation is due to the presence of a partitive formulation in frequencies rather than to a more ecological format, as claimed by the frequentist approach. The partitive type of formulation highlights the relationships between subsets of data (such as between true positives and the base rate), so it is possible to produce accurate estimates (i.e., Bayesian reasoning), not only with frequencies but also with percentages, as long as it is in the partitive format. Most importantly, it helps to avoid confusion, which, according to me, is the primary culprit causing the errors made by the doctors in Eddy's study. When this formulation is used—whether in terms of relative frequencies expressed as percentages (e.g., "80% of women with breast cancer got a positive mammogram") or as natural frequencies (e.g., "8 out of 10 women with breast cancer got a positive mammogram")—the relationships between the data in the problem are clarified and can therefore be correctly interpreted (as in the real-world example involving third-generation birth control pills discussed earlier). The partitive formulation that Barbey and Sloman (2007) renamed "nested sets" can be seen as the linguistic equivalent of the graphical representation of the Venn diagram (Figure 5.4) or the tree diagram (see Figure 5.5). In a task that is couched partly in specialised terms and partly in everyday language, the

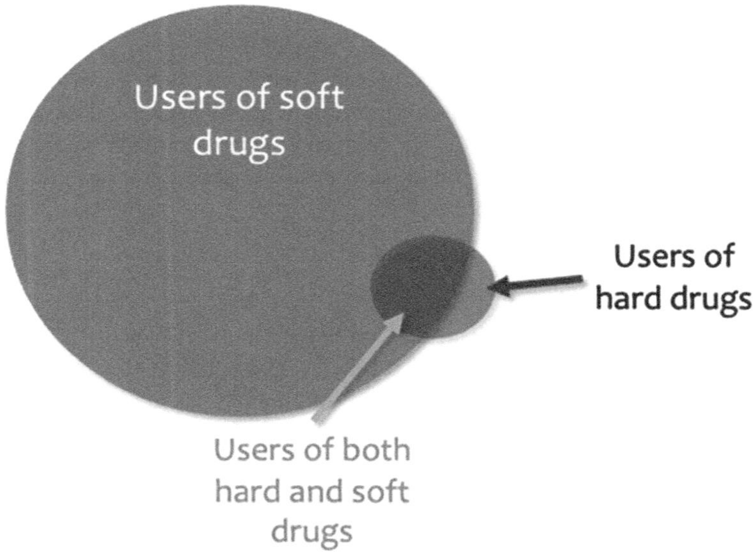

FIGURE 5.4 A Venn diagram showing users of hard and soft drugs.

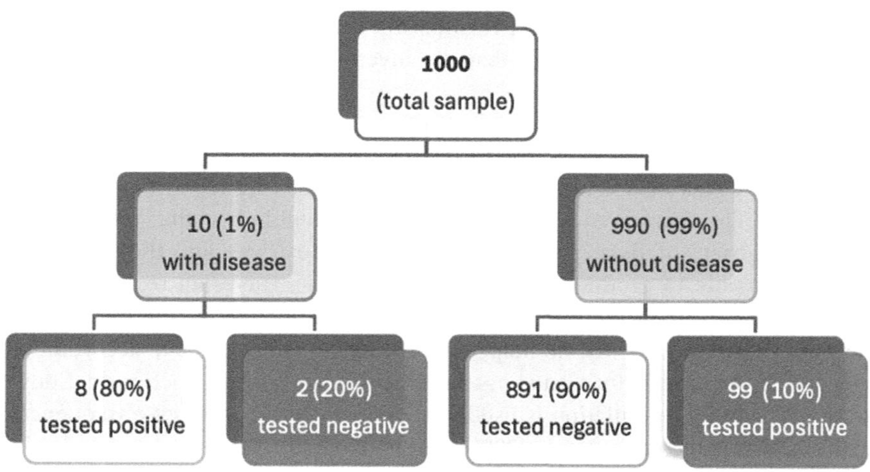

FIGURE 5.5 Tree diagram.

partitive formulation is a way of translating a specific language into everyday terms (Macchi & Bagassi, 2007).

The predictive power of this hypothesis is evident when we compare responses to different versions of problems that contain the same natural heuristic principles and the same information, but which differ in the way this is presented (partitive vs. non-partitive), and regardless of whether it is given in numbers or in percentages. Irrespective of whether the information is expressed in percentages or in frequencies, the bias is almost completely eliminated in the partitive versions but continues to be present when non-partitive versions are used (Macchi, 1995, 2000, 2003). A number of well-known problems are illustrated in Text Box 5.3.

In this light, results showing the use of Bayesian reasoning by naïve subjects (Tversky & Kahneman, 1980, using the heuristic of causality; Gigerenzer & Hoffrage, 1995, using frequentist formulations) do not depend on the principles (the presence of certain heuristics or probabilistic formats) proposed by the authors, but on the partitive expression of the hit rate.

In line with this perspective, the results I obtained are summarized below:

1. Partitive formulations prevent the confusion of probabilities.
2. No difference in performance emerged between texts formulated in frequencies or in percentages, provided that these are partitive.
3. Frequencies (if partitive) and percentages (relative frequencies) both lead to performances that are different and better than those obtained using versions relating to single events (Tversky & Kahneman, 1980), insofar as these are not partitive.
4. Even when probabilities are expressed as frequencies, eliminating the partitive formulation leads to the reemergence of the error.

If we take two of Tversky and Kahneman's classic problems—*Taxi-cab* problem and *Suicides* problem—and compare these with their *Books* problem, we can see that the base-rate fallacy is greatly reduced (to 35% of the participants) or even practically disappears (to less than 10% of the participants) when it is clear what the percentage refers to (partitive formulation) from how the text is formulated (Macchi, 1995, 2000). An exhaustive illustration comparing the partitive and non-partitive versions of the classical experimental designs used is provided in Text Box 5.3.

TEXT BOX 5.3 THE ROLE OF THE TEXT-PROBLEM FORMULATIONS

The results below were obtained by modifying certain elements in the text (in italics), but without changing the specificity and causality (heuristics) of the information: (a) the formulation of the true and false positives or (b) how the question itself was formulated (when this refers exclusively to specific information).

A) In this example, we will look at **how the specific information is formulated** (true positives and false positives):

The Taxi-cab Problem (non-partitive version, Tversky & Kahneman, 1980)
A taxi-cab was involved in a hit-and-run accident at night. Two taxi-cab companies, Green and Blue, operate in the city. You are given the following data:

1. *85% of the taxi-cabs in the city are Green and 15% are Blue.*
2. *A witness identified the taxi-cab as a Blue taxi-cab. The court tested his ability to identify taxi-cabs under the appropriate visibility conditions. When presented with a sample of taxi-cabs (half of which were Blue and half Green),* the witness made correct identifications in 80% of the cases and erred in 20% of the cases.

What is the probability that the taxi-cab involved in the accident was Blue rather than Green?

The Taxi-cab Problem (partitive version, Macchi, 2000)
A taxi-cab was involved in a hit-and-run accident at night. Two taxi-cab companies, Green and Blue, operate in the city. You are given the following data:

1. *85% of the taxi-cabs in the city are Green and 15% are Blue.*
2. *A witness identified the taxi-cab as a Blue taxi-cab. The court tested his ability to identify taxi-cabs under the appropriate visibility conditions. When presented with a sample of taxi-cabs (half of which were Blue and* half Green), the witness correctly identified 80% of the Blue taxi-cabs and misidentified 20% of the Green taxi-cabs as Blue taxi-cabs.

What is the probability that the taxi-cab involved in the accident was Blue rather than Green?

Approximately 70% of the participants gave Bayesian responses with the partitive version (74% on the taxi-cab version, compared to only circa 30% with the non-partitive version).

B) In this example, we will look at **how the question is formulated** in the *Suicides* and *Books* problems:

Causality is another heuristic investigated through the study of the base-rate fallacy; information is considered causal when it is regarded as the source of the event to be evaluated or as the process that generated it. According to Tversky and Kahneman, evidence of the role that causality plays in the use of the base rate is brought to light by a problem in which the causal nature of the specific information provided leads to the base rate being overlooked. The problem is as follows:

The Suicides Problem (Tversky & Kahneman, 1980)
Consider the following assumptions regarding suicide:

In a population of young adults, 80% of the individuals are married and 20% are single.

The percentage of deaths by suicide is three times higher among single individuals than among married individuals. What is the probability that an individual, selected at random from those who had committed suicide, was single?

Most of the participants (approximately 70%) in Tversky and Kahneman's study considered only the specific information, judging the probability of the suicide being single to be three times greater (the median and modal answers are, in fact, equal at 75%). The authors interpreted this result as the consequence of the perception of there being a causal link between being single and the motivations that can lead to committing suicide.

To test this hypothesis, they ran another experiment with the *Books* problem, which has an identical structure but no causal links, expecting to find an increase in the number of correct responses.

The Books Problem (Tversky & Kahneman, 1980)
A speciality bookstore stocks books in both German and French: 80% of the books in stock are in German, and the remaining 20% are in French.

The proportion of paperbacks is three times higher among the French books than among the German books.

What is the probability that a paperback, selected at random from the stock, will be in French?

Here, 61% of the participants used a Bayesian-type reasoning, combining the two types of information.

In 1992, I ran an experiment that showed that the differences in results obtained with the two problems do not depend on the presence or absence of causality, but on factors related to how the discourse is structured, and specifically to "asymmetries in the formulation" of the question. I modified the wording of the question in the *Suicides* problem to match that of the *Books* problem, and vice versa, so that they were effectively identical (the next paragraph shows exactly how this was done). I hypothesized that when a question refers only to specific information (in this case, the set of suicides) and not to the general population (that of young adults), the participants would tend to treat the smaller group as if it were already the result of taking the base rate into account. By referring only to the category of suicides, the question nudges the participants to interpret this specific information as if it related to a subset made up solely of those who committed suicide, 75% of whom are single and 25% married (the posterior probability).

If, on the other hand, the question explicitly refers to the entire population (as in the *Books* problem), it is clear that the probability relating to the specific information does not already incorporate the base rate, which therefore needs to be considered to solve the problem.

Rewording of the questions in the Suicides and Books Problems:

I took the original wording of the question in the *Suicides* problem:

1a. What is the probability that an **individual**, *selected at random from those who had committed* ***suicide***, was single? and reworded it to match the *Books* problem:

1b. What is the probability that a **suicide**, *selected at random from the* ***population*** *of young adults*, was single?

Similarly, I took the original question from Tversky and Kahneman's *Books* problem:

2a. What is the probability that a **paperback**, *selected at random from the* ***stocks***, is in French? and reworded it to match the *Suicides* problem:

2b. What is the probability that a **book**, *selected at random from the* ***paperbacks***, is in French?

The questions **1a** from the Tversky and Kahneman version of the *Suicides* problem and **2b** from my version of the *Books* problem are similarly structured, and accordingly, the results obtained from these two questions are almost identical. The responses based on the specific information (base-rate fallacy) corresponded to 62% in Tversky and Kahneman's version and 66% in my version. The same pattern emerged for **2a** from the Tversky and Kahneman version of the *Books* problem and **1b** from my version of the *Suicides* problem: responses based on the specific information corresponded to just 33% and 30%, respectively. This occurred independently of the causal relevance that could be attributed to the data (the explanatory factor traditionally proposed).

The experimental results appear to depend instead on how the discourse is structured and on the psychorhetorical properties of the text (in this case, of the question).

5.3 Partitive Formulation in Court: Same Data, Different Verdicts

Using the partitive format to present probabilistic data allows us to get a better grasp of the information and make more accurate predictions than when using a

single-case probability format. Indeed, if we compare data presented in a partitive or frequentist format with the same data given as a single-case percentage, it becomes clear that not only the *statistical form* changes but also the reference set to which the statistical data refers, the so-called *target*.
An example will help to clarify this:

- *Single case*: "There is a 0.08% chance that the lottery ticket I bought will win".
- *Partitive*: "8% of the tickets sold for the lottery will win".
- *Frequentist*: "8 out of 100 tickets sold for the lottery will win".

In the first case, the target to which probability refers is the single ticket I purchased; in the latter two cases, the target is the entire number of tickets sold. According to Kahneman and Tversky's Prospect Theory (1979), low probabilities tend to be systematically overestimated (whereas medium and high probabilities are underestimated). By contrast, Koehler and Macchi's Exemplar-Cuing Theory (2004) explains how the weight given to the low probabilities depends on the mental representation triggered by different data-presentation modes. According to this theory, the importance we attribute to unlikely events depends on how readily we can recall exemplars (similar events) from memory. The way an event is described affects how quickly and easily these examples come to mind.[5] Thus, both the data format (percentage vs. frequentist) and the target type (single vs. multiple) influence the importance attributed to low-probability events. Although research has rather overlooked the role of the target, prioritizing the statistical format, it is crucial when evaluating low-probability events.

One of the most interesting applications of this theory can be found in a legal setting. In our research we saw that reasoning along the lines of a multiple target (partitive formulation) encourages the inclusion of the accused in the population of the "false positives", which led the participants in our experiments to think that everyone who possesses the same DNA profile of the accused and as a result, if there is no other evidence, the number of acquittals increases.

On the other hand, focusing on a single-case target does not encourage consideration of similar exemplars. Let us take the following scenario as an example:

> A masked man bursts into a hardware store and announces his intent to rob it. However, the owner of the store resists and punches the robber in the nose. The robber flees the store, but not before a small drop of blood falls from his nose. DNA analysis of the blood reveals a match with a saliva sample taken from one of several suspects. The matching suspect is charged with attempted robbery and brought to trial.

Koehler and Macchi (2004, 2009) have examined how different formulations of the statistical format and the target regarding DNA evidence affect our mock

TABLE 5.1 The Four Conditions in Experiment 1

Target	Format	Description of DNA-match statistic
Single	Probability	The chance that the suspect would match blood drops if he were not their source is 0.001%.
Single	Frequency	The chance that the suspect would match blood drops if he were not their source is 1 in 100,000.
Multiple	Probability	0.001% of the people who are not the source would nonetheless match the blood drops.
Multiple	Frequency	1 in 100,000 people who are not the source would nonetheless match the blood drops.

jurors' decision-making, showing that the same data, presented in different forms as shown in Table 5.1, can indeed lead to completely opposite verdicts.

In trials involving DNA evidence, jurors are presented with the "*random match probability*" (RMP)—that is, the probability that the accused would by chance have the same DNA profile found at the crime scene. A low RMP (e.g., 0.001%) implies a very high probability that the suspect is the source of the DNA, and vice versa. When the formulation facilitates the availability/evocation of exemplars, examples of other people who share the same DNA profile (a multiple-target formulation), mock jurors tend to view this evidence as weak and are therefore more inclined to acquit. On the other hand, when the exemplars that come to mind are few and far between (a single-target formulation), our mock jurors perceive the DNA evidence as a virtually irrefutable proof of guilt. The characteristic of the single-target is that it focusses the mock jurors' attention exclusively on the accused, inhibiting consideration of false positives, i.e., all the other individuals in the population who might coincidentally share the same profile as the accused, thus impeding them from considering the possibility that the suspect might be innocent.

Both prosecution and defence can exploit this effect by choosing the formulation of the same scientific evidence that best supports their desired verdict. Under the "target effect" hypothesis, the prosecution will employ a single-target formulation to concentrate jurors on the defendant and foster a guilty verdict, whereas the defence will use a multiple-target formulation to link the defendant to the broader population of potential matches and encourage acquittal.

Notes

1 *This Week*, August 27, 1967.

2 Similarly, if we want to establish the probability of heads landing face up when tossing a coin, we have to divide the probability of heads landing face up (*favourable outcome*) by the total of the *possible heads and tails outcomes*, 1 out of 2.

3 Various authors—Duncker, Simon, Tversky, and Kahneman—have used the term *heuristics*, though with differing meanings. For both Duncker and Simon, heuristics mean strategies for arriving at a solution: in Simon's case, they were convenient shortcuts, while for Duncker, their connection to the *essence* of intelligent solutions and their origins made them appropriate tools. Tversky and Kahneman, by contrast, offered a markedly different interpretation, pointing out that such an approach to probability judgement could lead to serious errors, since the heuristics that guide intuitive assessments are often insensitive to factors that should, normatively, influence probability estimates. In other words, heuristics are not merely simplified or abbreviated procedures; they follow their own internal criteria and mechanisms, which may be unrelated to the logic of the problem at hand or the nature of the judgement required.
4 This explanation was later taken up by Girotto and Gonzalez (2001), Gigerenzer (2002), and Barbey and Sloman (2007).
5 This approach is in accordance with Tversky and Kahneman's availability heuristic.
6 According to Grice, the maxim of quantity can be divided into two sub-maxims: (a) make your contribution as informative as required for the current purposes of the exchange; (b) do not make your contribution more informative than is required.
7 Giovanni "Gianni" Agnelli (1921–2003) was an Italian industrialist and principal shareholder of Fiat. As the head of Fiat, he controlled 4.4% of the country's GDP. He is said to have been the richest man in contemporary Italian history.

Appendix

The Role of Pragmatic Rules in the Conjunction Fallacy

It would be possible to trace the history of psychological research into reasoning by following the thread of the increasing attention dedicated to pragmatic factors and their influence on experimental methodology. We have come a long way from the time when it was possible to propose syllogisms to participants without even clarifying the particular meaning of "some" in logical terminology (Woodworth & Sells, 1935; Sells, 1936) or the particular nature of a logical conclusion (Sells, 1936), or when the vast majority of said syllogisms were invalid and only a few were valid (Sells, 1936; Chapman & Chapman, 1959). However, heightened awareness does not seem to have even touched the presupposition of the legitimate dominance of the logical structure underlying a text (or the experimental situation in general), which was glaringly evident in the above examples; nor has it challenged the presupposition of a legitimate expectation—or, better still, insisted—that participants should interpret it according to the logical code rather than in a pragmatic manner based on the rules and psychological requirements of natural language. A more complicated but similar case is Tversky and Kahneman's well-known *Linda Problem* (1983), which is a paradigmatic example of the so-called *conjunction fallacy*, the term they attributed to the serious error in reasoning we tend to make when comparing the conjunction of two events (A and B) with one of the constituent events (for example, A), by saying that the first is more likely to occur than the second. To illustrate this, they devised a brief personality profile:

> Linda is 31 years old, single, outspoken, and very bright. She majored in philosophy. As a student, she was deeply concerned with issues of discrimination and social justice, and also participated in anti-nuclear demonstrations.

to which they added eight statements regarding Linda to be placed in the order of their probability, including "Linda is a bank teller" (A) and "Linda is a bank teller and she is active in the feminist movement" (A+B). According to Tversky and Kahneman, the judgement required of the participants revolves around an axiom of the theory of probability, according to which the conjunction of two events (A and B) cannot be greater than the probability of one of its parts (for example, A): $p(A+B) \leq p(A)$. Those who consider that "Linda is a bank teller and a feminist" (A+B) is more probable than "Linda is a bank teller" commit a grave error of judgement and have fallen into the trap of the conjunction fallacy. Indeed, most people (89%) do respond that "Linda is a bank teller and a feminist" is more probable than just "Linda is a bank teller". The explanation given for the error (or the presumed error) is that we allow our judgement to be swayed by the representative heuristic: we assume that the conjunction of "bank teller and feminist" is more representative of Linda's character as described in the profile than the simple "bank teller".

In a paper written with Mosconi in 2001, we attempted to demonstrate that the participants' replies to experiments of this type cannot be correctly interpreted as a violation of a rule of logic, because they conform to criteria and rules of discourse that differ from those of logic, to the extent that they respect requirements that logic legitimately does not consider. If we accept that conversational rules are descriptive of the speakers' natural language, then the apragmatic nature of discourses that do not respect these rules is similar to the agrammatical nature of phrases that do not conform to grammatical rules: in other words, such discourses do not pertain to the universe of discourses that can be produced and accepted in common communication.

There are cases which apparently violate these conversational principles (in this case, it would be the quantity maxim)[6] and may consequently be considered as counterexamples of their descriptive character, but a careful examination shows that this is not the case. A typical general critical case, which is strictly pertinent to our research, is that of affirmative and interrogative tautological sentences that per se seem to violate the maxim of quantity insofar as they assert or ask something redundant, because it is already contained in the meaning of the term referred to in the predicate. Take, for example, stereotype expressions such as "war is war" or "business is business" that I mentioned in Chapter 2. Tautological phrases such as these are informative in the sense that they isolate and accentuate a part of the global meaning of the term. The subject corresponds to the general concept; the predicate highlights one particular element of this general concept to the exclusion of others. Far from simply acknowledging an identity of the type "war = war" or "business = business", these proverbial phrases provide specific information, i.e., that the rules applied during a war are different from those of normal civilised society, and that behaviour which would be reprehensible in other contexts are allowed when it comes to business (or at least, they are not subject to the same degree of censure). Statements such as these cannot be represented as "A is equal to A", but as "A implies X". In such cases, it is only the form and not the message that is tautological and as a result, these utterances actually are informative. Then there is the case of riddles or conundrums. "Which is heavier: 1 kg of straw or 1 kg of iron?" is pure tautology, a pseudo-question that can only be asked rhetorically if it is limited to the information that both items weigh 1 kg. However, for the more ingenuous, this becomes a real question, as they see the information introduced by the activated knowledge of the different specific weights of the two substances as implying a change in the question, which becomes something like "Which weighs most: straw or iron?" or "Which is heavier: a certain quantity (volume) of straw or the same quantity (volume) of iron?". The same is true for those who see the contraposition of the information relating to weight (1 kg) and that relating to the activated knowledge of the different specific weights of the two substances (with the addition of the interrogative form that implies a request for a piece of information that is not known, or in any case is not contained in the question itself) as creating a situation of paradoxical incompatibility requiring a solution: in this sense the question becomes a real question. Finally, we can consider the use in *argumentative discourse* of propositions that are already known and shared ("obvious"). In such cases, the propositions usually have the precise and important function of rendering the agreement of the speakers explicit in view of the future development of the argument. It is not the content of the proposition that is informative, but the recognition that the content is shared (*rhetoric argumentation*).

None of the tautologies considered above violate any of the conversational maxims (least of all the maxim of quantity), because they are *informative* either objectively, insofar as the statement is effectively informative in terms of meaning (e.g., "War is war"), or functionally, insofar as the enunciation or reminder of shared knowledge (taken as shared) plays a well-defined and justified role in the development of a discourse.

Even such paradoxical cases therefore support the assumption of the descriptive nature of conversational rules. Furthermore, to prevent predictable objections, it should be noted that codified forms of discourse or those which fall within the competence of the speakers, such as figurative language or "special discourses" such as witticisms, are clearly not effective violations of conversational rules. There are also some classical experimental situations, such as those used by the cognitive psychologist Jean Piaget, involving inclusion and conjunction, in which the participants are asked tautological questions. These generally involve the simultaneous presence of the assumption of the predominance of the logical code and the inobservance of conversational rules. This can be easily illustrated with a case such as that of the question "Are there more Germans or blond Germans?" (a question of the type produced by Piaget to study the inclusion rule in children), containing an including set (Germans) and a subset (blond Germans). A comparison between a set and one of its parts that relates to the greater or lesser extension of the two terms is not informative in itself, because the extension ratio between the part (the subset) and the whole (the including set) is given or constitutively implicit in the concepts of the part and the whole themselves. The request to make such a comparison, as well as the question regarding its outcome, involves a violation of conversational rules (the quantity maxim), and, assuming that these rules are descriptive, they should therefore be considered "apragmatic".

This is not the case only if the question is "signalled " in some way—in the sense that it appears to be a question concerning "fundamentals" (informative not because of its evident content but because of its function of making consensus explicit or ascertaining knowledge, etc., for example, "Are all men mortal"?). Otherwise the proposition is unacceptable, unless the question is interpreted in a light that makes it pragmatically acceptable, as could be the case of younger participants for whom, precisely because they are less competent pragmatically, the most obviously informative reading of the question prevails (for example, the transformation of the question into "Are there more blond Germans or other Germans?"). Given the assumption that the only correct answer is the one that respects the logical code, and that it cannot be otherwise, such a reading is judged an error (or proof that the subject is at an early stage of logical development, without considering the possibility that the main element involved is pragmatic-discursive competence). Adults, on the other hand, see the question as a sort of trap or test that can be overcome by avoiding a natural reading and moving on to a literal interpretation.

In the *Linda* problem too, at least in the mind of who posed the question, the issue substantially hinges on the relationship between the including and the included term, and the same general considerations made in relation to the previous case also apply. What makes it different from traditional inclusion experiments is the fact that the question is formulated in terms of probability. This logically irrelevant difference is important from the pragmatic point of view. It is said that something is probable (more or less probable) when it is not certain (at least as far as the speaker knows). As can be seen from dictionaries, the word "probable", in addition to being used in contraposition to "improbable", is used in common speech as an intermediate term in contraposition to "certain". The formulation of the task in terms of probability disguises the logical nature of the question asked and, above all, is tautological and apragmatic in itself.

The evaluation of the probability of a given event is probabilistic in the true sense of the word and cannot be reduced to a "logical" judgement, at least not in the sense that it can be reached by means of a process of deduction on the basis of the meanings of the terms involved. On the contrary, a judgement about the relationship between a conjunction of events and the events that constitute the conjunction, or between an including term and an included term, is a logical judgement that can be (and can only be) reached through deduction, without uncertainty. This could explain why the results obtained on the *Linda* problem with adult participants differ from those obtained in traditional inclusion tasks.

On the basis of the Gricean maxims of quantity and relevance, participants working on the *Linda* problem should first of all regard the personality sketch as an important element of the problem itself, not as a red herring. This makes it unlikely that they would consider "bank teller" (the probability of which they have been asked to evaluate in comparison with "bank teller active in the feminist movement") as an including term, or as a term to be compared with itself plus the restriction "feminist". There is an incompatibility between considering the Linda personality sketch as an element of the problem (and therefore informative) and considering the question posed as relating to the axiom P (A) = P (A & B). Moreover, interpreting the question in these latter terms is itself apragmatic (at least in the context in which it is asked), because it is tautological and therefore unproposable.

In an experiment (Experiment 1) conducted with Mosconi in 2001, we showed that when given the choice of reading natural language in either the logical or the pragmatic code, the latter code is universally adopted, and the former, which is formally unexceptionable, is rejected (rightly so, in our opinion) precisely because it does not conform to conversational rules. This is the opposite of what is assumed in the majority of studies on reasoning and the *Linda* problem in particular. We asked the participants in this study to imagine they were jurors, with the task of evaluating a statement made by a witness who had been asked to consider the following question:

"Which of the following two statements do you judge to be more probable? 'Gianni Agnelli[7] has one billion lire' or 'Gianni Agnelli has one hundred billion lire'?". The witness answered that Gianni Agnelli has one billion lire. Our participant-jurors then had to decide whether this answer was correct, false, or reticent. Once they had submitted their answers, we then showed the witness's lawyer's statement below (the logical reasoning) to those who had answered "false" or "reticent" to see if it would make them modify their initial evaluation. The witness's lawyer's statement was couched in these terms: "in order to have one hundred billion lire, Agnelli must first have one billion lire, and it is therefore more likely that he has one billion lire. In this sense, my client's answer is correct. Now, how do you judge the answer?" The participants were then asked if they wished to modify their original evaluation; none did. They continued to evaluate the witness's statement as false or reticent and rejected the logical argumentation.

Although the witness's response was exemplary in its logic, the participants considered it to be false or reticent, claiming it was misleading and not informative (documented by their spontaneous justifications). No one would have said "a billion" based on the logical consideration corresponding to the lawyer's reasoning. The participants judged the logical answer to be incomplete, concealing pertinent information that should have been shared. So we can deduce that what would be the correct answer from a logical standpoint would not be acceptable for common usage. It should be kept in mind that this pragmatic criterion is actually adopted in court, when the person to be interrogated swears to tell "the truth, the whole truth and nothing but the truth"; indeed, a person who tells the truth, but not the whole truth, risks being accused of reticence.

Although it has a number of differences compared with the *Witness* problem, the *Linda* problem provokes a similar reaction in participants who will not answer just "bank teller" if they consider that she is probably "a bank teller and feminist" (= the whole truth). The same discursive rules that lead the participants to judge "a billion" to be "reticent" or "false" seem to be similar to those that make them consider "bank teller" as less probable than "bank teller and feminist" in the *Linda* problem. Such responses, given by the majority or even all the participants, are not "wrong"; they derived from the reasonable and consistent use of a code (that of natural discourse) which is simply different from the code that the researcher arbitrarily claimed should be used. This does not mean that people are not capable of using the logical code.

In the same study (Experiment 2), we showed that questions on basic logical relationships concerning inclusion or the conjunction of events do not give rise to errors that could be attributed to the conjunction fallacy as long as the conditions of speakability are given and the discursive norms are respected.

To conclude, the question about the judgement regarding the relationship between the included and including classes posed to the participants was purely logical in nature and not probabilistic; the information in the personality sketch was totally superfluous and irrelevant (and consequently misinforming and misleading) for the formulation of a judgement regarding this relationship; formulating the task in probabilistic terms was substantially inappropriate, and without a doubt misleading as the question was purely logical in nature. The essential point is that the decodification of the experimental discourse adopted by the authors, based on the logical code in correspondence with the hidden structure of the experiment, is not acceptable and indeed was not accepted by average speakers (and thinkers), and was not attributable to an error of judgement.

Despite the increasing attention to these pragmatic aspects and their influence on the results of experiments, the psychology of reasoning does not appear to have been influenced by this progress; indeed, it continues to uphold the presupposition of the legitimate dominance of the logical structure underlying experimental texts in the psychology of reasoning and consequently the presupposition that it is legitimate to expect that participants interpret such texts according to the logical code, rejecting basing their interpretation on a pragmatic reading complying with the rules of common discourse and the implicated psychological requirements. Consequently, only answers that conform to the logical code are considered to be correct; all the others are discarded as incorrect.

6

UNRAVELLING INCOHERENCE IN DECISION MAKING

The Critical Case of Disjunctive and Framing Effects

> Coherence is the last refuge of those who have no imagination.
>
> Oscar Wilde

6.1 Making Rational Choices in a World of Uncertainty

Almost all our decisions, from the most trivial to the most important, are taken while we are in a state of uncertainty. It may sound banal, but the states of certainty and uncertainty are psychologically different, and we attempt to overcome the latter as soon as possible. However, the results of our research indicated that uncertainty does not in itself lead to incoherent choices, contrary to what is often stated in the literature.

Given these premises, I will analyse here the outcomes of a series of studies (Bastardi & Shafir, 1998; Croson, 1999; Kühberger et al., 2001; Shafir, 1994; Shafir et al., 1993; Shafir & Tversky, 1992; Tversky & Shafir, 1992) that have illustrated the well-known phenomenon of incoherency in decision-making in conditions of uncertainty known as the *disjunction effect.*

One of the best-known of these problems is Tversky and Shafir's Gamble Problem (1992):

Imagine that someone has just taken part in a game of chance that gave them a 50% chance of winning $200 and a 50% chance of losing $100.

In the research conducted by these authors, both *winners* (69% of their participants) and *losers* (59% of their participants) chose to play a second game identical to the first. However, players who *did not know whether they had won or lost* (the

DOI: 10.4324/9781003680895-6

Disjunctive condition) tended to prefer not to participate in a second game identical to the first (only 36% accepted).[1] These participants behaved incoherently.
This form of incoherence violates one of the basic axioms of the rational theory of decision-making, that is, Savage's *sure-thing principle* (1954):

If A is preferred to B, whether knowing that either X occurred or that X did not occur, then A should be preferred to B even when it is not known whether X occurred or not.

If prospect x is preferred to y knowing that Event A occurred, and if x is preferred to y knowing that A did not occur, then x should be preferred to y even when it is not known whether A occurred (Tversky & Shafir, 1992).

The principle of certainty (the Expected Utility Theory) is not able to explain this phenomenon, as it treats the choices as being dependent on their anticipated consequences. According to this theory, each alternative is associated with an expected value and chosen according to the principle of value maximization.

Tversky and Shafir's model of reason-based choice (1992) provides an explanation for this phenomenon; according to them, it can be attributed to a lack of clear reasons for accepting an option (A) when we are in the Disjunctive condition. When gambling or playing games of chance, players have various reasons for accepting the second gamble in the Won and Lost conditions.

- In the Won condition, they have already won $200, so even a loss on the second gamble will still leave them ahead overall, making this option quite attractive.
- In the Lost condition, they are down $100, so playing the second gamble offers them a chance to "get out of the red", which many people find a more attractive option than accepting a sure loss of $100.
- In the Disjunctive condition, however, decision makers do not know whether they are up $200 or down $100: "Not knowing whether playing the second gamble amounts to a no-loss proposition or a chance to avoid a sure loss, the decision maker lacks a clear reason for playing the second gamble. The uncertainty concerning the first gamble, we suggest, makes it harder to contemplate the implications of each outcome". For example, the decision maker may be sure that he wishes to play the second gamble if he wins the first, but he may be unsure about his preference if he loses the first gamble. Only by focusing exclusively on the latter possibility does the decision maker realize that he wishes to play the second gamble in this case as well (Tversky & Shafir, 1992, p. 307).

Tversky and Shafir also cited the disjunction effect as being responsible for the fact that their participants sought information (and were even disposed to obtain it at an economic cost to themselves) even when it had no impact on their actual decision. In another study, structured on purchasing a vacation in Hawaii depending on the outcome of an exam, more than half of the students chose the vacation package when they knew that they passed the exam, and a slightly larger percentage chose the vacation when they knew that they had failed. However, when students did not

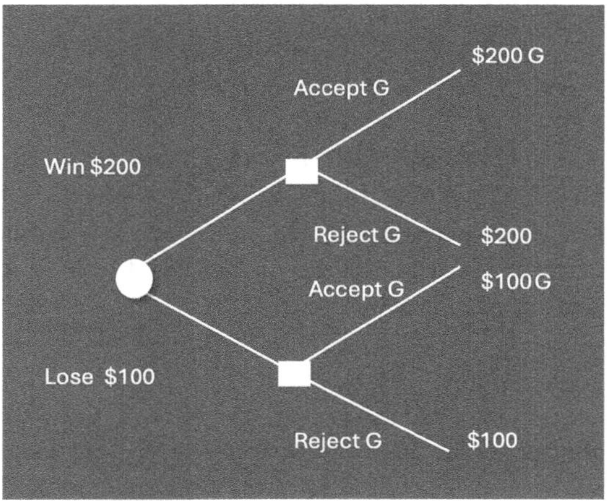

FIGURE 6.1 Decision tree.

know whether they had passed or failed, less than one-third chose the vacation, and 61% were willing to pay a fee to postpone the decision until the following day, preferring to wait until the results were known, paying extra to secure their right to purchase at a later date. Bastardi and Shafir (1998) provided a number of examples of this type of research in different contexts.

In line with the general perspective outlined by Tversky and Shafir, Croson (1999) identified the "various reasons" for deciding the cause of the disjunction effect, with a particular focus on the role of the complexity of the decision tree (Figure 6.1).

6.1.1 A Psychorhetorical Hypothesis

According to the perspective adopted in this book, everything communicated by the text of the problems being considered concurs in the representation of the decisional framework: not only what is said literally (the sentence) but also what is implied and then effectively communicated.[2] The phrases imply and mean more than they literally say. What is implied is the result of an inferential process, in which what is said is interpreted in the light of both the intentions attributed to the speaker and of the context that is inevitably activated and determined by any communicative act, the main idea being that communication is achieved when a recipient recognizes the particular type of intention with which a communicative act is produced. The intuition that inferential processes are influenced by the rules of discourse does not come as a surprise. Indeed, problems studied in reasoning are usually presented in verbal form. Nevertheless, however obvious it may seem, this intuition has not influenced the psychology of thinking and reasoning, at least not until some years ago. Numerous studies (Bagassi & Macchi, 2016; Dulany & Hilton, 1991; Macchi, 2000; Mosconi, 1990; Mosconi & Macchi, 2001; Politzer &

Macchi, 2000; Sperber et al., 1995; Mercier & Sperber, 2011, 2017) have shown the importance of the pragmatic approach for the study of thinking and reasoning, from problem-solving, and conditional and deductive reasoning to probabilistic reasoning.

We will now show that the disjunction effect is less general than has been supposed; to do this, we will make a pragmatic analysis of certain well-known tasks and the resulting reformulations, referring not only to Grice's theory but also to Sperber and Wilson's Relevance Theory (1986), which evolved from it, and to the psychorhetorical analysis of discourse (Mosconi, 1990).

6.1.1.1 The Gamble Problem

If we make a pragmatic analysis of the text of the Disjunctive version of the *Gamble* problem, it is evident that it is infelicitously phrased. In fact, according to our hypothesis, the following phrase

> … Imagine that the coin has already been tossed, but that you will not know whether you have won $200 or lost $100 until you take a decision concerning a second, identical gamble … [my underlining]

leads to a misunderstanding of the task; it implies that the aim of a second gamble is to *know the result of the first*. This would transform the aim of the second from "playing to win" ("again" or to "get out of the red") to "playing to know".

However, it is plausible to surmise that a person who is invited to risk decreasing a hypothetical win or increasing a hypothetical loss simply to find out whether they have made $200 or lost $100 would decline to take that risk. We hypothesized that, if the disjunction effect does in fact depend on the formulation of the text, coherent choices will be obtained by eliminating the irrelevant aim in the Disjunctive condition. Just like the participants in the Won/Lost conditions who agreed to play again, those in the Disjunctive condition should do the same. If, on the other hand, the *disjunctive effect* depends on the state of uncertainty and the different reasons for deciding, we would expect that the disjunction effect would also persist in the Disjunctive condition from which the irrelevant aim has been eliminated (see Text Box 6.1).[3]

An input is relevant to an individual at a certain time if it yields *cognitive effects* when processed. Examples of cognitive effects are the revision of previous beliefs or the derivation of contextual conclusions, i.e., conclusions that follow from the input taken together with previously available information. All else being equal, the greater the *cognitive effects* achieved by processing an input, the more relevant that input will be. On the other hand, the greater the effort involved in the processing, the lower will be the relevance. Thinking along these lines, the phrase: "but you will not know whether you have won $200 or lost $100 until you take the decision whether to make a second, identical gamble" implies a greater effort of cognitive processing than: "but you don't know whether you have won $200 or lost $100", in which the decision (to play or not to play) is not artificially influenced by knowing the outcome of the first gamble.

To test our hypotheses, we formulated a disjunctive experimental version, which we called the "Relevant Disjunctive version" (DR) (Bagassi & Macchi, 2006).[4] In this version, the choice to play a second time was not conditioned by the need to know the result of the first gamble (thereby eliminating the aim of "playing to know") but focused exclusively on winning. In this way, the goal of the second gamble becomes homogeneous with the won/lost control versions.

Each participant received a form that contained only one version of the problem. Four kinds of forms were prepared, defining the following versions: Control Won, Control Lost, Control Disjunctive, and the experimental Relevant Disjunctive version.

TEXT BOX 6.1 RELEVANT DISJUNCTIVE VS. NON-RELEVANT DISJUNCTIVE VERSIONS

Won/Lost Version

Imagine that you have just played a game of chance that gave you a 50% chance of winning $200 and a 50% chance of losing $100. The coin was tossed, and you have [won $200/lost $100].

You are now offered a second identical gamble: 50% chance to win $200 and 50% chance to lose $100.

- Accept the second gamble.
- Reject the second gamble.

[63% OF THE WINNERS AND 53% OF THE LOSERS DECIDED TO ACCEPT]

Disjunctive Version

Imagine that you have just played a game of chance with a 50% chance of winning $200 and a 50% chance of losing $100. Now imagine that the coin has already been tossed, but that you will not know whether you have won $200 or lost ***$100*** *until you make your decision concerning a second, identical gamble (my underlining and* ***bold****).*

You are now offered a second identical gamble: 50% chance to win $200 and 50% chance to lose $100.
Would you:

- Accept the second gamble.
- Reject the second gamble.

[*42% DECIDED TO ACCEPT*]

Relevant Disjunctive (RD)

Imagine that you have just played a game of chance with a 50% chance of winning $200 and a 50% chance of losing $100. The coin was tossed, but you don't know whether you have won $200 or lost $100 (my underlining and ***bold****).*

You are now offered a second identical gamble: 50% chance to win $200 and 50% chance to lose $100. Would you:

- Accept the second gamble.
- Reject the second gamble.

[*60% DECIDED TO ACCEPT*]

In the Relevant Disjunctive version, the disjunction effect disappears, showing that when the three conditions actually concern the same goal ("playing to win" again or to "get out of the red"), the participants' choices are the same. In the Disjunctive control version, "playing **[just]** to know" the outcome of the previous gamble is/**produces** an insufficient reason for playing a second time; indeed, it would be considered an ***irrelevant*** aim in a gambling context. In fact, the majority of the participants refused to play again. **The aim of knowing ("Playing to know") overshadows** the real aim of any gamble, which is to win; in the text of the control version, the real aim becomes secondary, **embedded, and not explicit,** and consequently an additional inferential effort is needed to make a decision.

In the original Disjunctive version, the participants should just play *to know*, while in the Relevant Disjunctive version they should play *to win* (the percentage of those who decided to play again rose to 60%). Therefore, it would appear that the results obtained with the original Disjunctive version are not due to uncertainty but to an irrelevant aim (playing to know). When the irrelevant aim was eliminated and the condition of uncertainty maintained, the fallacy disappeared, and the participants appeared to be coherent in their choices.

6.1.1.2 The Problem of the Hawaiian Vacation[5]

This is another well-known problem used in literature to illustrate the disjunction effect.

Disjunctive Version

Imagine that you have just taken a tough qualifying examination. It is the end of the fall quarter, you feel tired and run-down, and you are not sure that you passed the exam. If you fail, you will have to take the exam again in a couple of months—after the Christmas holidays. You now have an opportunity to buy a very attractive 5-day Christmas vacation package to Hawaii at an exceptionally low price. The special offer expires tomorrow, while the exam grade will not be available until the following day. Would you:

x. buy the vacation package.
y. not buy the vacation package.
z. pay a $5 non-refundable fee to retain the rights to buy the vacation package at the same exceptional price until the day after tomorrow—after you find out whether or not you passed the exam.

Pass/Fail Version
Imagine that you have just taken a tough qualifying examination. It is the end of the fall quarter, you feel tired and run-down, and you find out that you passed the exam [failed the exam. You will have to take it again in a couple of months—after the Christmas holidays]. You now have an opportunity to buy a very attractive 5-day Christmas vacation package to Hawaii at an exceptionally low price. The special offer expires tomorrow. Would you:

x. buy the vacation package.
y. not buy the vacation package.
z. pay a $5 non-refundable fee in order to retain the rights to buy the vacation package at the same exceptional price the day after tomorrow.

In this problem, most of the participants who knew the result of the exam (54% in the Pass condition and 57% in the Fail condition) chose to buy the vacation package (option x)—but only 32% made this choice when they were uncertain as to the outcome of the exam (Disjunctive version).

As the players in the *Gamble* problem, the participants faced with this dilemma seemed to prefer option *x* (to buy the vacation package) when they were **in a condition of certainty**, either having passed the exam or having failed it, but they refused option *x* (or preferred option *z*) when they did not know the outcome of the exam.

Once again, the phenomenon was explained by Tversky and Shafir as being due to a lack of clear reasons for accepting option *x* when in a condition of uncertainty (the Disjunctive condition). The authors speak about a sort of "loss of acuity" regarding the motivations for the decision, induced by the presence of the uncertainty condition. Once the outcome of the exam was known, all the participants had a good reason for taking the vacation: for those who passed, it was seen as a reward, for those who failed, as a consolation.

However, just as with the *Gamble* problem, according to our psychorhetoric analysis of the text of this problem, the choice seems to be affected by misleading goals resulting from how the text is formulated: "*playing to know*" in the *Gamble* problem, "*paying to know*" in the *Hawaiian vacation* problem—both of which are independent of the uncertainty condition that is due only to not knowing the outcome of the first gamble and by not knowing the result of the exam.

It would therefore seem plausible to assume that the incoherent choices (option *y* for the *Gamble* problem and option *z* for the Hawaii problem) do not occur as a consequence of uncertainty, but as the result of how the problem is formulated. If we take the *Hawaiian vacation* problem, the phrase:

> The special offer expires tomorrow, while the exam grade will not be available until the following day.

implies that it would be useful "*to know*" to be able "*to decide*", and it is this that brings the participants to choose option z. In fact, option z (i.e., *pay a $5 non-refundable fee to retain the rights to buy the package at the same special price the day after tomorrow* when you will have the results of the exam) satisfies the need "to know", induced by the text, because it allows the decision to be procrastinated until the outcome of the exam is known:

> *z. pay a $5 non-refundable fee in order to retain the rights to buy the vacation package at the same exceptional price the day after tomorrow*—***after you find out whether or not you passed the exam***.

It is important to note that the final part of the sentence (after you find out whether or not you passed the exam) stresses the surreptitious link between "to know" and "to decide". From this point of view, *z* is the best choice and is the solution to the problem created by the adversative phrase "*while the exam results will not be available until the day after tomorrow*".

All this makes the choice of option *z* relevant for the aim introduced in the original Disjunctive version. By eliminating the aim of "paying to know", our study of the behaviour of the participants in the Disjunctive version was "cleaner". As with the *Gamble* problem, after the surreptitious aim was eliminated from the Hawaii problem, the participants' choices in the three conditions did not differ, and there was no trace of incoherency of thought.[6]

The element of uncertainty and the different reasons for choice persist in our reformulation of the text of the Disjunctive version (see the "Pure and Simple" version, Experiments 2 and 3, Bagassi & Macchi, 2006). On the contrary, reasoning from Tversky and Shafir's point of view, it was to be expected that the majority of participants would have made an incoherent choice, selecting option z rather than x.

We created two different versions to explore this hypothesis. In the first, we wanted to eliminate the spurious connection between the "knowledge of the result" and the "decision" from the text and from option z, just leaving the element of uncertainty ("you are not sure that you passed the exam"). With this in mind, we reformulated the Disjunctive version, eliminating the connection between the decision to be made and the knowledge of the result of the exam, which was a critical and problematic element in the original version. Indeed, the revised text was very similar in form to the Pass/Fail conditions.

This reduced the number of choices (option z) in the experimental Disjunctive version that we called "Pure and Simple" (see below).

Imagine that you have just taken a tough qualifying examination. It is the end of the fall quarter, you feel tired and run-down, and you are not sure that you passed the exam. In case you failed, you have to take the exam again in a couple of months—after the Christmas holidays. You now have an opportunity to buy a very attractive five-day Christmas vacation package to Hawaii at an exceptionally low price. The special offer expires tomorrow, ~~while the exam grade will not be available until the following day.~~ Would you:

x. buy the vacation package.
y. not buy the vacation package.
z. pay a $5 non-refundable fee in order to retain the rights to buy the vacation package at the same exceptional price until the day after tomorrow – ~~after you find out whether or not you passed the exam.~~

In our experiment, in all three versions the majority of the participants (around 60%; no significant difference) decided to buy the vacation package, in contrast with the Control Disjunctive version (40%), where 6o% of the "Passes" and 62% of the "Fails" would have purchased the vacation, and the Pure and Simple Disjunctive (59%). The results show that the percentage of participants who chose to postpone the decision (option z) in the Pure and Simple Disjunctive version is substantially identical (18%) to the percentage of those who were not faced with the element of uncertainty (22% in the Pass and 15% in the Fail conditions). Actually, the majority of the participants in all three versions decided to buy the vacation package (option x, approximately 60%; no significant difference). On the contrary, almost 50% of the participants faced with the original Disjunctive version chose to postpone the decision (option z). The difference between the two Disjunctive versions—the original and the Pure and Simple—is significant. It would therefore appear that what determines the tendency to postpone the decision in the original Disjunctive version is the connection between the "knowledge of the result" and the "decision to be made", and not the element of uncertainty. When this connection between the "knowledge of the result" and the "decision to be made" is eliminated in the "Pure and Simple" version, the pattern of the participants' decisions is coherent once again.

In another experiment, we eliminated option z, thereby limiting the decision to just two options (as with the *Gamble* problem, see Text Box 6.2) to (x) "buy" or (y) "not buy" the vacation package. If the violation of the *sure-thing principle* was actually the result of the uncertainty in the Disjunctive condition then, according to Tversky and Shafir, incongruent choices were to be expected: i.e., that the majority of the participants faced with the Disjunctive condition would prefer (y), in (incoherent) contrast with those dealing with the certainty conditions (Pass/Fail) who should prefer (x).

In contrast, according to our hypothesis, incoherent choice depends on the irrelevant aim. Consequently, we expected that the choices of the three groups would not differ significantly (in accordance with the results obtained in the *Gamble* problem: Relevant Disjunctive D1, Experiment 1). In all three conditions, approximately 90% of subjects chose to go on holiday. Once again, we found no evidence for the disjunction effect, since we obtained coherent choices.[7]

6.1.2 Discussion

From the experiments above, it would appear that the disjunction effect is not a result of uncertainty but rather is a consequence of misleading goals in the text of the problem, "playing to know" in the *Gamble* problem and "paying to know" in the Hawaii vacation problem.

These two goals are not intrinsically connected to the condition of uncertainty. When they were eliminated, while still maintaining the uncertainty condition the disjunction effect disappeared, even though the element of uncertainty was still present. Evidently, the crucial factor is not certainty or uncertainty but the relevance of the whole discourse problem, of which option *z* is one element.[8]

Therefore, option *z* is not a "real" alternative to options x and y, but it becomes an additional premise that conveys information, changing the decisional context.

From a purely cognitive perspective, even the "complexity" factor indicated by Croson (1999) as characteristic of the condition of uncertainty does not seem to be a real explanation of the disjunction effect. Actually, when the complexity was equal to the original versions (see the Relevant Disjunctive version and the Pure and Simple Disjunctive version vs. the Control Disjunctive version), we also obtained coherent choices under uncertainty.

To sum up, if we simply do not know and are in a state of uncertainty (i.e., the link with misleading goals is introduced in the text of the problem), we do not make incoherent choices. Apparently, then, uncertainty itself does not induce either a "loss of acuity", or "a lack of clear reasons to decide", or an inability to consider each branch of the decision tree.[9]

The psychorhetoric approach appears to offer an alternative and more general explanation of the phenomenon, since it can predict and explain the kind of choices on the basis of what is actually communicated by the discourse problem. The text of any problem is a discourse, a conversation between a speaker and a listener; it is a cooperative venture: context, the identity of both speaker and listener, shared knowledge, and the aims of the speaker all contribute to determining how the problem should be interpreted, through sophisticated inferential processes that deeply influence the decisional processes.

6.2 The Framing Effect and the Choice between Surgery and Radiation Therapy

6.2.1 When the Numbers Do Not Add Up!

Providing patients with the possibility of making "informed choices" is held to be a fundamental requirement for guaranteeing dignity, allowing self-determination, and promoting rational decision-making (Annas, 2017). However, this requirement is challenged in some specific conditions, for example, when decisions involve different formulations of risk; for instance, research has shown that medical choices are "shaped" by how options are communicated and, in particular, that the way in which options are formulated may influence the decision as to whether a risk should be taken (Edwards et al., 2001). Tversky and Kahneman (1981) have shown how the preference for one option over another could be influenced by different formulations of logically equivalent choices.

On the one hand, people are likely to prefer a risky option when the issue to be decided is presented in a framework of loss, with the outcome being expressed in terms of lost resources. On the other hand, they are likely to prefer a safe option when the decisional problem is presented in a framework of gain by stating the results in terms of gain. This phenomenon is called the "framing effect", and it is traditionally considered to be a cognitive bias.

Rationality should satisfy some elementary requirements of consistency and coherence that, however, appear to be systematically violated in one classical framing effect problem, known as the *Asian Disease* problem (Tversky & Kahneman, 1981). Framing effects have been examined in a variety of studies, and their general robustness has been generally acknowledged in literature, with certain notable exceptions (see Text Box 6.3).

One of the areas that has seemed to be particularly critical is medical decision-making (Gong et al., 2013). Compared with the classical gain/loss framing effects, in the specific case of the framing of medical treatments, a reverse pattern of choice has been found; preferences for *risk* are elicited by a *positive* rather than by a negative *frame*.[10] For instance, research on choices between different medical treatments—such as surgery over radiation therapy—showed that treatments involving risk (e.g., surgery) are preferred when the outcomes are described in terms of saved lives. Conversely, support for the risky option decreases when the outcomes are described in terms of lives lost (Almashat et al., 2008; McNeil et al., 1982).[11]

To clarify the nature of this reverse pattern, in 2021, I conducted a study on framing in medical treatments with Edoardo Zulato, focusing on the contingencies associated with this particular choice, such as the formulation of the decision problem. In a paradigmatic study, McNeil and colleagues (1982) tested the framing effect by asking their participants to choose between two therapies (surgery and radiation therapy) based on the possible consequences these therapies could have in the specific case of an operable lung cancer. Half of the participants were assigned to a survival frame (positive), where outcomes were presented in terms of frequency of survival, while the other half was assigned to a mortality frame (negative), where outcomes were presented in terms of frequency of death:

Mortality frame: Of 100 people having surgery, 10 will die during treatment, 32 will have died by one year, and 66 will have died by five years. Of 100 people having radiation therapy, none will die during treatment, 23 will die by one year and 78 will die by five years. Which treatment do you prefer?

Survival frame: Of 100 people having surgery, 90 will survive during treatment, 68 will have survived by one year, and 34 will have survived by five years. Of 100 people having radiation therapy, all will survive during treatment, 77 will have survived by one year, and 22 will have survived by five years. Which treatment do you prefer?

Overall, the participants opted for surgery, but consistently with McNeil et al.'s hypothesis, they showed an inverse decision trend, choosing surgery less frequently in the mortality frame—10 will die (58%)—than in the survival frame—90 will survive (75%). The researchers interpreted the risk of perioperative death as the most salient disadvantage of surgery compared to radiation therapy.[12]

The different perceptions of perioperative mortality (0% for the radiation therapy, 10% for the surgical) between these two frames induced participants to choose the surgical alternative in the survival frame more frequently than in the mortality frame. By considering the risky option as that with *the highest perioperative risk* (*i.e., surgery*), these results have been interpreted as a reverse pattern of preference compared to Tversky and Kahneman's classical framing effect: in the positive frame (i.e., survival), the option with the higher risk (*i.e., surgery*) is preferred, whereas the option with the lower risk (*i.e., radiation therapy*) is preferred in the negative frame (i.e., mortality).

6.2.2 A Psychorhetorical Interpretation

In general, communication should allow an adequate perception of risk to promote informed decision-making, which is crucial in the medical context. This is particularly relevant for communications targeting laypersons, which means most of us, who are not familiar with statistical and probabilistic data. In such cases, a genuine understanding of information can only be guaranteed by adequate communication that takes the audience's psychological requirements into account (Koehler & Macchi, 2004). In other words, the transmission of objective information is a necessary condition in decision-making tasks, but in itself it is not sufficient to ensure understanding, because if the speaker (e.g., a physician, a policy-maker, or experimenters) does not respect the requirements of natural language, their communication may lead to an erroneous representation of the problem and, therefore, to a misleading interpretation (Bagassi & Macchi, 2006).

A pragmatic analysis of McNeil's texts led us to formulate an alternative hypothesis, attributing the shift of preference between the two conditions (from surgical to radiation therapy) to how the decisional problem was formulated. To be more precise, after analysing the options employed in the problem, we speculated that how they were formulated led the participants to misunderstand the numerical information, with the result that their choices were based on a misperception of the outcome of the two therapies. The negative version (i.e., the loss scenario) in particular interrupts the logical equivalence between the two frames.

The implicit part of an utterance contributes to the way in which we interpret information, whether it be numerical or verbal; in particular, when we are expressing ourselves in natural language our understanding is conditioned by the psychological expectation that the information transmitted by the communication adheres to Grice's Maxims of Quantity and of Relation, i.e., it is neither redundant nor irrelevant (Grice, 1975). For instance, in the research I am discussing here (McNeil et al.), the authors adopted a *cumulative format* (32 includes the 10 who already died at the beginning and 32 included in the 66), but the participants could instead consider the progression of numbers as an addition of new numerical information, relevant for each specified period (e.g., 10 + 32 + 66). In this case, the participants may have the conversational expectation that the ten who died during the treatment, the ones who died within one and five years, should be added (32 new deaths within one year, 66 new deaths within 5 years).

10 will die during treatment, 32 will have died by one year, and 66 will have died by 5 years.

Formulated in this way, the participants are led to expect that the 10 who died during treatment are to be added to the 32 patients who died within the year and the 66 who died within 5 years.

Regarding the positive frame, the outcome

90 will survive during treatment, 68 (of them) will have survived by one year,

is a nested formulation, which, by including one group within another, transmits the information with clarity. It allows the speaker to add new information about the subsets of patients who are still alive after one year and after five years.

We hypothesized that participants show a tendency to add numerical information sequentially in the negative frame. If this were the case, they would tend to calculate sequences of numbers in a *linear progression:*

Surgical: 10 + 32 + 66 *vs. Radiation therapy:* 0 + 23 + 78 instead of *cumulatively:*

Surgical: 10 included in 32 and 32 included in 66 vs *Radiation therapy:* 23 included in 78.

Therefore, it can be deduced that in the mortality frame, the participants made a calculation that differed from that of the researcher; they calculated the number of deaths as a linear addition, and as a result, their decision as to which of the two alternative therapies they wished to follow was based on erroneous outcomes. In my view, in this particular case, the outcomes of the therapies could be understood easily if Grice's maxims of quantity and relevance are respected. This can be done by employing a *linear progression format*, in which the results of the two therapies are given in terms of disaggregated rather than cumulative numbers. This formulation would respect this psychological need and expectation, and numbers relative to different periods can be added without misunderstanding the overall number of deaths in the mortality scenario:

For example: 10 + 22 + 34 = 66 (linear progression)
instead of 10 + 32 + 66 = 108 (cumulative)

We therefore decided to run a study with two objectives: the first being to verify whether possessing expertise in medicine can have a positive effect, supporting comprehension of the data, and the second to test the framing effect in the *linear progression* format to clarify the reasons behind the participants' choices.

6.2.3 Does Expertise Help the Comprehension of Numerical Communication?

We replicated the original paradigm used by McNeil and colleagues (1982) with 150 students[13] from the University of Milano-Bicocca, of whom 50 were from the faculty of Medicine, 50 were studying statistics, and 50 were from other faculties. We expected that our results would be the same as McNeil's, namely, a greater preference for surgery in the survival frame than in that of mortality. In addition to the original questions, we asked our participants to explain their choice, and we checked their comprehension of the data according to our theoretical perspective. Each participant was asked to read the problem, describing the outcome of two different therapies for treating lung cancer. The participants of each group (medical students, students of statistics, and students of other disciplines) were randomly assigned to one of two possible versions of this description. The first version presented the results in terms of life saved (survival frame), and the second version presented the same results in terms of loss of life (mortality frame). We used the original scenarios (see Chapter 1). At this point, the participants were asked to choose between the two alternatives, given that the quality of life would be the same in both conditions. After these descriptions, participants were asked to decide between the alternatives, and afterwards they were asked to explain their choice, stating which of the two options could have led to a higher number of deaths. We recorded all the spontaneous comments made by the participants during the task.

When the results were presented in the *survival frame*, 81.3% of the participants declared a preference for *surgery*, compared to the *mortality frame,* where the preference *decreased* to 20.0%. The results we observed confirmed the original results and showed an even greater effect than the original study.[14] The lack of differences among the three groups confirmed the presence of a framing effect and further corroborates the original results, since they all showed a significant difference in preferences across frames (Figure 6.2). Hence, we were able to support the hypothesis that students of medicine and statistics, who can realistically be expected to have greater competence in dealing with decisions of this kind, are influenced by the same bias as the students from other faculties when faced with a medical decision. In line with our hypothesis, we observed that several participants expressed doubts about their understanding of the data, and that this influenced their decision-making process. Following a pragmatic analysis of the decision problem, we speculated that the formulation could have resulted in errors due to a misperception of the results of the two therapies. This seemed to be the case in the mortality frame, in which most of the participants reported that there was a mistake in the calculations. Some were worried by the fact that in the surgical option, the total of the cases reported exceeded the starting pool of patients (100), and, for this reason, they believed *radiation therapy to be the best alternative* because the rate of deaths after five years was lower: "I would choose radiation therapy. Even though the result is more than 100. Look, 66+32 makes 98, +10 makes 108, and under (the radiation therapy results were in the line below) 78+23 makes 101. If we are

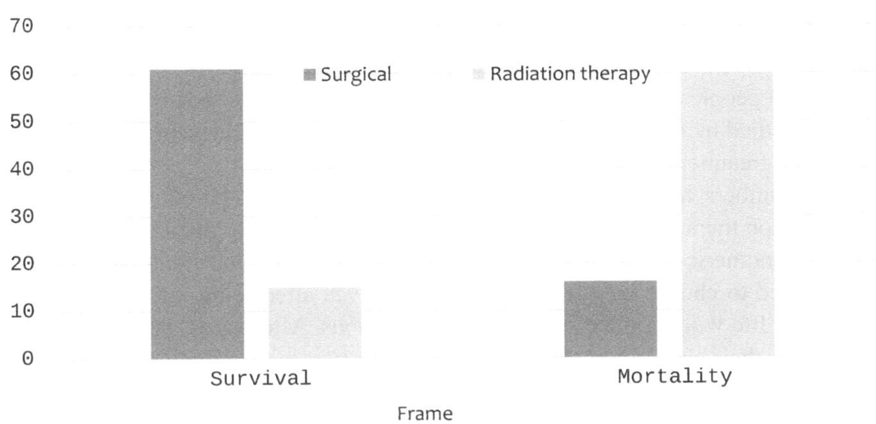

FIGURE 6.2 Preference frequencies (surgery versus radiation therapy) across frames (survival versus mortality).

talking about 100 people, that cannot be right". The negative frame version caused the participants to erroneously judge radiation therapy as the better alternative in the long term compared to surgical therapy: "My choice is radiation therapy because statistically surgery is too dangerous and, therefore, I do not consider it appropriate. I think surgery causes the highest number of deaths. I did a simple sum, and I would still prefer the radiation therapy because at least the patients do not die during the therapy" (the participants' responses for the mortality frame).

6.2.4 Psychorhetoric and Numbers

The results of our first study confirmed the phenomenon noted by McNeil et al. (1982). Therefore, the objective of our second study was to verify the effect of what we considered to be a pragmatically adequate presentation of the information, in other words, a communication that respects the participants' psychorhetorical expectations. Given the tendency of the participants to spontaneously organize the outcomes of the original version in the *linear progression mode*, formulating the problem in this mode permitted them to avoid misinterpreting the data. Having thus re-established the correct understanding of the options, we were able to explore whether the pattern of preferences was still producing a framing effect, which, according to our hypothesis, should have disappeared.

The participants were randomly assigned to one of the two conditions: a control condition, in which the problem was presented in the original cumulative frequency format (*"10 will die during treatment, 32 will die by one year"*) identical to that used in the previous study, and an experimental condition, in which the problem was presented in a *linear progression* format (*"10 will die during treatment, another 22 will die by one year"*) as shown below.

Mortality Frame:
Of 100 people undergoing surgery, **10** will die during treatment, **22 more** will have died by one year, and **34 more** will have died by five years.

Of 100 people having radiation therapy, none (0) will die during treatment, **23** will have died by one year, and **55 more** will have died by five years.

Which treatment do you prefer?

The numbers were changed to add up to 66 for surgery (10 + 22 + 34) and 78 for radiation therapy (0 + 23 + 55) after five years, in order to avoid any confusion over the numerical representation of the problem.[15] At this point, participants were asked to choose between the two alternatives after being informed that the quality of life would be the same in both conditions. Afterwards, they were asked to explain their choice and to state which of the two options they thought would result in a greater loss of life.

We observed that choice and frame appeared to be significantly related in the *cumulative frequency* condition (see Figure 6.3).

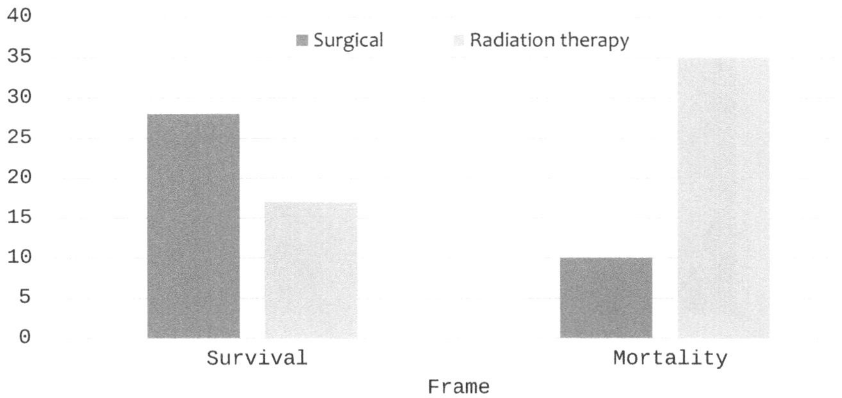

FIGURE 6.3 Preference frequencies (surgery versus radiation therapy) in the cumulative frequency condition.

When the results were presented in the survival frame, 64.4% of the participants showed a preference for surgery, while when the results were presented in the mortality frame, the preference decreased to 22.2% of the participants.

Conversely, in the *linear progression* condition, choice was observed to be independent of the frames. The lack of difference of preference between frames (Figure 6.4) confirmed the absence of a reverse pattern of choices. These results supported our hypothesis as, once the correct understanding of the options was reestablished, we found decisional coherence across frames. While the original formulation of the data interrupted the essential equivalence requirement across frames, the new formulation reestablished it. As a consequence, the reverse pattern of choices disappeared.

In point of fact, the results that emerged from this study brought an even more radical fact to light, as can be clearly seen in Figure 6.4. The participants showed full decisional coherence, indicating a preference for surgery in the survival frame based on the greater number of patients who will survive in the five-year range. Therefore, not only was the inverse framing effect, found by MacNeil et al., absent from our results, but the classical framing effect reported by Tversky and Kahneman—that predicted an aversion to risk in the positive frame and a propensity to risk in the negative frame—was also missing. When text versions were presented that were adequate in a pragmatic and psychorhetorical perspective, no significant differences emerged between the two frames. Indeed, the participants with both survival (73.3%) and mortality (71.1%) frames preferred surgery to radiation therapy.

The participants dealing with the *linear progression* version, unlike those dealing with the *cumulative frequency* version, had no difficulty in understanding

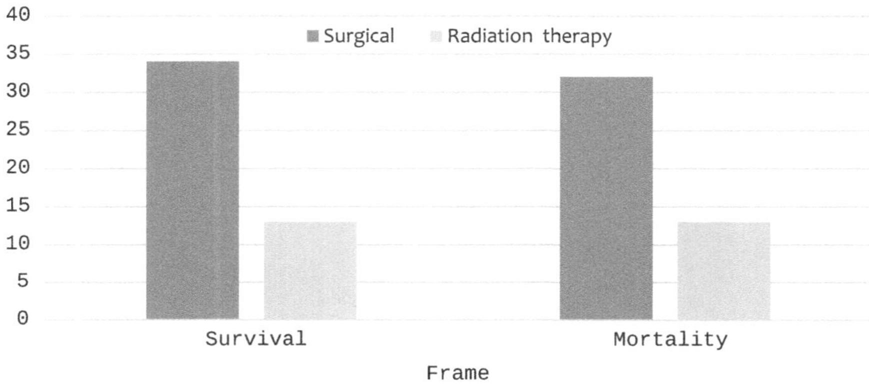

FIGURE 6.4 Preference frequencies (surgery versus radiation therapy) in the *linear progression* condition.

the data correctly. This supported our interpretation, namely that the framing effect could be the result of an erroneous perception of the data supplied in the *cumulative frequency* format. Finally, the higher survival rates at five years after treatment seemed to be the major motivation for their decisions, as evidenced by the spontaneous justifications offered by participants.

In conclusion, these results could have implications for healthcare, particularly when drafting communications that are suited to the psychological mechanisms of understanding data, to avoid biases in medical decision-making. This leads us to the next chapter, which deals with communications to the public.

TEXT BOX 6.2 THE PROBLEM OF THE HAWAIIAN VACATION: THE TWO-CHOICE VERSION

To verify our general hypothesis, we put the Disjunctive and the Pass/Fail versions to three groups of participants, offering only two options (just as in the *Gamble* problem), limiting the decision to:

x = "buy the vacation package"
or
y = "don't buy the vacation package"

If, as according to Tversky and Shafir, uncertainty was the reason for the disjunction effect, the choices in this scenario should also be incongruent; in other words, y should be chosen in the disjunctive condition compared to x in the condition of certainty (Pass/Fail).

According to our hypothesis, on the contrary, the choice that appears incoherent in the original experiment depends on the *irrelevancy* of the goal. Consequently, we expected that the choices of the three groups would not differ significantly (in line with the results that emerged in the *Gamble* problem: Relevant Disjunction). Three forms were prepared with the two-choice versions below; each participant received one form with only one problem.

Disjunctive Version (Two Choices)

Imagine that you have just taken a tough qualifying examination. It is the end of the fall quarter, you feel tired and run-down, and you are not sure that you passed the exam. If you failed, you have to take the exam again in a couple of months—after the Christmas holidays. Now you have the opportunity to buy a very attractive 5-day Christmas vacation package at an exceptionally low price. The special offer expires tomorrow. Would you:

x. buy the vacation package.
y. not buy the vacation package.

Pass/Fail Format with Certain Results

Imagine that you have just taken a tough qualifying examination. It is the end of the fall quarter, you feel tired and run-down, and you find out that you passed the exam [failed the exam, and you will have to take it again in a couple of months—after the Christmas holidays]. Now you have the opportunity to buy a very attractive 5-day Christmas vacation package at an exceptionally low price. The special offer expires tomorrow. Would you:

x. buy the vacation package.
y. not buy the vacation package.

In all three versions, approximately 90% of the participants chose to buy the vacation package (we did not find any significant differences: Pass = 91%, Fail = 82%, Disjunctive = 94%). Once again, we did not find any evidence of the disjunction effect, given that the choices were perfectly coherent.

TEXT BOX 6.3 COMBATTING A RARE DISEASE

The framing effect (Tversky & Kahneman, 1981) is another paradigmatic case illustrating the effect of different ways of describing the same objective reality. It shows how a change in perspective can alter the desirability of decision options, provoking a preference inversion across different frames. Specific expressions, such as percentages, can easily become subjective evaluation indicators. Consider this example: "75% lean meat" can be perceived as a very desirable cut, while "meat with 25% fat" (the same meat) could be considered as being too fatty and therefore not desirable (Levin & Gaeth, 1988). Although the information provided is objectively identical, the descriptive context in which it is contained is different. Therefore, the effect describes a cognitive bias that causes people to react differently when choosing between two options that are objectively the same but presented in different contexts of gain or loss, or more generally, of positive or negative aspects. People are strongly influenced by the context, or frame, in which information is presented. The most classic example of the framing effect is the *Asian Disease* problem. In the positive frame, the results of the programs to combat the disease are given in terms of lives saved, while in the negative frame they are couched in terms of lives lost.

The Unusual Disease Problem

Imagine that the US is preparing for the outbreak of an unusual Asian disease, which is expected to kill 600 people. Two alternative programs to combat the disease have been proposed. Assume that the exact scientific estimates of the consequences of the programs are as follows:

Version 1

If Program A is adopted, 200 people will be saved.

If Program B is adopted, there is a one-third probability that 600 people will be saved, and a two-third probability that no one will be saved.

72% of the respondents expressed a preference for Program A.

Version 2

If Program C is adopted, 400 people will die.

If Program D is adopted, there is a one-third probability that nobody will die, and a two-third probability that 600 people will die.

About 78% of the respondents preferred Program D. In this experiment, the authors noted a tendency to take greater risks when the choices focus on the possibility of avoiding losses, as opposed to the possibility of making gains. Therefore, it appears that the respondents were strongly influenced by the way in which the choices were presented, which is in contrast to the invariance principle. Jou and colleagues (1996) and McKenzie and Nelson (2003) conducted studies that concentrated on the pragmatic analysis of framing effect based on the assumption that the choice of a particular frame transmits a communication that is quantitatively and qualitatively different compared to the literal communication, thus influencing the choice and judgement of the decision-maker. In 1980, Thaler observed that credit card companies, which in those days were just starting to make their appearance on the market, were exerting pressure on retailers to use the wording "cash discount" instead of "credit card supplement" to indicate the price difference between the two methods of payment. In the first case, the credit card price is the point of reference, while in the second, it is the price when paying cash, the assumption being that people are more inclined to pass up a discount (an added advantage with respect to the base price) rather than pay a supplement. The value of an option, therefore, is always determined by a point of reference. The phenomenon of the "point of reference", studied by McKenzie and Nelson (2003), can be simplified as the maxim "seeing the glass half-full or half-empty". When we talk about a medical treatment (such as in the *Asian Disease* problem) in terms of mortality or survival, this not only provides the audience with an absolute frame of reference but also with a level from which to start, a point on which to anchor their expectations of gain or loss. The frame used to describe an object or a situation is never casual. Let's take the example of the glass of water that is half-full or half-empty: most people—asked to describe a half-full glass using one of the objectively equivalent descriptions "half-full" or "half-empty"—will opt for the first if the glass was originally empty and then filled halfway but will opt for the second if the glass was originally full and someone drank half the content. The choice of the frame, therefore, is influenced by the point of reference. We tend to describe an object using a particular property (such as "empty" or "full") when this property increases rather than diminishes with respect to its point of reference. From the point of view of communication, the speaker's choice of frame transmits the point of reference they have adopted; in this way, they implicitly supply information that transcends its purely literal content and thus influences the message received by the listener.

Notes

1 To state this in more formal terms, it could be said that the decision-makers preferred option A to option B when they were in a certain condition (winning the game) and also preferred option A when they were not in that condition (losing the game), but rejected option A (or preferred option B) when they were not aware of the outcome of the game they had just played.

2 The distinction between "sentence" and "utterance" lies at the very heart of Grice's theory of communiation; he held that sentences imply and mean more than they say

literally. The meaning must be attributed to the intention to communicate, and, therefore, the semantics must be attributed to psychology.

3 In fact, in subsequent studies in which the Game of Chance is studied, Shafir and Tversky (Shafir, 1994; Shafir & Tversky, 1992) omitted this part of the text as if it were irrelevant.
4 The test was held at the beginning of a lecture; 110 students received a form with one of the three control versions (Control Won, Control Lost, and Control Disjunctive), and 35 received a copy of our experimental Relevant Disjunctive version.
5 For obvious geographical reasons, Hawaii (which cannot be a reasonable destination for a five-day holiday from Europe) was changed to "a nice destination".
6 Given the fact that the state of uncertainty persists and the existence of different "reasons for deciding", this is opposite to what Tversky and Shafir would have predicted.
7 Furthermore, notice that in the experiment by Tversky and Shafir (and also in our Control version, Experiment 2), in addition to around 55% of the subjects who made the same choice x (in the Pass and Fail versions), a further one third of the subjects chose option z, indicating that almost all of the subjects (90%) potentially were favourably disposed to buy the offered package. The same happened in the disjunction condition, where 32% chose option x, and 61% chose option z. Again around 90% were potentially buyers of the holiday package (see Tversky & Shafir, 1992, p. 305).
8 Actually, when option z is a sensible choice most people will opt for it; on the other hand, when it is onerous or simply not advantageous, it is generally ignored as shown in other experiments (5 and 7, Bagassi & Macchi, 2006).
9 Even when they were certain of their results, as, for example, in the Pass/Fail versions, the majority of the participants chose option z when it was relevant to the decision. Obviously, this cannot be attributed to a lack of clear reasons for deciding, nor to the complexity of the decision tree given that in this condition the tree has only one branch.
10 According to Kahneman and Tversky's Prospect Theory, if the context is positive (gain), there will be an aversion to risk, while in a negative context, (loss), the propension to risk increases. This explains the well-known phenomenon of gamblers who take greater risks when they are losing, the aim being to avoid the certain loss they will incur if they stop playing.
11 This is not the case in other medical contexts such as an assessment of medicinal therapy or preventive behaviour, when the preferences are in line with the classic framing effect.
12 These authors therefore concluded that the perception of perioperative risk could be influenced by the numerical difference perceived between the mortality rates (0% for radiation therapy and 10% for surgery) and the survival rates (100% for radiation therapy and 90% for surgery). They surmise that the difference between 0% and 10% is psychologically greater than the difference between 100% and 90%, which is in line with Tversky and Kahneman's Prospect Theory.
13 Average age = 22.67; SD = 2.26; males = 73; females = 77.
14 Overall, the choice and the frame were found to be significantly correlated. In addition, the fact that the choice depended on the frames was also observed within each group.
15 We managed to highlight the nested nature of the data in the survival frame, though it must be said that the original formulation was neither misleading nor ambiguous.

7

PROMOTING ACTION BY DISCOURSE

The Power of Psychorhetoric in Behavioural Insight and Public Communications

> For the Greeks, to be political was to be able to speak [...], finding the right words at the right moment means acting.
>
> Hannah Arendt

7.1 Nudge and Communication in Public Policy

Red circles appeared on the grass of Milan's *Biblioteca degli Alberi* park during the Covid-19 pandemic (Figure 7.1). What were they for? They were designed to help the population enjoy being outdoors in full respect of the social distancing imposed by law. The space was modelled based on the characteristics of our cognitive system and indirectly supported and guided our social behaviour; they helped the population to avoid forming large groups, to maintain an appropriate distance, and so reduce the risk of spreading infection.

Every day we make decisions in conditions of risk or uncertainty. In certain contexts, for example, the recent pandemic, our decisions as individuals have an impact on the entire community. Take, for example, environmental sustainability, climate change, vaccinations, obesity, and there are many more. Understanding how we make decisions in contexts such as these—in conditions of uncertainty or risk, whose consequences do not necessarily affect us immediately or directly—is of the utmost importance for communication, education, and public policies (see Text Box 7.1 on climate change).

DOI: 10.4324/9781003680895-7

FIGURE 7.1 Red circles on the grass of Milan's *Biblioteca degli Alberi* park during the Covid-19 pandemic.

TEXT BOX 7.1 COMMUNICATING CLIMATE CHANGE

What makes communicating climate change so difficult? Cognitive and emotive difficulties seem to impede understanding of the fundamental issues and risks that we are facing. The so-called *discounting effect*, i.e., the distance in time (2050) and space (the Indian Ocean), would appear to be one of the elements contributing to this under-estimation of the climate emergency and is closely related to another psychological phenomenon, our tendency to normalize the situation, as when we think that a 1.5° increase in temperature isn't all that much. This, of course, takes on quite a different complexion when considered in connection with climate and weather, as it means an irreversible rather than a reversible change of state (as if our normal body temperature were to increase permanently to a febrile 38°, rather than being the exception to the rule). Finally, this tendency to normalize the situation and to avoid perceiving the phenomenon as something that affects us directly makes us unreasonably optimistic. Communications regarding this issue, therefore, should take these effects into consideration, avoiding catastrophic announcements that could evoke feelings of impotency or put people on the defensive, provoking them into refuting the existence of the problem altogether. Several strategies are being studied: the CMCC (Euro-Mediterranean Center on Climate Change) has tried to make climate change more understandable by comparing what the climate in our cities will be like in 30 years with the present climate in other urban conglomerations. This has provided the basis for "Understanding climate change from a global analysis of city analogues", realized by climatologists of the ETH Zurich.[1] The report provides a projection of how the climate will have changed in most European cities by 2050, to help represent the concept of climate change. "Despite our use of a highly optimistic climate change scenario [...], we show that the climate conditions of over 77% of world's major cities will change to such a great extent that they will resemble more closely the conditions of another major city". Here are just a few examples, and they are quite disturbing. London in 2050 could have the same climate that Barcelona has today, while the climate in Paris will be that of Istanbul. Things will be worse in Stockholm, where the climate in 2050 could be similar to that of Vienna, 1200 km to the south. Madrid will be like Marrakech, and Lisbon will be like Malta's La Valletta. Temperatures in Rome will be similar to those in Antalya today, while temperatures in Milan will be similar to those in Austin, Texas.

In line with this approach, I was the scientific director of the EduS4EL Project (a European Union project) with an intervention whose objective was to improve Environmental Literacy among secondary school students by means of innovative strategies and methodologies. The novelty of the project was its use of a cognitive and communication psychology approach to promote overcoming the difficulties related to how climate change is perceived by increasing awareness of cognitive and communication biases, developing adequate risk perception, and increasing critical thinking with respect to the polarized arguments present in the public debate. In particular, the development of critical thinking and psychorhetorical analysis of fallacious arguments appears to be crucial to promote a better understanding of climate change and other environmental issues, as these disciplines aim at rendering the public more adept at uncovering fallacies and rhetorical tricks that can be implicit in communication, helping to formulate correct opinions based on reliable data and sources, and developing deliberative skills. Our intervention—composed of sessions on three main sections (Education on the key topics of climate change, Critical Thinking and Psychorhetorical intervention, and Debate)—was conducted in an Italian secondary school with 11th and 12th-grade students. After the sessions, the participants were given a questionnaire to complete, and their performance was compared with a control group who had not attended the sessions. Critical thinking was measured by the level of accuracy in the evaluation of syllogisms and selection tasks, while psychorhetorical skills were assessed by whether the implicit denialist messages contained in newspaper articles were rejected or not. Overall, our results evidenced a better performance by participants who attended the intervention than that of those who did not (Macchi et al., 2023). Another interesting finding was the type of communication the participants considered to be the most effective in promoting awareness about climate change (Figure 7.2).

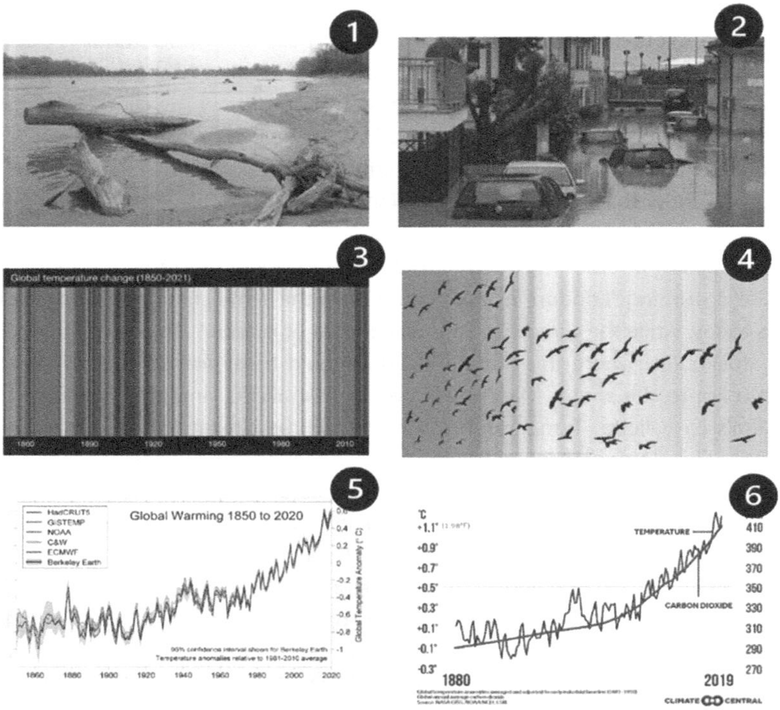

Fig. 5. Six images presented to participants who were asked to evaluate which, according to them, *would most promote awareness of climate change?*

FIGURE 7.2 Six images presented to participants who were asked to evaluate *which*, according to them, *would most promote awareness of climate change*.

Before the intervention, the participants favoured the catastrophic images (1 and 2), as having the greater impact and communication potential, but after listening to the intervention, the majority changed their preference to 3, global warming. This suggests that this image is more effective in representing the importance of conveying the evolution of the phenomenon in public communication compared to isolated extreme weather events. Such events, when viewed as isolated incidents, are often perceived as fatalistic and are less effective at making the phenomenon understandable in its entirety and prospective nature. The global warming image, on the other hand, enables the public to grasp the fundamental aspect of climate change, which is its progression and worsening over the years, and so conveys the urgency of coping with it without further loss of time.

Nowadays, policymakers have numerous ways of encouraging/discouraging individual behaviour that may improve the well-being of the community. Not only can they resort to classical methods such as laws, regulations, and economic incentives, they can also use other options with behavioural impact that derive from a fruitful collaboration of economy, cognitive, and communication psychology, whose origins lie in the behavioural sciences. Depending on the approach being considered, there are various behavioural science models that can be applied to public policies, one of which is the nudge (Text Box 7.2), which has given rise to considerable interest and heated debate, significantly more so than the other models, which arrived on the scene later.[2]

TEXT BOX 7.2 NUDGE

The origins of the word "nudge" are uncertain, but its roots are possibly to be found in the Norwegian "*nyggje*", to jostle, to rub. It indicates a gentle gesture, an almost imperceptible touch of the elbow that means, "go on, it's your turn" or "you'll be fine". It is a conventional gesture that helps you remember something, suggests you do something, without any obligation. It can be used to encourage the population to make better and more advantageous choices in critical areas of social life, such as welfare, health insurance, maternity issues, and energy saving. It shot to fame in the first decade of the second millennium with Thaler and Sunstein's book, *Nudge*—a book on choice architecture.

The nudge theory is a concept that takes its place in the field of behavioural economics and political philosophy; it maintains that positive support, suggestions, and indirect help can influence motivations and incentives of the decision-making process to the same extent as laws, instructions, and enforced compliance.

The application and diffusion of nudging represents an important innovation for evidence-based policy, that is, using policies based on empirical evidence and experimental tests, and promoting the use of more robust methods to evaluate the efficacy of the policies.

Choice architecture, which includes criteria, strategies, and methods that set the physical and social environment in which we make our choices, plays an important role in the use of cognitive nudges. It indicates that there are many ways to construct an option and present it to the decision-maker, and that what is actually chosen often depends on how the options have been presented.

Just as architects can modify the behaviour of the inhabitants of a building by where they position stairs, corridors, doors, so choice architects study tiny, seemingly insignificant details that can have a significant impact on the behaviour of decision-makers; they create a specific choice scenario, for example, by changing the default option or changing the quantity and order of the alternatives.

They use various instruments to do this, including structuring the options—what should be presented to the decision-makers, how many alternatives, and the use of the default. A default is a predefined setting that automatically becomes effective if the person involved does not make an active choice, exploiting the *status quo bias*. A status quo bias induces us to repeat a previously taken choice out of inertia, to avoid actively changing our preferences and thinking systems. We let ourselves be guided by the default option to avoid actively making a decision. An emblematic example of this is the automatic renewal option for subscriptions to magazines that we never read.

There are many fields in which the nudge could be applied to improve individual choices, ranging from how food is laid out in school cafeterias (to discourage the choice of caloric foods), to the choice of a pension plan, the donation of organs, and energy-saving programs.

The nudge is defined as a non-coercive behavioural intervention that steers a third path between those of libertarianism and paternalism, the so-called "libertarian paternalism". Indeed, this possibility of leaving the population with the freedom to choose while leveraging on well-known cognitive mechanisms is possibly one of the most debated aspects of the nudge theory. My objective here, however, does not include solving the libertarian paternalism oxymoron, but I can recommend the following texts to those readers who are interested in investigating the question further: Sunstein (2015) *Nudging and Choice Architecture: Ethical Considerations*; Sunstein (2025) *Nudges and Nudging: A User's Manual*. As Thaler and Sunstein (2008, 2021) suggest, the nudge can justifiably be used in all those situations that are too complex or rare for learning to be an option, when the distance between the choice and its consequences is not directly perceivable or is ambiguous, and when people do not usually make a decision actively but let themselves be guided by habit or routine.

In my opinion, the theory of the nudge, generally speaking and at least as far as heuristics and biases are concerned, is not limited to an application of these cognitive mechanisms; however, having detected how they can influence a decision positively, the nudge causes a shift in focus, weakening the decidedly irrational connotation of the original literature about heuristics and biases. What Thaler and Sunstein describe are no longer "erroneous cognitive tendencies", but *psychological characteristics*, of which we must be aware and must take into consideration to promote choices that lead to well-being. The principles that describe the functioning of human thought are not limited abilities that in themselves can only lead to error, to cognitive illusions; they are characteristics that we use to perceive, to think, to communicate.

There is no doubt that nudges are based on old methods and knowledge, but these are linked together by a substantially new purpose, the promotion of "wise" behaviour (Figure 7.3). The difference between exploiting know-how to guide purchasing choices (marketing) and building an architecture of choice to help people make decisions that will favour a healthier lifestyle and more socially responsible behaviour that respects the environment, over and above the utopic halo all this evokes, lies in their end purpose.

What I want to emphasize, however, is that the nudge cannot and should not be considered as a "universal solution". While the idea of having a list of ready-to-use and efficacious interventions to hand is tempting, it must be kept in mind that—as some recent non-completely positive assessments[3] of the nudge have pointed out—it is important to keep in mind the complexities of the contextual and individual characteristics of the situation for which the nudge is intended to be used.

The *framing effect* (Tversky & Kahneman, 1981), which I have described at length in the previous chapter, is a paradigmatic example of how a concept that has been known for more than 40 years can become an integral part of choice architecture techniques. It explains, for instance, the impact that presenting information in different ways can have on the desirability of the various options available, showing that when we are in a losing situation, we are more inclined to take risks, compared to when we are in a gain frame. However, I must stress once again that using frames in behavioural interventions without duly considering the characteristics of the context can only reduce their efficacy. From the point of view of communication, our choice of a particular form of presentation of information, whether it be a frame or default, inevitably transmits our own point of view, thus implicitly supplying information that goes beyond the literal content and

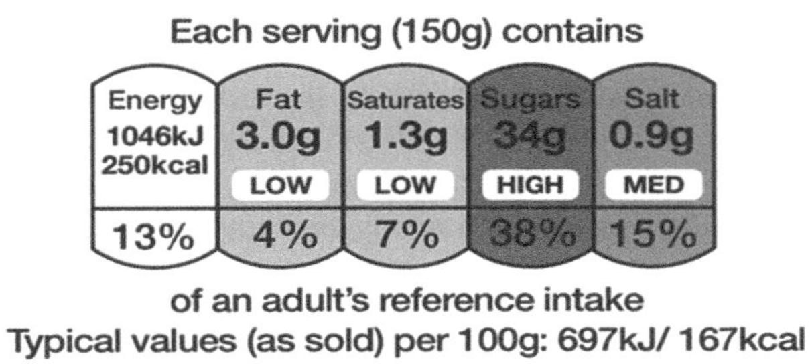

Image credit: https://www.food.gov.uk

FIGURE 7.3 Traffic Light labelling and Traditional labelling: a comparison.

consequently influencing the message that our audience receives, in terms of trust and perceived intentions of the speaker (see Section 7.3.2).

Take, for example, the question of increasing post-mortem organ donations described by Johnson and Goldstein (2003), where the use of a default option implicitly transmits the prospective and the intentions of the communicating institution. As well as representing an *a priori choice* (opt-in for non-donators and consent given for opt-out), the default option, which comes into force if a person does not officially express their choice, conveys the majority position (see Section 7.3.3).

What, in my opinion, is particularly worthy of attention is the interpretative dimension elicited by the specific interlocutors and the contexts involved. All the activities of the human cognitive system are characterized and focussed on a search for meaning, in the context of a specific goal. The interpretative function is based on universal interactional abilities: the capacity to create representations of others and understand the intentions underlying their actions and communications. Indeed, it is possible that the key to the success of certain public policy interventions could be the correct combination of the communicator, the message itself, and the audience. A study we conducted at the University of Milan-Bicocca (Macchi, 2019) revealed that the same nudge techniques used by two different sources for a blood donor campaign (and also for the reduction of alcohol consumption among youth) did not obtain the same effect, confirming that what contributes to the success of the nudge is, in fact, the dynamics between these various factors.

The persuasive intent of the nudge acts implicitly, which is why it can be more efficacious than explicit discourse. That said, if it is to be efficacious, it must be perceived as being legitimate, and there must be a sharing of assumptions between the proposer (the choice architect) and the decision maker. If the implicit plan is not shared, the behavioural intervention must be able to stimulate aspects that are only partially shareable, as long as they are justifiable, as in an act of persuasion.

Now, this is possible when we move within what Mosconi (1978) called our *cognitive complex*, the knowledge, the ideas, and attitudes that characterize us as a person. In his words:

> The supporting framework of the persuasive discourse must rest on one or more elements that have been accepted by the listener, by the audience. The cognitive complex is not a coherent and organic system. It is composed of partial systems, which in turn are more or less coherent and organic internally that tend to establish relationships of compatibility or integration among themselves (with the possible consequence that parts of the cognitive complex may be modified or rejected). [...] The cognitive complex, which is a product of culture and personal experience, is always composed of heterogeneous elements or parts and is characterized by levels of organization of the significantly differing individual parts. [...] If the cognitive complex were a coherent and organic system, most persuasive processes would not be possible. It is the very heterogeneity of the material that

> makes up the cognitive complex, the various levels of organization and integration of its parts that provides the possibility of constructing or activating a different subsystem [...] by introducing a different interpretation, a different scheme of reference [...] that opens the way for new elements, information and criteria that were not present in the preceding system to establish new and different links among the elements, to change the value, the weight and so on.
>
> (Mosconi, 1978, pages 18-20)

The way a discourse, problem, or dilemma is interpreted depends not only on the context and the identity of the interlocutors but also on their shared knowledge—both implicit and explicit—and on the speaker's communicative goals. These elements activate sophisticated inferential processes and shape the attribution of meaning.

If we treat the nudge as a communicative act, we move beyond the notion that it is just a standard strategy to be repeated and see it as something that should be shaped by context, shared understanding, and interpretation. All communication relies on a background of tacit knowledge, presuppositions, and implications, and the way these are handled influences not only how effective the communication is but also how effective a behavioural intervention will be. In this light, one factor that deserves particular attention when designing a nudge is the recognition that implicit aspects of communication—aspects that may be unnoticed by one or even both parties—are always at play.

7.2 Public Communication

Nudges, and behavioural policies in general, which are the focus of most behavioural units worldwide, are essentially about communication (Dianoux, 2019; Singler, 2015). As many of these interventions and messages are intended to avoid risky behaviour, as well as reminding us of our duties (such as paying taxes), it is important that the people who are entrusted with their formulation make them efficacious, easy to understand, and not misleading. Halpern (2015) emphasizes that most of a behavioural centre's activity includes "informing, encouraging, and persuading". Therefore, it is a question of "simply" making the communication "efficacious" (Cialdini, 1993). In my view, the nudge itself can be considered a form of communicative act, in a general sense. However, Dianoux (2019) clarifies that the "nudge is different than persuasion" in the sense that rhetoric acts through persuasive discourse while the nudge, and *behavioural insights* in general, avoid doing this. They act indirectly, given that change is not always brought about by a conscious voluntary action.

That said, according to the view I am proposing here, the mechanisms that exploit the nudge are the same as those of rhetoric. Shaping opinions and prompting action by taking the interlocutors on board—acknowledging their cognitive, emotional, and ethical characteristics, their epistemic state, cultural assumptions, and value system—has always been the aim of rhetoric: a millennia-old discipline that, in fact, offers a sophisticated distillation of the general principles that underlie effective natural communication. Without this, the discourse loses its power. And yet this is precisely the task that those responsible for public policy must now take on.

Therefore, when designing public policies, it is not enough to analyse the cognitive mechanisms involved; this activity must also take into consideration the communicative factors that are intrinsically connected to these mechanisms. Closely related to the cognitive heuristics, we must also consider the heuristics or the principles that guide the communication, which involve the source-message dynamic, its goals, the context, and, finally, on a more general level, as mentioned above, the implicit design of the communication itself. The same cognitive mechanism could give rise to different effects if these factors are modified and invalidate its efficacy.

In general terms, in every discourse, it is "how" we speak about something that lets our listeners understand "what" we are talking about. There are aspects relative to the functioning of the mind in the production and reception of every discourse that are decisive for its comprehensibility, adequacy, and effectiveness of communication. When choice architects formulate a text, they formulate it exactly as a communicative exchange. The intention of the person who is speaking or is structuring decisional options (the choice architect or the person they are representing), more or less consciously conveys aims that can guide the listener, the person to whom the message is directed.

In spite of this increasing awareness, the behavioural intervention is still susceptible to being understood as the adoption of general *debiasing* tools, or more precisely, of the exploitation of thought biases. However tempting it may be to have a list of ready-to-use interventions to hand that are effective transversally in various fields of application, the complexity of the individual and contextual characteristics of the intervention must be kept in mind. As I have mentioned earlier, the context (in all its nuances) and the objectives of the intervention contribute to determining how it will be interpreted, using sophisticated inferential processes of attribution of meaning. If we do consider the nudge as being on a par with a communicative act, it is possible to avoid perceiving it just as a valid intervention that reflects the concept of biases as general mechanisms independent of contextual factors (Stanovich & West, 2008). Fortunately, more frequently now than before, experts or groups of experts in communication are being included in behavioural insight teams (Mindspace-Behavioural Insight Team; COMBI Communication for behavioural impact—World Health Organization). The communicative mechanisms of some nudge typologies and other behavioural insights will be analysed in this chapter, with a separate section dedicated to messages that transmit numerical information, whether they be in numerical reports, percentages, or frequencies (unfortunately, space here does not permit an analysis of nonverbal public communications). I will consider the principal nudge interventions in the light of these characteristics that explain how they function and, sometimes, why they fail, to focus on the factors on which policy-makers should concentrate when they are planning their interventions. I will give some examples of international studies and interventions on public communication, with some insightful suggestions for possible future interventions.

7.3 Behavioural Biases, Nudges, and Communication

Ruggeri (2018) noted that there are both challenges and opportunities involved in the different forms of communication between the parties whose contributions are essential for creating successful public policy, i.e., on the one hand, the scientists, those responsible for drafting the policies (stakeholders and policymakers), in the middle, and finally, on the other side, the public. It is well-known that a government's policy messages that are not effectively communicated to the public will inevitably have little influence on the public's behaviour. Simple, salient messages that can also be communicated with a combination of images and narrative have been seen to be important above all for effective scientific dissemination with public policy communicators (through traditional communication channels such as academic articles and white papers or more contemporaneous methods such as scientific blogs). Indeed, the way information and issues are included in the policymakers' agenda depends largely on how scientists communicate them. It is often how the issues are presented rather than their content that determines whether they will be noticed at all and how they will be interpreted (Simon, 1947), regardless of their urgency, usefulness, or importance (Hallsworth et al., 2018). Frames, social norms, personalization, participation, trust, and a shortened temporal distance are just some of the instruments that contribute to developing effective public policies, through traditional or contemporary channels (mass media and web technologies, respectively). For reasons of space, I will discuss here the principles that are most commonly shared and adopted, analysing them from the point of view of communications. Tversky and Koehler, writing in 1994, noted that, generally speaking, it is evident that variations in the description of the options and the decisional context influence our choices and behaviour and frequently overturn choices. They explain this phenomenon with the inevitable relativistic assessment of the option, starting from the quantitative point of reference taken or the way that the options are contextualized in terms of gain and loss.

If we consider the phenomenon from the point of view of the psychology of communication it is even more general in nature: the assumption of a quantitative reference point (in the value function of Kahnemann and Tversky's prospect theory) is a particular case of a more general mechanism that consists in the fact that we always assume a point of reference when describing a fact, an option, and that the choice of description is never neutral but inevitably encompasses the point of view of the speaker or the choice architect. Indeed, adopting a particular description implicitly transmits not only a state of knowledge but also and above all the speaker's intention.

7.3.1 The Unpacking Effect

I will start with a very general and very simple observation: if we take three descriptions of the same phenomenon "death from natural causes" as "death from tumour, or heart disease, or other natural causes" or "death from pancreatic cancer, stomach cancer, breast cancer, ictus, stroke, or other natural causes" and ask people to assign a degree of probability to these three descriptions, we will find that the second description will be considered more probable than the first and the third most probable of all three. The more information is added, the higher will be the level of probability assigned. This is known as the *unpacking factor* (Tversky and Koehler's Support Theory, 1994), in which the unpacking of the event to be evaluated into its constituent parts (sub-events) results in an increase in the probability (p) attributed to the event itself (as the sum of the probability attributed to the sub-events), which results in differences in the decisions taken (from the availability to make donations, to taking out insurance policies, etc.). The authors identified a psychological mechanism that consisted of psychological "support" (translated into an estimate of the probability that the event would occur) that we attribute to events by simply mentioning them. Otherwise, these events would be implicit and remain in the shadows, so to speak, and only a few would come to mind. The choice of a certain description rather than another, however, also communicates the importance that the speaker attributes to that sub-event and, for example, could be exploited to communicate the risk involved in a particular event, such as an epidemic or a natural catastrophe, increasing the effective perception.

7.3.2 The Framing Effect

As we saw in Chapter 6, Tversky and Kahnemann described the consequences that a change in perspective (framing) has on the relative desirability of equivalent decisional options, resulting in an inversion of the preferences in the different frames adopted. Framing, therefore, has an implicit communicative dimension, and it is immediately evident that it can help to make a communication more persuasive. For example, if during an election campaign a candidate receives a 49% disapproval rating or a 51% approval rating from the electorate, the perception of their chances of winning the election will be greater in the second case, even though numerically the two values are complementary (and, of course, if these are the only two options present). Various studies have shown that positive frames that emphasize the advantages of a certain option are facilitators of positive attitudes to the environment and healthy behaviour towards smoking.

What I will describe now is a case showing that framing, combined with other basic communication strategies, can involve the public in virtuous behaviour. A collaboration was set up in 2013 between the Ontario Government's Behavioural

Insights Unit (BIU) and the Rotman School of Management's Behavioural Economics in Action Research Hub (BEAR) to encourage 626,212 automobile owners to renew their licences with a simple online procedure rather than going into the city to do it in person. The frame of the standard messaging used was reformulated, emphasizing (a) the advantages (gain) of renewing the licenses online or (b) the disadvantages (loss) of using the traditional method. Actually, both frames (a) and (b) produced a significant increase in online renewals in less than two months, but frame (a) stressed that the gain was even more effective. The savings in service costs and time were significant (Castelo et al., 2015).

The cases I have described above are examples of the *attribute framing effect* (Thaler, 1980; Tversky & Kahneman, 1981; Levin & Gaeth, 1988), in which there is an inversion of the preferences even where no risky choices are involved due to the different evaluation given to the salient attribute of the object. According to these authors, the framing effect of the attribute produces a process of codification of the information: a positive "label" leads to the information being codified so as to promote positive associations, while a negative "label" results in the information being codified with negative associations. From a qualitative point of view (see Text Box 7.3 for an analysis of the quantitative framing effect), the speaker's choice of a particular frame conveys their point of view, implicitly communicating information that goes beyond its literal content and becomes part of the message that is received by the listener. In general, a speaker's choice of a particular frame conveys their point of view: in fact, the inferences the listener produces regarding the properties of the object are based on the frame chosen to describe it. Yet again, the value of an option is determined based on a point of reference, and this phenomenon, which was studied by Craig McKenzie and colleagues (Sher & McKenzie, 2006; McKenzie & Nelson, 2003), can be condensed into the expression of "seeing the glass half full or half empty".

As I explained in Text Box 6.2, when asked to describe a glass in which the water reaches the half-way mark, most people will say that the glass is half full if they know that it was originally empty, and that it is half empty if originally it was full, as they are influenced by the variation in a property that becomes the initial reference (see page 143). Of course, this is not to be taken as a general rule, as if the context and the expectations change, the phenomenon could be inverted (Macchi, 2021). Take for example the case of a child who wants their glass filled with their favourite drink; if the glass is only partly filled, the child might well say, "but it's half empty!", or that of an adult who needs just a drop of water to dilute their medicine, who might say, "but it's still half full!" when given a glass that was full but was partially emptied on their request. So we can say that it is not only the starting point that counts, but also the context, the intentions, and expectations that contribute to the speaker's selection of one particular frame rather than another. The frame used to describe an object or a situation, then, is never neutral.

7.3.2.1 The Framing Effect and Public Policy

Therefore, using different frames can have a powerful effect on how we perceive a problem. It is particularly interesting to see that framing can be an efficacious tool in helping to make the communication of a public policy persuasive. An example of this is the 2015 Ipsos MORI survey in the UK regarding Brexit. Two groups of adults were asked for their opinion on the lowering of the minimum voting age. The results showed that the opinion of the majority changed depending on whether they were asked if they were in favour of "lowering the minimum voting age from 18 to 16 years of age" (37% in favour, 56% against) or whether the question was formulated as "extending the right to vote to persons of 16 and 17 years of age" (52% in favour, 41% against). The first formulation is perceived as a problem of liberalization and its inherent potential risks (which could implicate the loss of the *status quo*), while the second is seen as a question of recognizing the right to vote.

The shift in these responses underlines the importance of taking framing into account when designing forms of direct democracy or attempting to anticipate the outcome of controversial political decisions. Finally, there is a metaphorical dimension to the framing effect that goes beyond simply representing events in terms of gains and losses—it profoundly shapes how public policies are conceived and developed. In this case, the frame not only highlights certain positive and negative aspects of the question at hand, but it also links them together in a "coherent and comprehensible framework". In other words, a frame can offer a convincing unit that forms a basic picture of beliefs, perceptions, and values.

This is often done by supplying a suggestive image or metaphor; for example, in its 2018 Behavioural Government Report, the Behavioural Insights Team investigated to see if the metaphor used to represent crime influenced opinions regarding the policies implemented to fight it. Their participants were divided into two groups who received a report on the crime rates in a certain city. One report described crime as "a beast ravaging the city", while the other used the metaphor "a virus infecting the city". Both reports contained the same statistics on crime rates; at the end of the presentation, the participants were asked to decide on a program to reduce crime, the choice being between a social reform and the implementation of more severe sanctions. The preferred choice when "virus" was used as a metaphor for criminality was social reform to "vaccinate" the community (44% versus 26%), whereas the majority of the participants who received the report describing criminality as a beast opted for more severe sanctions (74% versus 56%). This type of frame has two problematic implications: the first being that the use of a metaphor seems to imply there is a "natural" and obvious solution (e.g., in the case of a virus, it is necessary to create a clean environment), while the second is that our use of these images is frequently unintentional. This may mean that those who use opposing frames not only strongly disagree about what needs to be done, but they also have difficulty in committing themselves to a line of action for reaching a compromise. If a common metaphor isn't found, an intense political conflict and an impasse may result.

7.3.3 Default

Another tool available to choice architects is the *default*. This is a predefined option that becomes the actual choice when we do not actively make a choice. According to Samuelson and Zeckhauser (1988), the use of this technique is based on the so-called *status quo bias*, our natural aversion to change even in those cases where the cost of modifying the status of the moment is minimal. This option depends on the reference population and works well only in contexts where the choices tend to be homogeneous. Take, for example, the case of organ donations that we saw earlier. In Germany, citizens are not donors by default; they become donors only by enrolling voluntarily on the donor register (the *opt-in* method). In Austria, on the other hand, the citizens are donors by default, but they can cancel their names from the register if they do not wish to donate their organs (the *opt-out* method). In Figure 7.4, Johnson and Goldstein compared intention to donate organs in various countries, distinguishing between explicit (opt-in) and presumed consent (opt-out). The percentages are very different,[4] at least as far as the intentions are concerned. These authors also conducted an experiment in which they asked a group if they would agree to becoming organ donors; they formulated the question in two different ways. In the first, the opt-in scenario, all the citizens were considered non-donors

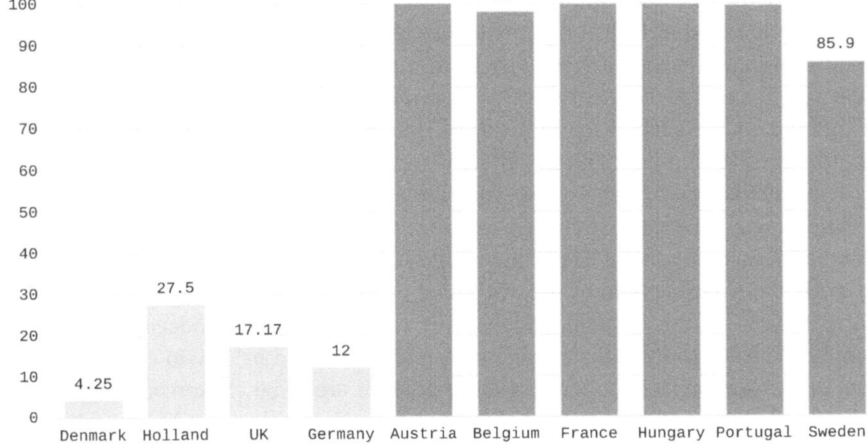

FIGURE 7.4 Effective consent rates by country. Explicit consent and presumed consent.
Source: Johnson and Goldstein (2013).

by default and were given the option of confirming or modifying their status. In the second, the presumed consent opt-out scenario, the participants were considered to be donors by default. Only 42% of the participants in the opt-in scenario decided to become donors, while in the opt-out scenario, the positive choice rate was as high as 82%. The *status quo bias* appeared to explain this significant difference; however, the authors ran a third, neutral condition in which no default was mentioned, and the participants were simply asked to choose whether they would become donors or not. In this condition too, a high number of participants (79%) chose to become donors, revealing a positive attitude to organ donation that can also be seen in the opt-out condition and that could be dampened in the opt-in condition by the implicit message transmitted, for example, by the fact that "the majority of people are not donors".

The explanation of a *status quo bias* or inertia regarding an action to be undertaken would not appear to fully justify the phenomenon, as it doesn't apply to the neutral condition that, in all effects, resembles the opt-in scenario. Indeed, in the neutral condition, approximately 80% of the participants were willing to become donors in spite of the fact that they would have to take action to change their status quo.[5]

The opt-in/opt-out default options, in addition to representing a choice taken a priori in the case that a person does not actively make a choice, would also appear to implicitly convey the position of the institution proposing the choice as, over and above inviting the individual to "do the right thing" it also provides information as to "what the majority of the population does". In the case of explicit consent, this information would be that "the majority of the population is not a donor", while in the case of presumed consent, the information being transmitted is that "the majority of the population is a donor". The default option, therefore, is the preferred choice of the institution (it transmits the institution's values as in the opt-out condition) and/or is the option that corresponds to the choice of the majority, to the extent that it is set automatically to favour/satisfy the majority (this applies to both opt-in and opt-out conditions). The question of organ donations usually falls within the competence of the Ministry of Health, which is generally trusted by the population and is in line with its mission.

It would be interesting to see what the effect of this strategy on the opt-out condition would be if the source (institution) were less acceptable or one perceived as being less trustworthy. Would the nudge still be just as efficient? For the nudge to work, the values upheld by the institution proposing the choice must be coherent with those who are allowing themselves to be "nudged". Indeed, the correct combination of institution, message, and recipient could be key to explaining the success of some public policies. If these policies are to be effective, the premises must be perceived as legitimate, and they must be implicitly shared by the proposer (the choice architect) and the person taking the decision, as well as being shared by the majority.

7.3.4 *Social Norms*

As we have just seen, people often seek validation of their opinions and decisions by social comparison, imitating the majority (Cialdini, 1993; Gigerenzer, 2001; van der Linden et al., 2015) on the basis of social norms, group rules that can direct the behaviour of the individual (Goldstein et al., 2008). Social norms have proven to be a powerful lever for effective communication, and they are often implicitly activated even through other types of nudges, as we have seen in the case of default options. In the social experiment on organ donation we have just seen, the default implicitly conveyed that the procedure had been simplified precisely because it represented the choice preferred by the majority. This phenomenon seems to satisfy Grice's maxim of quality communication theory by associating the behaviour of the majority and a foundation of truth: if the majority asserts (or does) something, its degree of truth is supported.

7.3.5 *Personalization*

Personalized messages are designed to respond to the characteristics of the recipient as opposed to standard communications that can be used for the entire population (Hirsh et al., 2012). The degree of personalization can range from simply adding the recipient's name to a standard message, to communications "tailored" to demographic characteristics, to messages drafted with specific psychological profiles in mind (leveraging various motivational traits associated with different personality characteristics).

These techniques are widely used in marketing and have already been adopted for public policies (Ruggeri, 2018) for the promotion of preventative medical care, such as breast cancer screening every two years for women over 40. Plohl and colleagues (2019) carried out a brief survey on personalized messages, in which the participants were asked to indicate the reason they had not attended the screening in previous years, based on one of two options: the conviction of personally not being at risk from breast cancer and the costs (economic and logistic) of attending. The authors drew inspiration from the Health Belief Model, which holds that people are more likely to take action if they perceive a serious risk to their health, and if the communication underlines that the future benefits outweigh the costs (Sohl & Moyer, 2007).

Three conditions were formulated: (1) no message, (2) a message with information about the medical procedure and the objective of the screening, and (3) message 2 integrated with a note mentioning the specific factors identified in the questionnaire that had impeded the successful outcome of the prevention campaign. The results showed that while in the short term (3 to 6 months) the efficacy of messages 2 and 3 was comparable, in the long term (16 to 22 months) message 3 was more efficacious (56.6% compared to 47%). These results were supported by a meta-analysis conducted by the authors.

7.4 Examples of Public Communication around the World

7.4.1 Behavioural Insights Team (BIT): Drawing a Line between Efficacious and Manipulative Communication

Governments have always had Psychological Operations Units and Ministries of Information, which more often than not have tended to manipulate public opinion (Halpern, 2015). Since its foundation in the UK in 2010, the mission of the Behavioural Insights Team is to ensure that the line of demarcation between efficacious communication and manipulation is not crossed. In the projects that the team undertakes, all statements must be based on real data; for example, if we were to say that "9 people out of 10 pay their taxes on time", exploiting Robert Cialdini's social normative, we would have to make sure that this statement corresponds to reality. The team also advocates transparency; it is open about the work it does, making public its research protocols and the relative documentation. Public reaction to the projects is recorded and is the subject of further reflections. Finally, the BIT makes sure it has a system of independent quality control composed of academics with behavioural science expertise.

7.4.2 COMBI: Contextualizing Communication

COMBI (Communication for Behavioural Impact) is an interagency toolkit produced by the World Health Organization (WHO), the Food and Agriculture Organization (FAO), and the United Nations Children's Fund (UNICEF) that integrates social and behavioural communication in the field of public health programs. It can provide essential information in the case of epidemics, representing a change in the communication procedure adopted. For example, during the outbreak of Ebola in Sudan, it focused on the behavioural and social aspects of prevention and control of the disease, an approach that can be adapted to local characteristics. Epidemic hotspots are frequently characterized by uncertainty and the need for urgency, so appropriate timing of communication is essential. Significant sums of money have been spent on communication campaigns for epidemic prevention and control but the impact of many of these campaigns has not been clearly demonstrated, often due to the divergence between the people who plan actions to control the disease in hotspots (for example, epidemiologists, vets and public health specialists) and those who actuate the actions and mobilize a community through communications.

These technical activities must be understood and applied in the social, political, economic, and cultural contexts. These are the contexts that determine the success of measures of control and prevention. The potential of methods such as COMBI emerges in projects to amplify and transmit preventative information, which is often in contrast with deeply rooted cultural practices that must be understood in order to have an impact on controlling the epidemic, but which cannot be identified from the usual interviews conducted on the hotspots.

The COMBI toolkit shows why it is not easy to change behaviour and how systematic communication programs can be planned with strategies that encourage dialogue with the community in the effort to bring the epidemic under control. These programs range from interviews with key informers to focus group discussions with social mobilizers, health care workers, and other members of the response team, such as law enforcement, religious leaders, and market operators. In parallel, information is collected from the population regarding their daily life—what they were doing and with whom they came into contact—to identify the appropriate approach to be taken and information channels to be used, as well as influential, trustworthy, and reliable sources of information that can best transmit the communication and promote the necessary activities for prevention and control. In the specific case of the Ebola outbreak in the Sudan, an observational study was conducted to understand how the social mobilizers operate and how best they could be supported.

7.4.3 Mindspace

The Mindspace model was developed from the findings of a behaviour change summit held in London in 2009, attended by politicians, senior policy, strategy, and insight officials from the British government, and academics. The Behavioural Insight Team (BIT) has its origins in this summit. Here too, we find the concept that public communication that is limited to providing information often results in modest or even undesired results. The factors that Mindspace identified as crucial for public policy are as follows:

- Messenger: We are heavily influenced by who communicates information.
- Incentives: Our responses to incentives are shaped by predictable mental shortcuts, such as strongly avoiding losses.
- Norms: We are strongly influenced by what others do.
- Defaults: We "go with the flow" of pre-set actions.
- Salience: Our attention is drawn to what is novel and seems relevant to us.
- Priming: Our acts are often influenced by subconscious cues.
- Affect: Our emotional associations can powerfully affect our actions.
- Commitments: We seek to be consistent with our public promises and reciprocate acts.
- Ego: We act in ways that make us feel better about ourselves.

All the above factors involve the sphere of communication more or less directly, and to a certain extent overlap what has already been said, compared to other models of public policies. However, here I will dedicate a few lines to one in particular, salience, that Mindspace defines in terms of novelty, accessibility (different labels and colours for differentiated waste collection), and simplicity (use of slogans). It goes without saying that we tend to be attracted by communications we can understand and encode easily; and it is much easier to encode information that relates directly to our own personal experience rather than information of a general nature (for example, the budget for the National Health Service is easier to comprehend if it is communicated in the form of a sum per individual rather than as the overall figure).

7.4.4 Social and Behavioural Sciences Team (SBST): Simplification and Salience

The fundamental elements of the communication model adopted by SBST, a government agency which was operative in the USA from 2015 to 2017 under President Obama, are very similar to the others described so far and focus on the simplification of the language used, a reduction in the quantity of data, a clarification of the procedures, and salience of the information to be transmitted. One example of the success of the SBST model was the improvement in the efficacy of the communications sent to those who took out student loans for higher education. The United States Department of Education offered flexible repayment options for borrowers so that they could respect the repayment terms. These included Income-based Repayment, Pay-as-you-earn, and Income-Contingent Repayment, which link the monthly payments to the debtors' income. Well aware that managing repayment plans can be complicated and challenging, the Federal Office of the Education Department collaborated with the White House's Social and Behavioural Sciences team to study effective communication strategies.

One such strategy was activated in November 2013 with the launch of an email campaign to raise public awareness regarding the theme of loan repayments based on income and to assist debtors in making repayment decisions based on better information about the options open to them on the basis of their income. The emails were sent to debtors who were behind with their repayments due to financial difficulties or lack of work, to those whose loans were higher than average, or any combination of these factors. During the campaign, emails were sent to a total of over three million people, of whom 221,000 accepted to reimburse the loan. The emails indicated the eligibility criteria for income-based debt repayment, the relative benefits that accrued from adopting that system, and the costs that not taking any action would entail, as well as web links and contact details for the loan servicer. The team used a strict randomized pilot check to measure the impact of the email based on behavioural science intuitions at 90 and 180 days.

The study showed that prompt, clear, low-cost messages of this type can help people to have a better understanding of the options available to them, to make more informed decisions that are in line with their intentions. The email campaign sent to borrowers who were behind with their payments resulted in a statistically significant increase in applications for loan repayments based on income, approximately 6,000 supplementary applications completed in just one month following the mailing to the 841,442 debtors of the pilot study.

The SBST also collaborated with the Department of Defence in a similar program, the objective of which was the formulation of an effective communication to the members of the Armed Forces, encouraging them to continue to pay into their savings plan (Roth IRA—Individual Retirement Account). In 2015, as a result of a change in the military salary system, almost 140,000 people were obliged to re-enrol in their savings plan online to avoid their contributions being suspended indefinitely. The SBST collaborated with the Department of Defence to reword the communication, making the language clear and concise, explaining what had to be done, and personalizing the email. At the end of the first week of the pilot study, the results clearly showed that compared to the original communication, there had been an increase of 22% (3770 individuals) in online registrations. The new text was then used for the entire military database.

7.4.5 Department for International Development (DFID)—Regarding the Ideal Amount of Information: Not Too Much, Not Too Little

Politicians are faced with a delicate balancing act when communicating; they need to provide sufficient information so that people know what to do, but they must be careful not to eclipse the essential with the superfluous. So, how much information is too much? In 2019, DFID conducted a randomized study with Unilever in Bangladesh on how to effectively wash one's hands, which is generally recognized as an essential strategy for controlling the transmission of Covid-19. A thousand public handwashing stations were set up in locations with high affluence throughout Bangladesh, outside mosques, markets, and at bus stops. Each station was equipped with three hand basins and a message board with posters encouraging the population to wash their hands (Figure 7.5). The study involved 2,196 adults, recruited from social media, who were tested for their ability to remember and understand the key messages posted on the boards. The posters varied in the quantity of information on handwashing, ranging from the basic function of the handwashing station with instructions to wash your hands for at least 20 seconds to messages describing how to wash your hands in 4 or 7 steps. The results showed that the step-by-step approach improved recall of the various phases of handwashing, but too much added detail tended to obscure the main message. After seeing the posters with the 4 or 7 phases, the respondents had an additional 10% probability (70%) of recalling the need to wash the palms of their hands and their thumbs than those who only saw the basic message without the step-by-step instructions (59%).

While it is difficult to see how it could be possible to wash one's hands without washing the palms, many people forget to wash their thumbs, so specifying this step could significantly improve results. That said, however, it was seen that in the case of the 7-phase poster, improvement came with a cost: there was a lower probability that the respondents would remember to wash their hands for 20 seconds, compared to those who only saw the basic posters. This is a case of "too much information": the extra details caused the participants to forget the elementary

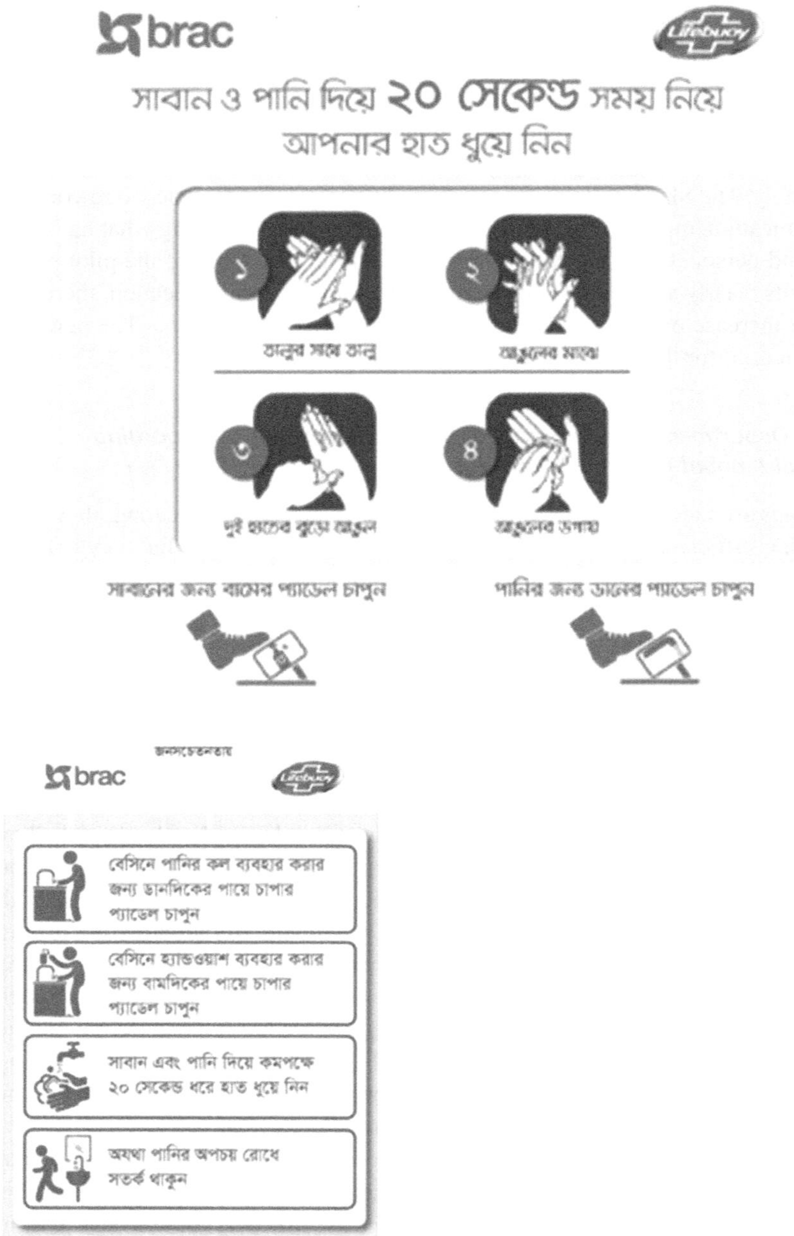

FIGURE 7.5 Messages affixed to public handwashing stations in Bangladesh during the pandemic.

FIGURE 7.5 (Continued)

information and the basic message. The availability of more information, time and cognitive resources does not in itself guarantee an increase in the accuracy of the responses (less-is-more effect) (Goldstein & Gigerenzer, 2002), the risk being that someone who is not familiar with the issue may put all the information on the same level and will have difficulty in identifying what is effectively relevant in a given context. For a communication to be effective, the person who is formulating it must take into consideration the inevitable limits of attention and working memory of the cognitive system, abandoning the illusion that an all-encompassing communication is informative because it contains every detail. Ideally, as well as reducing the amount of information included, the message should identify the most pertinent elements so that the recipient has less information to process, but what they have is the most relevant.

7.5 Communicating Numbers: Another Issue

When socially aware behaviour is to be encouraged—essential when attempting to eradicate the Covid-19 pandemic, for example—communications must be formulated in such a way as to convey an appropriate perception of the risks involved. This is particularly true when communicating statistics and probabilistic data to the lay public, inevitably conditioning their perception of risk. All the data are available, but when their specific meaning is couched in technical terms, the public will only be in a position to understand them if they are communicated appropriately. Therefore, if the data contained in the message is to be interpreted correctly, a "signalled" formulation is required. Continuing to supply information regarding new cases of infection, whether in absolute terms or in percentages, only rarely clarifies which base line or dataset is being referred to and how this changes with the increase in the number of tests carried out based on the type of population being tested (random or health workers or elderly residents in care), and so it is not possible to have a clear perception of what the data really means. The theoretical physicist, Giorgio Parisi, who was awarded the Nobel prize for physics in 2021, made the following statement regarding the need for clear and complete data during the Covid-19 pandemic:

> As a start, you have to know which numbers arrive and how. The data are not sufficiently transparent and complete. Each day we know there are +X patients occupying beds in intensive care. That said, if we want to understand how the pandemic is developing, it would be interesting to know how many new patients were accepted and how many were dismissed from intensive care (I would also add how many were dismissed because they were cured and how many died) [...] we only have the daily balance. Even the RT Index is not reliable: when calculating the RT you have to make statistical inferences on the data, which may have a series of approximations. The data is couched in a language that is incomprehensible to the lay person. In the latest monitoring it was indicated

> as RT: 1.73 (95% CI: 1.41-1.83). It doesn't even spark your curiosity to find out what we are talking about. Translating it into more comprehensible terms, it says that the range lies between 1.41 and 1.83 with the most probable value being 1.73. The following week the most likely RT value was 1.43, but the range widened enormously from 1.1 to 1.8 which shows how unstable the data are. An expert will realise this and the fact that the system has lost control (and consequently that the data cannot be relied upon). The layperson cannot.

The two points raised by Parisi regarded a lack of transparency and incomprehensibility, leading to the inefficacy of the communication. In the first case, the aggregate data do not provide a key to understanding the real trend of the pandemic, while in the second, the lack of clarity is to be ascribed to the use of overly technical terms that impede the layperson's understanding of the situation. The vague impression that remains gives only a very ephemeral sense of a change in the situation for better or for worse. While good intentions and scientific knowledge are necessary but not sufficient conditions, alone they are not enough to ensure that the message is really informative with the potential of persuasion. Specialized languages such as logic or statistics presuppose an exclusive and univocal interpretation of their content that is achieved through a shared code; natural language, on the other hand, must be interpreted by inferential processes, in the light of the interlocutors' attribution of intentions. In Chapter 5, we explored the confusion in the inverse conditional probabilities (p(H|D) versus p(H|D), the lack of awareness of the importance of defining the base line in understanding percentages and the correct denominators for frequencies (Barbey & Sloman, 2007; Macchi, 1995, 2000) and how we formulate probability judgement on low probability events (Koehler & Macchi, 2004; Macchi et al., 1999).

Generally speaking, there is a divergence between technical-specialized language and natural language. They do have an objective in common, that of conveying a meaning clearly and effectively, or, in other words, of communicating, but they have different ways of attaining it. Specialized languages, such as logic or statistics, attempt to achieve univocal communication through simplification, eliminating all aspects that could interfere with the unambiguity of the meaning to be communicated (by de-psychologizing the language), while natural language exploits the expressivity of the terms used and the information that derives from the specific content and its pertinence to the context. So, when we want to communicate scientific terms or data in a discourse in natural language outside the technical field, we have to reintroduce psychological aspects that characterize the communication, and so "translate" the technical discourse into natural language. In official communications, the intent is elevated, the data used is generally obtained from reliable and accredited sources, and even if the explanation given is exhaustive, the message may still not be fully understood. Objective information on its own is not sufficient to make an impact on the subjective level. The truth alone is not enough!

7.5.1 The Statistical Format: Frequencies and Percentages

As we have seen in Chapter 5 (page 106), using frequencies and percentages is without doubt advantageous for thought, it saves cognitive resources and increases knowledge, as well as offering the possibility of making inferences and predictions regarding samples to which we have no direct access. That said, it must be remembered that if used incorrectly, these same frequencies and percentages can lead to misunderstandings (as in the case of the contraceptive pill alarm in the United Kingdom, see pages 99 to 110).

It is worthwhile here to comment again on that well-known and widely studied phenomenon, the *base-rate fallacy* (Tversky & Kahnemann, 1974), which we examined in Chapter 5, i.e., the tendency to neglect the primary probability or base rate in probability judgements of conditioned events, causing serious judgemental biases and errors in decision-making. Robyn Dawes cited a number of examples of mass media communication in which the failure to clarify the base rate generated confusion between inverse conditional events (see Chapter 5).

TEXT BOX 7.3 FREQUENCIES AND PERCENTAGES

Certain classic experiments, such as Eddy's problem of medical diagnosis (1982), contain an error of judgement, the *base-rate fallacy*, even though the base rate is specified. A group of doctors were supplied with a series of data and then asked to estimate the probability of a woman with a positive mammogram having a breast tumour. The data supplied were as follows:

The probability that a 40-year-old woman participating in a routine screening would have breast cancer is 1%. If a woman has breast cancer, the probability that her mammogram will be positive is 80%. If the woman does not have breast cancer, the probability that her mammogram will still be positive is 10%. What then is the probability that a woman who has a positive mammogram really has breast cancer?

If the problem is solved by correctly applying Bayesian reasoning, the result is 7%. The majority of the doctors in the group estimated it to be approximately 75%–80%. Of the 100 doctors, experts in their field who are faced with this situation on a daily basis, only 5 gave the correct answer. The remaining 95 had not considered the base rate, most of them using it merely as an indicator to tweak the data of the genuine positives and incorrectly using it as the final response. Generally, confusing the conditional probability p (tumour | mammograph +) with its inverse p (mammograph +|tumour) is a very common error:

- 80% of women with breast cancer had a positive mammogram.
- 80% of women with a positive mammogram had breast cancer.

These two sentences seem to say the same thing as they both associate having breast cancer with a positive mammograph, but actually they are saying something quite different. The frequentist approach (Gigerenzer & Hoffrager, 1995) adopted the following formulation to express the real positives and obtained much better results: "8 out of 10 women with breast cancer had a positive mammograph". The pragmatic perspective offered a different explanation. According to Macchi (1995, 2000), the improvement in the results when using the frequentist formulation is not to be attributed so much to a more ecological format as to how the information was structured, the partitive formulation. This particular structure brings to light the relations between subsets of data (i.e., between the data and the baseline), which makes it possible to calculate a correct estimate with both frequencies and percentages: "80% of women who have breast cancer have a positive mammograph". When this formulation is used, both in terms of relative frequencies expressed as percentages, as in the experiment above, and in terms of natural frequencies, the relationships between the data are clarified so they can be correctly used. The importance of this was evident in the case of the third-generation contraceptive pill reported in Chapter 5. As we have seen, the partitive formulation can be considered as the linguistic equivalent of a graphic representation and is a way of translating a specific language into natural language in tasks that are structured partly in natural language and partly in specialized language (see pages 109 and 110).

Thinking back to the examples given in Chapter 5 regarding where road accidents happen most frequently and the use of drugs in high schools, we have to agree with Dawes when he says, "words are poor vehicles for discussing inverse probabilities". Awareness of this fact leads inevitably to reintroducing psychological aspects—which were eliminated from the technical-specialized communication—into communications to the public.

7.6 Conclusions

Nudging can be considered a prototypical approach to behavioural change that takes into consideration human cognitive characteristics. This strategy functions on various levels using implicit factors, bypassing defensive attitudes and exploiting inferential and adaptive communication processes without overloading the cognitive system. All the same, it appears evident that the suggestion induced by the nudge is not sufficient in itself to explain a change in behaviour. The acceptance of any suggestion, whether it be explicit or implicit, implies that it is congruous with the receiving system: the "way of reasoning" or the rules by which the suggestion has been produced must be the same as those used by the receiver. What I want to underline here is that the nudge cannot be considered a universal solution. As

I mentioned earlier in this chapter, although the idea of having a list of ready-to-use interventions available for any eventuality is undoubtedly tempting, there is the question of the complexity of the individual and contextual characteristics of the intervention that must be kept in mind and investigated. The context, the identity of the persons involved, the shared knowledge, and the objectives of the speaker all contribute to determining how an utterance, a speech, a problem, or a decision to be taken, will be interpreted through sophisticated inferential processes and attributions of meaning. The context, the identity of the interlocutors, common knowledge, and the intentions of the speaker, all contribute to the interpretation of an utterance, a discourse, a problem, or a decisional dilemma, using sophisticated inferential processes and attribution of meaning. If we consider the nudge to be on a par with a communicative act, it is possible to go beyond the mere repetition of a strategy and, based on tacit knowledge, assumptions, and implications, structure a behavioural intervention. The persuasiveness of implicit messaging has always been widely exploited by advertising and political propaganda. Implicit constructs can, in fact, reduce the audience's critical attention, and as Anne Reboul says: "implicit communication evolved to allow senders to obscure their communicative intent, enabling content to bypass the recipient's critical scrutiny".

As Mercier (2009) maintains, when somebody says something to us from which we draw an inference, we think that the conclusions we reach are our own, and we accept them more readily than if they were communicated to us directly: "the less important the role of the speaker in determining the conclusion by the interlocutor, the easier it will be for the audience to accept that conclusion". This effect is explained by the egocentric bias that leads us to prefer our own beliefs and to use less critical thinking, or, as Sperber and colleagues (2010) put it, we exercise less epistemic vigilance. An aspect regarding the use of the nudge that is worthwhile considering in greater detail, is that the implicit aspects of a communication, even if unknown to one or both parties involved, are always present and can be exploited, not to be manipulated as in advertising or political propaganda, but to be creative, to participate in the construction of the meaning to be attributed to an intervention. As we have seen in the various social experiments illustrated earlier, in order for this to happen, policy-makers must be made more aware of the importance of the communicative dimension in each specific context in which the nudge can be deployed. Therefore, the appearance of the theme of choice architecture becomes a new opportunity for research and creative application of a very general phenomenon that has always existed.

Notes

1 Bastin J-F, Clark E, Elliott T, Hart S, van den Hoogen J, Hordijk I, et al. (2019). Understanding climate change from a global analysis of city analogues. *PLoS ONE* 14(7): e0217592. https://doi.org/10.1371/journal.pone.0217592

2 As well as the *nudge* (Thaler & Sunstein, 2008, 2021), there is the *boost* (Hertwig & Grüne-Yanoff, 2017), and the *budge* (Oliver, 2013), *Behavioral Change Insights* (see *Behaviour Change Wheel*, Michie et al., 2011, for example).

3 See, for example, Chater and Loewenstein (2022); Hallsworth (2023).

4 As reported in later studies, these are not real donations (Arshad et al., 2019).

5 This is the case in Italy where the option of becoming a donor is offered when the identity card is being renewed. Currently, 53% of those renewing their ID have accepted to become a donor. While the presumed consent model, adopted by countries such as Austria and France, is seen as a potential tool to increase donation, its efficacy remains debated. Countries such as Spain and Italy, although not formally implementing such a system, have achieved outstanding results through organizational strategies and awareness-raising campaigns. The Spanish model in particular, with its multi-level structure and the support of a national health system, has shown that factors such as staff training and the inclusion of donors with broader criteria are crucial to success. In an article in course of publication, I have suggested that, in addition to legislative change, an integrated approach that considers different organizational and cultural aspects is needed to improve organ donation rates (Panizza & Macchi, 2025).

REFERENCES

Ahn, W. K., & Graham, L. M. (1999). The impact of necessity and sufficiency in the Wason four-card selection task. *Psychological Science*, *10*(3), 237–242.

Almashat, S., Ayotte, B., Edelstein, B., & Margrett, J. (2008). Framing effect debiasing in medical decision making. *Patient Education and Counseling*, *71*(1), 102–107.

Annas, G. J. (2017). Informed consent: Charade or choice?. *The Journal of Law, Medicine & Ethics : A Journal of the American Society of Law, Medicine & Ethics*, *45*(1), 10–11. https://doi.org/10.1177/1073110517703096

Arnheim, R. (1989). *Parables of sun light: Observations on psychology, the arts, and the rest*. Berkeley and Los Angeles: University of California Press.

Arshad, A., Anderson, B., & Sharif, A. (2019). Comparison of organ donation and transplantation rates between opt-out and opt-in systems. *Kidney International*, *95*(6), 1453–1460.

Ash, I. K., & Wiley, J. (2006). The nature of restructuring in insight: An individual-differences approach. *Psychonomic Bulletin & Review*, *13*, 66–73.

Baars, B. J. (1989). *A cognitive theory of consciousness*. Cambridge, MA: Cambridge University Press.

Bagassi, M., & Macchi, L. (2006). Pragmatic approach to decision making under uncertainty: The case of the disjunction effect. *Thinking & Reasoning*, *12*(3), 329–350.

Bagassi, M., & Macchi, L. (2016). The interpretative function and the emergence of *Unconscious Analytic* Thought. In L. Macchi, M. Bagassi, & R. Viale (Eds.), *Cognitive unconscious and human rationality* (pp. 43–76). Cambridge, MA: MIT Press.

Baird, B., Smallwood, J., Mrazek, M. D., Kam, J. W. Y., Franklin, M. S., & Schooler, J. W. (2012). Inspired by distraction: Mind wandering facilitates creative incubation. *Psychological Science*, *23*, 1117–1122.

Ball, L. J., & Stupple, E. J. (2016). Dual reasoning processes and the resolution of uncertainty: The case of belief bias. In L. Macchi, M. Bagassi, & R. Viale (Eds.), *Cognitive unconscious and human rationality* (pp. 143–165). Cambridge, MA: MIT Press.

Barbey, A. K., & Sloman, S. A. (2007). Base-rate respect: From ecological rationality to dual processes. *Behavioral and Brain Sciences*, *30*(3), 241–254.

Bar-Hillel, M. (1980). The base-rate fallacy in probability judgments. *Acta Psychologica*, *44*(3), 211–233.

Barsalou, L. W. (2009). Simulation, situated conceptualization, and prediction. *Philosophical Transactions of the Royal Society of London. Series B, Biological Sciences*, *364*(1521), 1281–1289. https://doi.org/10.1098/rstb.2008.0319

Bastardi, A., & Shafir, E. (1998). On the pursuit and misuse of useless information. *Journal of Personality and Social Psychology*, *75*(1), 19–32.

Behne, T., Liszkowski, U., Carpenter, M., & Tomasello, M. (2012). Twelve-month-olds' comprehension and production of pointing. *British Journal of Developmental Psychology*, *30*(3), 359–375.

Betsch, T. (2007). The nature of intuition and its neglect in research on judgment and decision making. In H. Plessner, C. Betsch, & T. Betsch (Eds.), *Intuition in judgment and decision making* (pp. 3–22). Mahwah, NJ: Lawrence Erlbaum Associates.

Betsch, T., & Held, C. (2012). Run and jump modes of analysis. *Mind and Society*, *11*(1), Special issue on: Dual process theories of human thought: The debate, 69–80.

Bowden, E. M., Jung-Beeman, M., Fleck, J., & Kounios, J. (2005). New approaches to demystifying insight. *Trends in Cognitive Sciences*, *9*, 322–328.

Braine, M. D. S., Connell, J., Freitag, J., & O'Brien, D. P. (1990). Is the base rate fallacy an instance of asserting the consequent? In K. Gilhooly, M. Keane, R. Logie, G. Erdes (Eds.), *Lines of thought: Reflections on the psychology of thought* (Vol. 1, pp. 165–180). Chichester, England: Wiley.

Bulbrook, M. E. (1932). An experimental study into the existence and nature of "insight." *The American Journal of Psychology*, *44*, 409–453.

Caravona, L., & Macchi, L. (2023). Different incubation tasks in insight problem solving: Evidence for unconscious analytic thought, *Thinking & Reasoning*, *29*(4), 559–593.

Castelo, N., Hardy, E., House, J., Mazar, N., Tsai, C., & Zhao, M. (2015). Moving citizens online: Using salience & message framing to motivate behavior change. *Behavioral Science & Policy*, *1*(2), 57–68.

Chapman, L. J., & Chapman, J. P. (1959). Atmosphere effect re-examined. *Journal of Experimental Psychology*, *58*(3), 220–226.

Chater, N., & Loewenstein, G. (2022). The i-frame and the s-frame: How focusing on individual-level solutions has led behavioral public policy astray. *Behavioral and Brain Sciences*, *46*, e147.

Cheng, P., & Holyoak, K. (1985). Pragmatic reasoning schemas. *Cognitive Psychology*, *17*, 391–416.

Chronicle, E. P., MacGregor, J. N., & Ormerod, T. C. (2004). What makes an insight problem? The roles of heuristics, goal conception, and solution recoding in knowledge-lean problems. *Journal of Experimental Psychology: Learning, memory, and cognition*, *30*(1), 14–27.

Cialdini, R. B. (1993). *Influence: Science and practice* (3rd ed.). HarperCollins College Publishers.

Cohen, L. J. (1981). Can human irrationality be experimentally demonstrated? *Behavioral and Brain Sciences*, *4*(3), 317–331.

Croson, R. T. (1999). The disjunction effect and reason-based choice in games. *Organizational Behavior and Human Decision Processes*, *80*(2), 118–133.

Dawes, R. M. (1988). *Rational choice in an uncertain world*. New York: Harcourt Brace Jovanovich.

De Neys, W. (2012). Bias and conflict: A case for logical intuitions. *Perspectives on Psychological Science*, *7*(1), 28–38.

Dehaene, S., & Changeux, J.-P. (2011). Experimental and theoretical approaches to conscious processing. *Neuron, 70*, 200–227.

Dianoux, C., Heitz-Spahn, S., Siadou-Martin, B., Thevenot, G., & Yildiz, H. (2019). Nudge: A relevant communication tool adapted for agile innovation. *Journal of Innovation Economics & Management, 28*(1), 7–27. https://doi.org/10.3917/jie.028.0007

Dulany, D. E., & Hilton, D. J. (1991). Conversational implicature, conscious representation, and the conjunction fallacy. *Social Cognition, 9*, 85–110.

Duncker, K. (1945). *On problem solving. Psychological monographs* (Vol. 58, p. 270). Berlin: Springer. (Original work in German, *Psychologie des produktiven Denkens*, published 1935.)

Eddy, D. M. (1982). Probabilistic reasoning in clinical medicine: Problems and opportunities. In D. Kahneman, P. Slovic, & A. Tversky (Eds.), *Judgment under uncertainty: Heuristics and biases* (pp. 249–267). New York: Cambridge University Press.

Edwards, A., Elwyn, G., Covey, J., Matthews, E., & Pill, R. (2001). Presenting risk information—A review of the effects of "framing" and other manipulations on patient outcomes. *Journal of Health Communication, 6*(1), 61–82.

Ericsson, K. A., & Simon, H. A. (1984). *Protocol analysis: Verbal reports as data.* Cambridge: MIT Press.

Esteve-Gibert, N., Prieto, P., & Liszkowski, U. (2017). Twelve-month-olds understand social intentions based on prosody and gesture shape. *Infancy, 22*(1), 108–129.

Evans, J. S. B. T. (2010). Dual-process theories of reasoning: Facts and fallacies. In K. J. Holyoak & R. G. Morrison (Eds.), *The Oxford handbook of thinking and reasoning.* Oxford: Oxford University Press.

Evans, J. S. B. T. (2012a). Dual-process theories of reasoning: Facts and fallacies. In K. J. Holyoak & R. G. Morrison (Eds.), *The Oxford handbook of thinking and reasoning* (pp. 115–133). Oxford: Oxford University Press.

Evans, J. S. B. T. (2012b). Spot the difference: Distinguishing between two kinds of processing. *Mind & Society*, Special issue on: Dual process theories of human thought: The debate, *11*(1), 121–131.

Evans, J. S. B. T., Barston, J. L., & Pollard, P. (1983). On the conflict between logic and belief in syllogistic reasoning. *Memory & Cognition, 11*(3), 285–306.

Evans, J. S. B. T., & Curtis-Holmes, J. (2005). Rapid responding increases belief bias: Evidence for the dual-process theory of reasoning. *Thinking & Reasoning, 11*(4), 382–389.

Evans, J. S. B. T., Handley, S. J., & Harper, C. (2001). Necessity, possibility and belief: A study of syllogistic reasoning. *Quarterly Journal of Experimental Psychology, 54*, 935–958.

Evans, J. S. B. T., Handley, S., Neilens, H., & Over, D. E. (2007). Thinking about conditionals: A study of individual differences. *Memory & Cognition, 35*, 1772–1784.

Evans, J. S. B. T., Newstead, S. E., Allen, J. L., & Pollard, P. (1994). Debiasing by instruction: The case of belief bias. *European Journal of Cognitive Psychology, 6*(3), 263–285.

Evans, J. S. B. T., & Stanovich, K. E. (2013). Dual-process theories of higher cognition: Advancing the debate. *Perspectives on Psychological Science, 8*, 223–241, 263–271.

Fairley, N., Manktelow, K., & Over, D. (1999). Necessity, sufficiency, and perspective effects in causal conditional reasoning. *The Quarterly Journal of Experimental Psychology Section A, 52*(3), 771–790.

Fleck, J. I. (2008). Working memory demands in insight versus analytic problem solving. *European Journal of Cognitive Psychology*, *20*, 139–176.
Fleck, J. I., & Weisberg, R. W. (2004). The use of verbal protocols as data: An analysis of insight in the candle problem. *Memory & Cognition*, *32*, 990–1006.
Fleck, J. I., & Weisberg, R. W. (2013). Insight versus analysis: Evidence for diverse methods in problem solving. *Journal of Cognitive Psychology*, *25*(4), 436–463.
Floridi, L. (2011). *The philosophy of information*. Oxford University Press eBooks.
Frankish, K. (2012). Dual systems and dual attitudes. *Mind and Society*, *11*(1), Special issue on: Dual process theories of human thought: The debate, 41–51.
Frankish, K., & Evans, J. St. B. T. (Eds.) (2009). *In two minds*. Oxford: Oxford University Press.
Frederick, S. (2005). Cognitive reflection and decision making. *Journal of Economic Perspectives*, *19*(4), 25–42.
Gardner, E. P., & Johnson, K. O. (2013). Sensory coding. In E. R. Kandel, J. Schwartz, T. Jessell, S. Siegelbaum, & A. J. Hudspeth (Eds.), *Principles of neural science* (p. 455). New York: Mc-Graw Hill.
Gardner, H. (1983). *Frames of mind: The theory of multiple intelligences*. New York: Basic Books.
Gigerenzer, G. (2000). *Adaptive thinking: Rationality in the real world*. New York: Oxford University Press.
Gigerenzer, G. (2001). The adaptive toolbox. In G. Gigerenzer & R. Selten (Eds.), *Bounded rationality: The adaptive toolbox* (pp. 37–50). Cambridge, MA: MIT Press.
Gigerenzer, G., Gaissmaier, W., Kurz-Milcke, E., Schwartz, L. M., & Woloshin, S. (2007). Helping doctors and patients make sense of health statistics. *Psychological Science in the Public Interest*, *8*(2), 53–96. https://doi.org/10.1111/j.1539-6053.2008.00033.x
Gigerenzer, G., & Hoffrage, U. (1995). How to improve Bayesian reasoning without instruction: Frequency formats. *Psychological Review*, *102*(4), 684.
Gilhooly K. J., Ball L. J., & Macchi L. (Eds.) (2018). *Creativity and insight problem solving*. Oxford: Routledge.
Gilhooly, K. J., Fioratou, E., & Henretty, N. (2010). Verbalization and problem solving: Insight and spatial factors. *British Journal of Psychology (London, England: 1953)*, *101*(Pt 1), 81–93.
Gilhooly, K. J., Georgiou, G. J., & Devery, U. (2013). Incubation and creativity: Do something different. *Thinking & Reasoning*, *19*, 137–149.
Gilhooly, K. J., Georgiou, G. J., Sirota, M., & Paphiti-Galeano, A. (2015). Incubation and suppression processes in creative problem solving. *Thinking & Reasoning*, *21*(1), 130–146.
Girotto, V., & Gonzalez, M. (2001). Solving probabilistic and statistical problems: A matter of information structure and question form. *Cognition*, *78*(3), 247–276.
Goldstein, D. G., & Gigerenzer, G. (2002). Models of ecological rationality: The recognition heuristic. *Psychological Review*, *109*(1), 75.
Goldstein, N. J., Cialdini, R. B., & Griskevicius, V. (2008). A room with a viewpoint: Using social norms to motivate environmental conservation in hotels. *Journal of Consumer Research*, *35*(3), 472–482.
Gong, J., Zhang, Y., Yang, Z., Huang, Y., Feng, J., & Zhang, W. (2013). The framing effect in medical decision-making: A review of the literature. *Psychology, Health & Medicine*, *18*(6), 645–653.

Grice, H. P. (1975). Logic and conversation. In P. Cole & J. Morgan (Eds.), *Syntax and semantics* (Vol. 3). *Speech acts* (pp. 41–58). New York: Academic Press.

Griggs, R. A., & Cox, J. R. (1982). The elusive thematic-materials effect in Wason's selection task. *British Journal of Psychology*, *73*, 407–420.

Hacking, I. (1975). *The emergence of probability*. Cambridge: Cambridge University Press.

Hallsworth, M. (2023). A manifesto for applying behavioural science. *Nature Human Behaviour*, *7*(3), 310–322.

Hallsworth, M., Egan, M., Rutter, J., & McCrae, J. (2018). Behavioural government. Using behavioural science to improve how governments make decisions. Behavioural Insights, London, UK. www.bi.team/wp-content/uploads/2018/08/BIT-Behavioural-Government-Report-2018.pdf

Halpern, D. (2015). *Inside the nudge unit: How small changes can make a big difference*. Random House.

Handley, S. J., Newstead, S. E., & Trippas, D. (2011). Logic, beliefs, and instruction: A test of the default interventionist account of belief bias. *Journal of Experimental Psychology: Learning, Memory, and Cognition*, *37*(1), 28–43.

Hayes, J. R., & Simon, H. A. (1974). Understanding written problem instructions. In L. W. Gregg (Ed.), *Knowledge and cognition*. Mahwah, NJ: Lawrence Erlbaum.

Hélie, S., & Sun, R. (2010). Incubation, insight, and creative problem solving: A unified theory and a connectionist model. *Psychological Review*, *117*(3), 994–1024.

Henle, M. (1962). On the relation between logic and thinking. *Psychological Review*, *69*, 366–378.

Hertwig, R., & Grüne-Yanoff, T. (2017). Nudging and boosting: Steering or empowering good decisions. *Perspectives on Psychological Science*, *12*(6), 973–986.

Hirsh, J. B., Kang, S. K., & Bodenhausen, G. V. (2012). Personalized persuasion: Tailoring persuasive appeals to recipients' personality traits. *Psychological Science*, *23*(6), 578–581.

Johnson, E. J., & Goldstein, D. (2003). Do defaults save lives? *Science*, *302*(5649), 1338–1339.

Johnson-Laird, P. N., Legrenzi, P., & Sonino Legrenzi, M. (1972). Reasoning and a sense of reality. *British Journal of Psychology*, *63*(3), 395–400.

Jou, J., Shanteau, J., & Harris, R. J. (1996). An information processing view of framing effects: The role of causal schemas in decision making. *Memory & Cognition*, *24*, 1–15.

Jung-Beeman, M., Bowden, E. M., Haberman, J., Frymiare, J. L., Arambel-Liu, S., Greenblatt, R., et al. (2004). Neural activity when people solve verbal problems with insight. *PLoS Biology*, *2*(4), 1–11.

Kahneman, D. (2003). A perspective on judgment and choice: Mapping bounded rationality. *American Psychologist*, *58*(9), 697–720.

Kahneman, D., Slovic, P., & Tversky, A. (1982). *Judgement under uncertainty: Heurustics and biases*. Cambridge: Cambridge University Press.

Kahneman, D., & Tversky, A. (1972). Subjective probability: A judgment of representativeness. *Cognitive Psychology*, *3*(3), 430–454.

Kahneman, D., & Tversky, A. (1973). On the psychology of prediction. *Psychological Review*, *80*(4), 243.

Kandel, E. R. (2012). *The age of insight*. New York: Random House.

Kanizsa, G. (1980). *Grammatica del vedere*. Bologna: Il Mulino.

Kaplan, C. A., & Simon, H. A. (1990). In search of insight. *Cognitive Psychology*, *22*, 374–419.

Killingsworth, M. A., & Gilbert, k.D. T. (2010). A wandering mind is an unhappy mind. *Science*, *330*, 932.

Klauer, K. C., Stahl, C., & Erdfelder, E. (2007). The abstract selection task: New data and an almost comprehensive model. *Journal of Experimental Psychology. Learning, Memory, and Cognition*, *33*(4), 680–703. https://doi.org/10.1037/0278-7393.33.4.680

Koehler, J. J. (1996). The base rate fallacy reconsidered: Descriptive, normative, and methodological challenges. *Behavioral and Brain Sciences*, *19*(1), 1–17.

Koehler, J. J., & Macchi, L. (2004). Thinking about low-probability events: An exemplar-cuing theory. *Psychological Science*, *15*(8), 540–546.

Koehler, J. J., & Macchi, L. (2009). Comments on "Getting scarred and winning lotteries: Effects of exemplar cuing and statistical format on imagining low-probability events," By Newell, Mitchell, and Hayes (2008). *Journal of Behavioral Decision Making*, *22*(5), 523–527.

Kühberger, A., Komunska, D., & Perner, J. (2001). The disjunction effect: Does it exist for two-step gambles? *Organizational Behavior and Human Decision Processes*, *85*(2), 250–264.

Levin, I. P., & Gaeth, G. J. (1988). How consumers are affected by the framing of attribute information before and after consuming the product. *Journal of Consumer Research*, *15*(3), 374–378.

Levinson, S. C. (1995). Interactional biases in human thinking. In E. N. Goody (Ed.), *Social intelligence and interaction* (pp. 221–261). Cambridge: Cambridge University Press.

Levinson, S. C. (2000). *Presumptive meanings: The theory of generalized conversational implicature*. Cambridge, MA: MIT Press.

Levinson, S. C. (2013). Cross-cultural universals and communication structures. In M. A. Arbib (Ed.), *Language, music, and the brain: A mysterious relationship* (pp. 67–80). Cambridge, MA: MIT Press.

Lindley, D. V. (1985) *Making decisions* (2nd ed.). London: Wiley.

Macchi, L. (1995). Pragmatic aspects of the base-rate fallacy. *The Quarterly Journal of Experimental Psychology. A, Human Experimental Psychology*, *48*(1), 188–207.

Macchi, L. (2000). Partitive formulation of information in probabilistic problems: Beyond heuristics and frequency format explanations. *Organizational Behavior and Human Decision Processes*, *82*(2), 217–236.

Macchi, L. (2003). The partitive conditional probability. In D. Hardman & L. Macchi (Eds.), Thinking: Psychological perspectives on reasoning, judgment and decision making (pp. 165–188). Chichester, UK: Wiley.

Macchi, L. (2019). *Nudge and communication: Implicit layers of language, thought and decision making*. AISC 2019, 16th Annual Conference of the Italian Association of Cognitive Science, The complexity of cognition: Multidisciplinary approaches to human behaviour. December 11–13, Università degli Studi di Roma Tre.

Macchi, L. (2021). La comunicazione pubblica. In R.Viale & L. Macchi (Eds.), *Analisi comportamentale delle politiche pubbliche. Nudge e interventi basati sulle scienze cognitive*. Bologna: Il Mulino.

Macchi, L., & Bagassi, M. (2007). The underinformative formulation of conditional probability. *Behavioral and Brain Sciences*, *30*(3), 274–275.

Macchi, L., & Bagassi, M. (2012). Intuitive and analytical processes in insight problem solving: A psycho-rhetorical approach to the study of reasoning. *Mind & Society*, Special issue on: Dual process theories of human thought: The debate, *11*(1), 53–67.

Macchi, L., & Bagassi, M. (2014). The interpretative heuristic in insight problem solving. *Mind & Society*, *13*(1), 97–108.

Macchi, L., & Bagassi, M. (2015). When analytic thought is challenged by a misunderstanding. *Thinking & Reasoning*, *21*(1), 147–164.

Macchi, L., & Bagassi, M. (2018). A new test for rationality: Contributions and outstanding issues. *The American Journal Of Psychology*, *131*(2), 237–240 [10.5406/amerjpsyc.131.2.0237].

Macchi, L., & Bagassi, M. (2019). The Argumentative and the Interpretative Functions of Thought. *Teorema: Revista internacional de filosofía*, *38*(1), 87–96.

Macchi, L., Bagassi, M., & Ciociola, P. B. (2019). *Normative performances in classical reasoning tasks: High cognitive abilities or interactional intelligence*? Unpublished manuscript.

Macchi, L., Bagassi, M., & Passerini, G. (2006). *Biased communication and misleading intuition of probability*. International Workshop on "Intuition and affect in risk perception and decision making," Bergen (Norway), November 3–4, oral presentation.

Macchi, L., Caravona, L., Poli, F., Bagassi, M., & Franchella, M. A. G. (2020). Speak your mind and I will make it right: The case of "selection task." *Journal of Cognitive Psychology*, *32*(1), 93–107. DOI: 10.1080/20445911.2019.1707207

Macchi, L., Osherson, D., & Krantz, D. H. (1999). A note on superadditive probability judgment. *Psychological Review*, *106*(1), 210.

Macchi, L., Over, D., & Viale, R. (Eds.) (2012). Special issue: Dual process theories of human thought: The debate. *Mind & Society*, *11*, 1.

Macchi, L., Poli, F., & Caravona, L. (2025). Dissociable effects of verbalization on solving insight and non-insight problems. *Journal of Intelligence*, *13*(3), 36.

Macchi, L., Poli, F., Caravona, L., Vezzoli, M., Franchella, M. A., & Bagassi, M. (2019). How to get rid of the belief bias: Boosting analytical thinking via pragmatics. *Europe's Journal of Psychology*, *15*(3), 595.

Macchi, L., & Zulato, E. (2021). Numbers do not add up! The pragmatic approach to the framing of medical treatments. *Judgment and Decision Making*, 16(3), 596–613.

MacGregor, J. N., Ormerod, T. C., & Chronicle, E. P. (2001). Information- processing and insight: A process model of performance on the nine-dot and related problems. *Journal of Experimental Psychology: Learning, Memory, and Cognition*, *27*, 176–201.

Mach, E. (1914). The analysis of sensations. Chicago: Open Court.

Maffei, L. (2012). *La libertà di essere diversi*. Bologna: Il Mulino.

McKenzie, C. R., & Nelson, J. D. (2003). What a speaker's choice of frame reveals: Reference points, frame selection, and framing effects. *Psychonomic Bulletin & Review*, *10*(3), 596–602.

McNeil, B. J., Pauker, S. G., Sox Jr, H. C., & Tversky, A. (1982). On the elicitation of preferences for alternative therapies. *New England Journal of Medicine*, *306*(21), 1259–1262.

Mercier, H. (2009). *La théorie argumentative du raisonnement* (Doctoral dissertation, Ecole pratique des hautes études-EPHE PARIS).

Mercier, H., & Sperber, D. (2011). Why do humans reason? Arguments for an argumentative theory. *Behavioral and Brain Sciences*, *34*, 57–111.

Mercier, H., & Sperber, D. (Eds.) (2017). *The enigma of reason*. London: Penguin Random House.

Metcalfe, J. (1986). Feeling of knowing in memory and problem solving. *Journal of Experimental Psychology: Learning, Memory, and Cognition*, *12*(2), 288–294.

Michie, S., Van Stralen, M. M., & West, R. (2011). The behaviour change wheel: A new method for characterising and designing behaviour change interventions. *Implementation Science*, *6*(1), 1–12.

Mosconi, G. (1978). *Il pensiero discorsivo*. Bologna: Il Mulino.

Mosconi, G. (1990). *Discorso e pensiero*. Bologna: Il Mulino.

Mosconi, G., & D'Urso, V. (1974). *Il farsi e il disfarsi del problema*. Firenze: Giunti-Barbera.

Mosconi, G., & D'Urso, V. (1975). The selection task from the standpoint of the theory of double code. International Conference on "Selection Task," Trento.

Mosconi, G., & Macchi, L. (2001). The role of pragmatic rules in the conjunction fallacy. *Mind & Society*, *2*, 31–57.

Newell, A., & Simon, H. A. (1972). *Human problem solving*. Englewood Cliffs, NJ: Prentice-Hall.

Oakhill, J., Johnson-Laird, P. N., & Garnham, A. (1989). Believability and syllogistic reasoning. *Cognition*, *31*(2), 117–140.

Ollinger, M., Jones, G., & Knoblich, G. K. (2008). Investigating the effect of mental set on insight problem solving. *Experimental Psychology*, *55*(4), 270–282.

Over, D. E. (2009). New paradigm psychology of reasoning: Review of "Bayesian Rationality." *Thinking & Reasoning*, *15*, 431–438.

Panizza, A., & Macchi, L. (2025). Organ donation strategies: The effect of presumed consent and organisational models in Spain and Italy. *Giornale Italiano di Psicologia* (in press).

Parisi, G. (2024). *In a flight of starlings: The wonder of complex systems*. London: Penguin Press.

Pennycook, G., Newton, C., & Thompson, V. A. (2022). *Base-rate neglect*. In R. F. Pohl (Ed.), *Cognitive illusions: Intriguing phenomena in thinking, judgment, and memory* (3rd ed.). London: Routledge.

Perkins, D. N. (1981). *The mind's best work*. Cambridge, MA: Harvard University Press.

Piaget, J. (1953). How children form mathematical concepts. *Scientific American*, *189*(5), 74–79.

Plohl, N., Ruggeri, K., Stuhlreyer, J. P., & Matz, S. C. (2019). Communication and public engagement. In K. Ruggeri (Ed.), *Behavioral insights for public policy: cases and concepts* (pp. 174–199). Abingdon: Taylor & Francis Routledge.

Politzer, G., & Macchi, L. (2000). Reasoning and pragmatics. *Mind & Society*, *1*, 73–93.

Raichle, M. E., MacLeod, A. M., Snyder, A. Z., Powers, W. J., Gusnard, D. A., & Shulman, G. L. (2001). A default mode of brain function. *Proceedings of the National Academy of Sciences of the United States of America*, *98*(2), 676–682.

Reboul, A. (2011). A Relevance-theoretic account of the evolution of implicit communication. *Studies in Pragmatics*, *13*, 1–19.

Ricoeur, P. (1969). *Le conflit des interprétations: Essais d'herméneutique*. Paris: Éditions du Seuil; translated into English as *Conflict of Interpretation* (Ed. Don Ihde), Evanston, IL: Northwestern University Press, 1974.

Rizzolatti, G., & Strick, P. L. (2013). Cognitive functions of the premotor systems. In E. R. Kandel, J. Schwartz, T. Jessell, S. Siegelbaum, & A. J. Hudspeth (Eds.), *Principles of neural science* (pp. 412–425). New York: McGraw-Hill.

Ruggeri, K. (2018). *Behavioral insights for public policy. Concepts and cases*. New York: Routledge.

Sá, W. C., West, R. F., & Stanovich, K. E. (1999). The domain specificity and generality of belief bias: Searching for a generalizable critical thinking skill. *Journal of Educational Psychology*, *91*(3), 497–510.

Samuelson, W., & Zeckhauser, R. (1988). Status quo bias in decision making. *Journal of Risk and Uncertainty*, *1*, 7–59.

Savage, L. J. (1954). *The foundations of statistics*. Hoboken, NJ: Wiley.

Schelling, T. C. (1960). *The strategy of conflict*. Cambridge, MA: Harvard University Press.

Schooler, J. W., Ohlsson, S., & Brooks, K. (1993). Thoughts beyond words: When language overshadows insight. *Journal of Experimental Psychology. General*, *122*(2), 166–183.

Schooler, J. W., Smallwood, J., Christoff, K., Handy, T. C., Reichle, E. D., & Sayette, M. A. (2011). Meta-awareness, perceptual decoupling and the wandering mind. *Trends in Cognitive Sciences*, *15*, 319–326.

Segal, E. (2004). Incubation in insight problem solving. *Creativity Research Journal*, *16*, 141–148.

Seifert, C. M., Meyer, D. E., Davidson, N., Patalano, A. L., & Yaniv, I. (1995). Demystification of cognitive insight: Opportunistic assimilation and the prepared-mind perspective. In R. J. Sternberg & J. E. Davidson (Eds.), *The Nature of insight* (pp. 65–124). Cambridge: MIT Press.

Sells, S. B. (1936). The atmosphere effect: An experimental study of reasoning. *Archives of Psychology (Columbia University)*, *200*, 72.

Shafir, E. (1994). Uncertainty and the difficulty of thinking through disjunctions. *Cognition*, *50*(1–3), 403–430.

Shafir, E., & Tversky, A. (1992). Thinking through uncertainty Nonconsequential reasoning and choice. *Cognitive Psychology*, *24*, 449–474.

Shafir, E., Simonson, I., & Tversky, A. (1993). Reason-based choice. *Cognition*, *49*(1–2), 11–36.

Sher, S., & McKenzie, C. R. (2006). Information leakage from logically equivalent frames. *Cognition*, *101*(3), 467–494.

Simon, H. A. (1947). *Administrative behavior a study of decision-making processes in administrative organization*. New York: Macmillan.

Simon, H. A. (1955). A behavioral model of rational choice. *Quarterly Journal of Economics*, *69*, 99–118.

Simon, H. A. (1966). Theories of decision-making in economics and behavioural science. *Surveys of Economic Theory* . London: Palgrave Macmillan.

Simon, H. A. (1979). Information processing models of recognition. *Annual Review of Psychology*, *30*, 363–396.

Simon, H. A. (1986). The information processing explanation of gestalt phenomena. *Computers in Human Behavior*, *2*, 241–255.

Simon, H. A., & Hayes, J. R. (1976). The understanding process: Problem isomorphs. *Cognitive Psychology*, *8*(2), 165–190.

Simon, H. A., & Newell, A. (1971). Human problem solving: The state of theory. *American Psychologist*, *21*(2), 145–159.

Singler, E. (2015). *Nudge marketing English version: Winning at behavioral change*. London: Pearson.

Sio, U. N., & Ormerod, T. C. (2009). Does incubation enhance problem solving? A meta-analytic review. *Psychological Bulletin*, *135*(1), 94–120.

Sloman, S. A. (1996). The empirical case for two systems of reasoning. *Psychological Bulletin*, *119*, 3–22.

Smallwood, J., & Schooler, J. W. (2006). The restless mind. *Psychological Bulletin*, *132*, 946–958.

Smallwood, J., McSpadden, M., Luus, B., & Schooler, J. W. (2008). Segmenting the stream of consciousness: The psychological correlates of temporal structures in the time series data of a continuous performance task. *Brain and Cognition, 66*, 50–56.

Smith, S. M., & Blankenship, S. E. (1991). Incubation and the persistence of fixation in problem solving. *The American Journal of Psychology, 104*(1), 61–87.

Smith, S. M., Fox, P. T., Miller, K. L., Glahn, D. C., Fox, P. M., Mackay, C. E., Filippini, N., Watkins K. E., Toro, R., Laird, A. R., & Beckmann, C. F. (2009). Correspondence of the brain's functional architecture during activation and rest. *Proceedings of the National Academy of Sciences of the United States of America, 106*(31), 13040–13045.

Sohl, S. J., & Moyer, A. (2007). Tailored interventions to promote mammography screening: A meta-analytic review. *Preventive Medicine, 45*(4), 252–261.

Sperber, D., Cara, F., & Girotto, V. (1995). Relevance theory explains the selection task. *Cognition, 57*(1), 31–95.

Sperber, D., Clément, F., Heintz, C., Mascaro, O., Mercier, H., Origgi, G., & Wilson, D. (2010). Epistemic vigilance. *Mind & Language, 25*(4), 359–393.

Sperber, D., & Wilson, D. (1995). *Relevance: Communication and cognition*. Oxford: Blackwell. (Original work published 1986.)

Stanovich, K. E., & West, R. F. (1998). Individual differences in rational thought. *Journal of Experimental Psychology. General, 127*, 161–188.

Stanovich, K. E., & West, R. F. (1999). Individual differences in reasoning and the heuristics and biases debate. In P. L. Ackerman, P. C. Kyllonen, & R. D. Roberts (Eds.), *Learning and individual differences: Process, trait, and content determinants* (pp. 389–411). Washington, DC: American Psychological Association.

Stanovich, K. E., & West, R. F. (2000). Individual differences in reasoning: Implications for the rationality debate? and Advancing the rationality debate. *Behavioral and Brain Science, 23*(5), 645–665 and 701–717.

Stanovich, K. E., & West, R. F. (2008). On the relative independence of thinking biases and cognitive ability. *Journal of Personality and Social Psychology, 94*, 672–695.

Stanovich, K. E., West, R. F., & Toplak, M. E. (2016). *The rationality quotient: Toward a test of rational thinking*. New York: MIT Press.

Sternberg, R. J., & Davidson, J. E. (Eds.) (1986). *Conceptions of giftedness*. New York: Cambridge University Press.

Stupple, E. J. N., & Ball, L. J. (2008). Belief–logic conflict resolution in syllogistic reasoning: Inspection-time evidence for a parallel-process model. *Thinking & Reasoning, 14*(2), 168–181.

Stupple, E. J. N., Ball, L. J., Evans, J. S. B. T., & Kamal-Smith, E. (2011). When logic and belief collide: Individual differences in reasoning times support a selective processing model. *Journal of Cognitive Psychology, 23*(8), 931–941.

Tarski, A. (1969). Truth and proof. *Scientific American, 220*(6), 63–77.

Thaler, R. (1980). Toward a positive theory of consumer choice. *Journal of Economic Behavior & Organization, 1*(1), 39–60.

Thaler, R. H., & Sunstein, C. R. (2008). *Nudge: Improving decisions about health, wealth, and happiness*. New Haven, CT: Yale University Press.

Thaler, R. H., & Sunstein, C. R. (2021). *Nudge: The final edition*. New Haven, CT: Yale University Press.

Thompson, V., & Morsanyi, K. (2012). Analytic thinking: Do you feel like it? *Mind & Society, 11*, 93–105.

Thüring, M., & Jungermann, H. (1990). The conjunction fallacy: Causality vs. event probability. *Journal of Behavioral Decision Making*, *3*(1), 61–74.

Tomasello, M. (2009). *Why we cooperate*. Cambridge, MA: MIT Press.

Tomasello, M., & Barton, M. E. (1994). Learning words in nonostensive contexts. *Developmental Psychology*, *30*(5), 639.

Trevarthen, C. (1979). Communication and cooperation in early infancy: A description of primary intersubjectivity. In M. Bullowa (Ed.), *Before speech: The beginning of human communication* (pp. 321–347). Cambridge, UK: Cambridge University Press.

Tversky, A., & Kahneman, D. (1974). Judgment under uncertainty: Heuristics and biases. *Science*, *185*, 1124–1131.

Tversky, A., & Kahneman, D. (1980). Causal schemata in judgments under uncertainty. In M. Fishbein (Ed.), *Progress in social psychology* (Vol. 1, pp. 49–72). Hillsdale, NJ: Erlbaum.

Tversky, A., & Kahneman, D. (1981). The framing of decisions and the psychology of choice. *Science*, *211*, 453–458.

Tversky, A., & Kahneman, D. (1983). Extension versus intuitive reasoning: The conjunction fallacy in probability judgment. *Psychological Review*, *90*(4), 293–315.

Tversky, A., & Koehler, D. J. (1994). Support theory: A nonextensional representation of subjective probability. *Psychological Rreview*, *101*(4), 547.

Tversky, A., & Shafir, E. (1992). The disjunction effect in choice under uncertainty. *Psychological Science*, *3*(5), 305–310.

Van Damme, D., & Zahner, D. (Eds.) (2022). *Does higher education teach students to think critically?* Paris, FR: OECD Publishing.

Van der Linden, S., Maibach, E., & Leiserowitz, A. (2015). Improving public engagement with climate change: Five "best practice" insights from psychological science. *Perspectives on Psychological Science*, *10*(6), 758–763.

Verschueren, N., Schaeken, W., & d'Ydewalle, G. (2005). A dual-process specification of causal conditional reasoning. *Thinking and Reasoning, 11*(3), 239–278.

Wallas, G. (1926). *The art of thought* (Vol. 10). Brace: Harcourt.

Wason, P. C. (1966). Reasoning. In B. M. Foss (Ed.), *New horizons in psychology* (Vol. 1). Harmondsworth: Penguin. LCCN 66005291.

Wason, P. C. (1983). Realism and rationality in the selection task. In J. Evans (Ed.), *Thinking and reasoning* (pp. 45–75). London, UK: Routledge and Kegan Paul.

Wason, P. C., & Evans, J. (1974–1975). Dual processes in reasoning? *Cognition*, *3*(2), 141–154. https://doi.org/10.1016/0010-0277(74)

Wason, P. C., & Johnson-Laird, P. N. (1972). *Psychology of reasoning: Structure and content* (Vol. 86). Cambridge, MA: Harvard University Press.

Wason, P. C., & Shapiro, D. (1971). Natural and contrived experience in a reasoning problem. *Quarterly Journal of Experimental Psychology*, *23*(1), 63–71.

Weidenfeld, A., Oberauer, K., & Hörnig, R. (2005). Causal and noncausal conditionals: An integrated model of interpretation and reasoning. *The Quarterly Journal of Experimental Psychology Section A*, *58*(8), 1479–1513.

Weisberg, R. W. (2006). *Creativity: Understanding innovation in problem solving, science, invention, and the arts*. New York: Wiley.

Weisberg, R. W. (2015). Toward an integrated theory of insight in problem solving. *Thinking & Reasoning*, *21*, 5–39.

Wertheimer, M. (1925). *Drei Abhandlungen zur Gestalttheorie*. Erlangen: Verlag der Philosophischen Akademie.

Wertheimer, M. (1945). *Productive thinking.* New York: Harper.

Wertheimer, M. (1985). A Gestalt perspective on computer simulations of cognitive processes. *Computers on Human Behavior*, *1*, 19–33.

Wertheimer, M. (2020). Max Wertheimer productive thinking. In *Classic texts in the sciences*. https://doi.org/10.1007/978-3-030-36063-4

Woodworth, R. S., & Sells, S. B. (1935). An atmosphere effect in formal syllogistic reasoning. *Journal of Experimental Psychology, 18*(4), 451–460.

INDEX

Note: Figures are indicated by *italics*. Tables are indicated by **bold**. Endnotes are indicated by the page number followed by 'n' and the endnote number e.g., 20n1 refers to endnote 1 on page 20.